Contents

The staircase to the Ceramics Gallery, from a drawing by John Watkins *c.*1876–81

The Victoria & Albert Museum

British Art

MICHAEL DARBY

European Art

ANTHONY BURTON AND
SUSAN HASKINS

Oriental Art

JOHN AYERS
(with contributions by Andrew
Topsfield and John Lowry)

Published in association with
the Victoria & Albert Museum

Scala/Philip Wilson

© 1983 Philip Wilson Publishers Ltd and
Summerfield Press Ltd

First published in 1983 by Philip Wilson
Publishers Ltd and Summerfield Press Ltd
Russell Chambers, Covent Garden, London WC2E 8AA

Designed by Paul Sharp
Edited by Philip Wilson Publishers Ltd
Produced by Scala Istituto Fotografico Editoriale, Firenze
Phototypeset by Tradespools Ltd, Frome, Somerset
Printed in Italy

ISBN 0 85667 129 0

Abbreviations
D = Depth
Diam = Diameter
H = Height
L = Length
W = Width

FRONT COVER: *Madame de Pompadour* by François Boucher, 1758

BACK COVER: Tin-glazed earthenware plate, Italian, c.1510

ORIENTAL ART *continued*

British Art
in the Victoria and Albert
Museum

Introduction

Osterley House. Osterley was completed in 1577 for Sir Thomas Gresham, but altered by Robert Adam in 1761 for Francis Child. Adam's work, which is based primarily on Roman classical interior architecture, also included the furnishings, most of which survive intact.

The façades which the Victoria and Albert presents to the public, designed by (Sir) Aston Webb in the 1890s, give a beguiling sense of uniformity to the Museum, which is perpetuated in the main entrance hall and surrounding galleries. When one penetrates further, however, one becomes aware of odd changes of level, unhappy junctions between galleries and corridors, different constructional materials, and areas decorated with polychrome tiles, enamelled tin, or spirit fresco. It becomes apparent that the story of the Museum's architectural development is not as straightforward as it seems. When one also discovers that some of the curatorial departments are based on media, ceramics, textiles, and metalwork, for example, whilst the Indian and Far Eastern Departments are based on cultures and the Museum of Childhood and the Theatre Museum relate to activities, one's comprehension of the V & A is further confounded. That a decorative arts museum should house the national collection of water-colours and the Constable collection, which would seem more appropriate to the Tate or the National Galleries, complicates the issue still more.

The picture becomes clearer when one looks at the history of the Museum. The V & A came into being in the aftermath of the Great Exhibition of 1851, as the brain-child of the Prince Consort and of Henry Cole (1808–82), the principal promoters of the Crystal Palace. They were concerned about the low standard of design in British industry, and set out to establish not only the inseparability of art and manufacture, but also to expound the theory and practice of design in a simple, logical manner so as to make it comprehensible to manufacturers, designers, and public alike. This radical, utilitarian approach was reflected in the title of a new section of the Board of Trade called the Department of Practical Art (the forerunner of the present Department of Education and Science), which was set up in 1852 in Marlborough House with Cole as General Superintendent to administer both a museum and the metropolitan School of Design.

The Museum, called at first the Museum of Manufactures but renamed the Museum of Ornamental Art when it opened to the public in September 1852, initially comprised two quite separate collections. Some of the models, casts, and prints acquired for teaching purposes by the head school of design at Somerset House, including copies of Raphael's decorations of the Vatican Loggia and a miscellaneous collection of contemporary items purchased at the Paris Exhibitions of 1844 and 1845, were transferred to the Museum, and displayed alongside several hundred objects purchased at the Great Exhibition with the aid of a Government grant of £5,000 and a number of loans from the Royal and other prominent collections. The Museum immediately proved popular with the public, and it was not unusual for as many as 5,000 persons to visit Marlborough House when admission was free (6d entrance was otherwise charged).

The Museum's collections grew rapidly, and Cole could already boast by the end of 1853 of the ceramics, for example, that 'within its moderate compass there is probably no European collection more complete or comprehensive'. Under J. C. Robinson, whom Cole appointed as Superintendent of Art, the Bernal Collection of porcelain, maiolica, glass, and metalwork, and the Gherardini Collection of sculptors' models, including waxes attributed to Michaelangelo, were purchased in 1855. Important acquisitions were made at the Paris Exhibition in this year, and negotiations commenced for acquiring the large collection of medieval and Renaissance art belonging to the Toulouse lawyer, Jules Soulages.

With the intention of making the Museum more useful to the provinces and of encouraging the setting up of other museums throughout the country, a

Ham House. Originally built for Sir Thomas Vavasour, Ham House now stands as a monument to Elizabeth, Countess of Dysart, and her husband the Duke of Lauderdale. Recently restored, it is one of the most lavishly decorated and furnished seventeenth-century houses to have been preserved almost intact.

'Circulating Museum' of about four hundred objects was lent for study and exhibition to the provincial schools of art. This was later to become the Museum's Circulation Department. An expanding library of art books was also begun, which, like the Museum, was only open to the public on payment of a fee. Both Cole and Prince Albert were anxious that the Museum should, as far as possible, pay for its own running costs.

The difficulties of housing the collections and of providing adequate facilities for students was so acute by 1856 that Parliament agreed to transfer the entire Department to South Kensington. The Prince Consort succeeded in obtaining a vote from Parliament for £15,000, to which the Commissioners for the 1851 Exhibition added a further £3,000, and work was commenced on a 'temporary' corrugated and cast iron structure. The choice of site for the Department's move was perfectly logical because several years earlier the Prince had employed architects to plan a museum on the Commissioner's estate as part of a vast cultural centre, but the scheme had fallen through owing to lack of funds.

With the opening on 22 June 1857 of the 'Iron Museum', quickly renamed the 'Brompton Boilers' by the local inhabitants, who ridiculed its utilitarian appearance, began a new phase in the Department's history. The ground floor housed three quite different museums. The Educational Museum filled the major part, while the Museum of Ornamental Art under Robinson, and a Museum of Construction under the sapper-architect Francis Fowke, occupied

The Quadrangle. The northern side of the quadrangle was designed by Francis Fowke in 1863 and served for some time as the front entrance of the Museum. The pediment includes a mural commemorating the Great Exhibition of 1851.

smaller areas. Above these were situated several other museums and collections. The Architectural Museum was located in the western gallery, and included over 7,000 casts, principally of Gothic art. The eastern gallery contained the Museum of Animal Products, inherited from the 1851 Exhibition, and the popular food Museum arranged by Lyon Playfair, intended to provide 'lessons in household and health subjects, especially addressed to the working classes'. The northern gallery was given over to changing displays of recent work by members of the Institute of British Sculptors. Lastly, there was the collection of patent models administered by the Commissioners of Patents who objected to Cole's policy of charging for admission and had their own separate cottage-like entrance. Later, collections of marine models and of fish culture were added.

Thus, in this heterogeneous assemblage of Gothic casts and wax pork chops, of Renaissance sculpture and model boats, and of French furniture and stuffed animals, lay the ancestors of many modern institutions, including the Building and Design Centres, the National Maritime and Science Museums, and the Royal College of Art. Since John Sheepshanks had also given his collection of contemporary British art to the Department in 1856, the Tate Gallery could be added to the list. As the art collections continued to grow and space became more critical, so some of these collections were moved to new sites, and others disbanded; but the process was a long one, not completed until 1909 when those devoted to science were moved to the opposite side of Exhibition Road.

One of the conditions of the Sheepshanks gift was that a gallery should be erected to house the paintings within twelve months. The task of designing this was given to Francis Fowke, who had previously built a large refreshment room and photographic gallery elsewhere on the Department's site. When in 1859 the 'Iron Museum' was found 'unsuitable in every respect for the conservation of articles of value', many of the more precious objects were removed into the ground floor of the Sheepshanks Gallery. The Department's involvement with painting was given further impetus when one evening late in December 1856, while Cole was in Italy, Fowke was informed over dinner that they could begin a new building to house the Turner and Vernon collections (now in the National Gallery). To forestall bureaucratic interference Fowke began immediately, and these buildings continued the line of the Sheepshanks Gallery northwards, but formed an awkward junction with it, and were criticized on aesthetic grounds.

The collections of the Museum of Ornamental Art continued to grow. It must be remembered that in the first decade or so after the Department's foundation the Museum experienced little competition from other collectors. Art history as we know it today did not exist. A steady stream of important Renaissance and earlier works of art, such as would be inconceivable nowadays, flowed into the Museum: terra cottas and marbles by Donatello, Giambologna, and other Renaissance sculptors from the Gigli and Campana collections in 1860; the Gloucester candlestick from the Soltikoff Collection in the same year; the Eltenberg reliquary in 1861; the Syon Cope in 1864; the Raphael Cartoons on loan from the Queen in 1865; and hundreds of others.

By 1860 attendance had risen to more than 610,000 per annum and extra accommodation was again required for the collections. Cole rejected further piecemeal development and asked Fowke to draw up plans for major new buildings to incorporate or replace most of those already on the site. Building work was to last for more than twenty years and resulted in the appearance of much of the Museum as we know it today.

The Green Dining Room. This room, which was designed and decorated by Morris, Marshall, Faulkener and Company in 1863, was one of the first important commissions received by the firm, which quickly became famous for the production of textiles and wallpapers designed by its founder William Morris.

The Gamble Room. Like the Green Dining Room, the Gamble Room formed part of the original Museum restaurant. The ceramic columns and tiles were made by Minton, Hollins and Company of Stoke on Trent to the designs of Godfrey Sykes and James Gamble, and the room was opened in 1868.

In the decoration of the new buildings Fowke was helped by Godfrey Sykes, who clothed Fowke's ingenious architecture with 'the craftsmanship and humanist idealism of the Renaissance'. At the same time Cole called upon other artists, including Owen Jones, Morris and Company, E. J. Poynter, and Frederick Leighton, to carry out decorative work too. Thus, the Department took seriously its role as a promoter of practical art, many of the galleries becoming, as their decoration progressed, didactic displays of techniques and methods.

By this time the 'Iron Museum' was beginning to look decidedly out of place in its polychrome Renaissance setting, and in 1867 the greater part was removed and re-erected at Bethnal Green as the interior of what is now the Museum of Childhood. In its place two huge courts were built, from 1868, to house the collection of casts. Their completion in 1873 marked another turning-point in the history of the Museum. A new Chancellor of the Exchequer terminated the funds for building and thereby provoked Cole's resignation. 'South Kensington' as a whole may not have been Cole's inspiration, but many of the details were certainly his, and it was largely through his endeavour that it was achieved. What was not to Cole's liking was the bias of the collections towards art history. He blamed Robinson for this, and forced him to resign. Even after retirement Cole attempted to reverse the trend, but by 1880 his was a lone voice. The principles of good design he had formulated with Owen Jones and emblazoned on the gallery walls had long since been removed and the original purpose of the Museum forgotten.

The first major building work carried out after Cole's retirement was the completion in 1884 of the south side of the quadrangle containing the National Art Library. This was followed by the fronts to Cromwell and Exhibition Roads, which had been commenced when Queen Victoria laid the foundation stone in 1889, and were officially opened by King Edward VII in June 1909. It was at this time that the South Kensington Museum, as it had become known, was re-titled the Victoria and Albert Museum. In the present century, the story of development has largely been one of altering, hiding, or removing the Victorian features— now, happily, a policy that has been reversed—and of infill building to accommodate the growing collections.

Many major acquisitions were made in the later nineteenth century. The famous collection of English ceramics formed by Lady Charlotte Schreiber and presented in 1885, and John Jones' tremendously important bequest in 1882 of eighteenth-century French furniture and applied art, recently re-displayed in new galleries to the left of the main entrance, were two of the most important. Thousands of other gifts, purchases, and bequests have continued up to the present. The V & A has acquired a special niche in the hearts of many of its visitors. Dr W. L. Hildburgh, a wealthy American amateur scholar, gave presents to the Museum at Christmas and on his birthday, and quite apart from hundreds of important purchases over many years for most of the departments, bequeathed further enormous collections in 1956. Other very important acquisitions in the present century were Gabrielle Enthoven's theatre collection in 1925, one of the bases of the present Theatre Museum, and the purchases of the George Eumorphopoulous Collection in 1936, which with the collection of George Salting acquired in 1909 firmly established the importance of the Far-Eastern collections. Since responsibility for the India Office Museum had been assumed by the Department in 1879, the representation of Oriental art is now very strong. In 1947 and 1948 the contents of Ham and Osterley Houses were given to the

V & A, and in 1952 Apsley House, the home of the Duke of Wellington, also came into its care. These three out-stations are now administered by the Department of Furniture and Woodwork. As an indication of the numbers of objects presently entering the Museum's collections it is worth recording that more than 12,000 were received in 1978 alone.

The twentieth century has also seen the introduction of new departments in the Museum not specifically related to scholastic activities: the Conservation Department in 1960; Public Relations (now part of Museum Services) in 1964; the Design Section in 1968; Education in 1970; and the Exhibitions Section in 1975. Perhaps the most significant developments on the curatorial side to parallel these were the setting up of the Far Eastern Section in 1970, the confirmation of Bethnal Green as the Museum of Childhood in 1974, the closing of the Circulation Department in 1976, and the recognition of photography by its incorporation in the Department of Prints and Drawings, and Paintings in 1977. The establishment of the primary galleries after 1945 by the then Director, Sir Leigh Ashton, presented the greatest change in the public face of the Museum.

Ashton was fortunate to begin work with an almost empty building, for most of the collections had been moved to safety during the War. Present plans to redesign the primary galleries and include twentieth-century objects will not be achieved so easily. Indeed, there is the added problem now that much of the building is 'listed' and cannot, therefore, be altered. The cast courts have been successfully re-opened after a major programme of restoration, and the Department of Prints and Drawings, Paintings and Photographs has moved to the Henry Cole building (previously the Huxley building). It is to be hoped that it will not be long before a new restaurant opens in the basement of this building so that the present restaurant may be stripped out to reveal Sykes' brilliant South Court.

The long term is more difficult to assess. Decentralization for part of the collections must surely become necessary if the present rate of expansion continues. The artificiality of the barriers separating the V & A from the other national museums, in particular the Science and British Museums, is more than ever obvious. Even the practice of collecting in the art historical field (or is it the design field?) is being questioned. Art historians themselves point to the arbitrary nature of the present selection process, and social historians to many utilitarian and decorative objects not presently collected by the Museum, which popular consensus suggests deserve a place. Issues such as these have recently been brought sharply into focus by Sir Derek Rayner's report on the Museum. 'Devolution' from the Department of Education and Science, which he recommended, has resulted in the need to draw up specific aims and to accept wider financial responsibilities which have far-reaching implications for the public and private faces of the Museum.

Apsley House. The home of the Duke of Wellington, Apsley House was presented to the Nation in 1947. The house, which was originally designed by Robert Adam for Lord Bathurst, was much altered by Benjamin Dean Wyatt for the Duke of Wellington, who purchased it in 1817. It is situated at Hyde Park Corner.

Interior of the Museum of Childhood at Bethnal Green. The building first stood in South Kensington, where its utilitarian appearance caused it to be ridiculed as the 'Brompton Boilers'. It was moved to Bethnal Green in 1867 as a Museum of Science and Art for East London, and was recently re-named the Museum of Childhood.

The Shannongrove gorget   Eighth century B.C.
This is one of some ten whole or fragmentary 'gorgets' or gold neck ornaments which come from the region of the Lower Shannon in Ireland. On the basis of similar gold ornaments found in the Gorteenreagh hoard, it can be dated to approximately the eighth century B.C. The workmanship is of an exceptional standard, and the method of joining the main sheet to the terminal discs by means of tabs and slots, and punched decoration, particularly interesting. Stylistically, the gorget probably owes as much to South West European influences as to Danish and West Baltic sources.   M.35–1948

Early Medieval and Gothic (to 1485)

In spite of its somewhat confused and arbitrary development, the Victoria and Albert Museum has succeeded in accumulating a collection of British art which now ranks as the finest in the world. Although this chapter opens with a consideration of some objects which are very early in date, it should be stressed that the Museum's interests, unlike those of the British Museum, are mainly post-medieval.

The Roman occupation of Britain ended during the first half of the fifth century, and with the Romans' departure classical art, which so depended on the stability and inherent knowledge of their leisured and cultured classes, departed too. What skills the Romans did leave behind were largely lost when new invaders from Northern Germany and Denmark fought their way into the country. When it did come, the revival in the arts was largely a result of the influence of Christianity: St Patrick's arrival in Ireland in 432 and St Augustine's in Canterbury in 597 both preceded periods of new creative activity. This was further encouraged by the Synod of Whitby in 663 and the re-establishment of links with a Roman world which was by that time heavily influenced by the Near East. Few British objects in the Museum's collection date from this period, and the seventh-century brooch illustrated here is secular. The ninth-century cross from Easby Abbey, near Richmond in Yorkshire depicts another form of Anglo-Saxon ornament. The carvings on the shaft are an elegant testimony to the birth of the art of sculpture in Britain.

Most of the objects displayed in Gallery 43 date from after the Norman conquest. The influx of northern-European Romanesque culture which followed Harold's defeat in 1066, however, did not exert as much influence in the decorative arts as it did in sculpture and architecture. Scrolling foliate forms with birds and biting beasts such as appear on the pectoral cross reliquary and the Gloucester candlestick owe far more to Saxon and Norse than to Norman, Carolingian, or Byzantine influences.

A single manuscript leaf from a Canterbury Psalter reminds us that it was in the workshops around the great schools of manuscript illumination associated with Canterbury and the cathedrals of St Albans, Winchester, and elsewhere that most of the ivories and metalwork displayed in the medieval galleries were made. One exception is the outstanding small whalebone relief of the Adoration of the Magi, which does not relate obviously to any particular school. Small-scale sculpture which could be easily carried was widely imported at this time, and although the relief is presently ascribed to a southern English workshop, it is quite possible that research will show it was carved on the Continent.

In 1174 a fire destroyed Canterbury cathedral, and during the next ten years it was rebuilt by William of Sens in the Gothic style of his native Île-de-France. As a result, Canterbury became the first major English building in the Gothic style which the Victorians called 'Early English'. Other cathedrals quickly followed, and as patrons demanded more elaborate and dramatic effects, so Gothic progressed through the 'Decorated' stage to its culmination in the 'Perpendicular' of the fourteenth and fifteenth centuries. Quite apart from the introduction of a new decorative and sculptural vocabulary, one effect of Gothic was to increase the size of windows, a great stimulus to stained glass designers.

While most English art and architecture at this time involved the importation of craftsmen and ideas from the Continent, the trend was different for English embroidery, *Opus Anglicanum*. Indeed, it has been said that no English artistic product has ever achieved wider fame than the embroidery of the Middle Ages.

The great Vatican inventory of 1295 lists far more pieces of *Opus Anglicanum* than any other type of embroidery. The bulk of this work was carried out in professional workshops, mostly situated in the City of London, and it involved not just the use of silk and silver-gilt thread, but also large quantities of pearls and precious stones, so that the finished pieces were often of immense value.

Superb embroidery had earlier been produced during the Anglo-Saxon period, such as the Bayeux Tapestry, but very few pieces have survived. All those displayed in the Museum date from after the Norman conquest. Perhaps the best-known are the fourteenth-century Syon and Butler-Bowden Copes and the thirteenth-century Clare Chasuble. All three, like the Jesse and Steeple Aston Copes shown in the same area, have been much altered, for like so many articles of Church property, *Opus Anglicanum* was refashioned or destroyed during the Reformation. Pieces still retaining their pearls and precious stones are almost non-existent, and much that has survived was preserved in the homes of Catholic families for occasional domestic use.

Of medieval gold and silversmith's work the Museum possesses several outstanding examples. The Gloucester candlestick is undoubtedly the best known. In the same case is a beautiful reliquary cross of *c.* 1000 made of gold with applied filigree work and plaques of cloisonné enamel. The art of enamelling is of great antiquity. It was fostered particularly in Byzantine workshops and at Limoges, so that many early pieces, like the famous Alfred jewel in the Ashmolean Museum in Oxford, were almost certainly importations mounted in this country. The Valence casket and the Warwick and Balfour of Burleigh ciboria are later examples.

The Studley bowl is a rare secular survival, and indicates the sumptousness of the last decades of the fourteenth century, when Richard II's interest in the arts created a court unequalled in taste and talent. But the story of secular patronage belongs to that era after 1485 when the Tudors succeeded the Plantagenets, and, more particularly, to the period after the Reformation.

Anglo Saxon brooch   Seventh century
Diam. 7.6 mm
This is one of a pair of brooches which were found on the breast of a skeleton at Milton North Field, near Abingdon in about 1832. The other is in the Ashmolean Museum at Oxford. It is made of gold and silver foil with enamel and garnet inlay, on a backing of copper and composition. The style of the brooch bears resemblance to pieces from the Sutton Hoo ship burial uncovered in 1939 and now in the British Museum. The latter included more than twenty pieces of gold jewellery set with several thousand cut garnets in a similar technique. On the evidence of coins found with these pieces they can be dated with some certainty to A.D. 625–30.
M.109–1939

Pectoral cross reliquary   *c. 1100*   *H. 11.8 cm W. 4.4 cm D. 2.6 cm*
The box is made of walrus ivory, carved and pierced in low relief with
foliate scrolls, birds and monsters, an anchor probably representing
Ishmael, son of Abraham and Hagar, the *Agnus Dei*, and the symbols
of the Evangelists. Attention was first drawn to the cross in 1855
when it was exhibited by Nathaniel Gould at a meeting of the British
Archaeological Association. Nothing further was heard of it (and in
1962 it was published as lost) until 1966, when it was sent to
Sotheby's for auction by a Bournemouth antique dealer. The
decoration of the cross with interlaces of biting beasts caught in coils
of foliage and tendril, and small human forms enmeshed in scrolls
bears close comparison with Canterbury manuscripts, and it is
thought that it was probably carved in the same school.   A.6–1966

The Transfiguration   Late tenth century   *H. 14.2 cm W. 7.9 cm*
On the other side of this ivory plaque is a depiction of the Last
Judgement. The plaque and a companion piece with a representation
of the Ascension also in the Museum were catalogued for many years
as Carolingian and related to the Rheims school of the ninth century.
They are now thought, however, with a book cover in the Bibliothèque
Nationale, Paris, to be copied from Rheims manuscripts in this
country in the tenth and eleventh centuries. Such copying was
considered quite acceptable at this time, the famous Utrecht Psalter
being copied meticulously at Canterbury in about the year 1000.
253–1867

Head of a pastoral staff *c. 1180*   *H. 121 cm*
This crozier head, which is carved with scenes from the Life of Christ and Life of St Nicholas, is one of the finest examples of English ivory carving of the period. The original provenance of the crozier is not clear, but one may assume that it was made either for the head of an institution consecrated to St Nicholas or for an abbot or bishop of that name. The carving is one of the exceedingly rare examples of the use of elephant tusk in this country before the Gothic period.   218–1865

The Adoration of the Magi   Eleventh or twelfth century
H. 36 cm W. 16 cm
Various suggestions have been made as to the origin and dating of this beautiful whalebone relief. Although usually accepted as English, some authors have suggested that it may have been made in Ireland and others that the style of carving relates most closely to that from Northern France and Belgium. More recently it has been suggested that the relief could be of Spanish origin. In general style the Adoration shows a certain resemblance to some English manuscripts of the twelfth century, and the awe-inspiring quality of the majestic figure of the Virgin has been specifically likened to the great figures of the stooping Christ on the rather earlier outline drawing of the Harrowing of Hell in an English Psalter in the British Museum.   142–1866

The Gloucester candlestick Early
twelfth century *H. 58.4 cm W. at base
20.3 cm*
First modelled in wax, then cast in bell-metal
by the *cire-perdue* process, this candlestick is
a splendid example of the technical skill of
the craftsman in the early years of the twelfth
century. The inscription round the stem tells
that it was given by Peter, Abbot of Gloucester, to the church (now Cathedral) over
which he ruled from 1104 to 1113. It is
possible that the Gloucester Candlestick was
looted from the church when it was destroyed by fire in 1122; a medieval inscription inside the grease-pan states that it was
presented by one Thomas de Poche (perhaps
not long after that date) to the Cathedral of
Le Mans, where it remained until the
French Revolution. It reappeared in the
possession of an antiquary at Le Mans, who
sold it to Prince Soltikoff, on the dispersal of
whose collection in 1861, it was acquired by
the Museum.   7649–1861

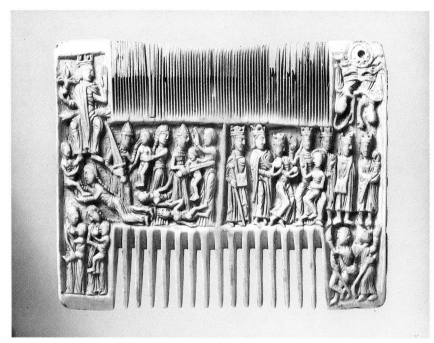

Liturgical comb *c. 1120 H. 7.5 cm W. 11.4 cm*
On one side the comb is carved with the Nativity, the Flight into Egypt, the Washing of the Feet of the Disciples, the last Supper, the Betrayal, the Crucifixion, and the Entombment; and on the other with the Massacre of the Innocents, the Adoration of the Magi, the Departure of the Magi, and the Annunciation to the Shepherds. The style of the carving compares closely with the historiated capital letters in the Psalter from St Albans, now at Hildesheim, which was completed before 1123. The comb of St Henry, now at Verdun, is also close in style and was probably produced in the same workshop.
A.27–1977

Leaf from a psalter *c. 1130–50*   ▷
H. 38 cm W. 26.7 cm
The forty-two pictures which cover both sides of the leaf illustrate the life of Christ from the Passion to Pentecost. It is one of four surviving leaves (the others are in the British Museum and in the Pierpoint Morgan Library, New York) which may have been part of the Eadwine Psalter, belonging to Trinity College, Cambridge, which was written at Canterbury in about 1147.   816–1894

The Warwick ciborium   Late twelfth century   *H. 120 cm Diam. 19.7 cm*
Copper gilt, engraved and enamelled, decorated with foliage enclosing figure subjects, representing various scenes from the Old Testament, including the Sacrifice of Cain and Abel, Moses and the burning bush, and Jonah issuing from the whale. The ciborium, which is missing its cover, was probably made in Winchester. There are no records of its whereabouts until 1717, when it was found in a brazier's shop in London. Later it entered the Warwick Castle Collection where it was burnt in the fire of 1871. It was probably as a result of this fire that much of the enamelling which originally decorated the ciborium was lost. Ciboria are receptacles used for the reservation of the Eucharist.   M.159–1919

The Valence casket 1290–6 *H. 9.5 cm L. 17.8 cm W. 13.3 cm*

The casket is made of copper engraved and gilt, decorated in champlevé enamel with a diaper of coats of arms representing William de Valence, Earl of Pembroke (d.1296), and some of his family connections, including the royal house of England, the Dukes of Brittany (Dreux), Angouleme, and Brabant, and Lacy, Earl of Lincoln. The marriage of Margaret of England with John, Duke of Brabant which accounts for the presence of his arms, took place in 1290. Four knobs are missing from the lid. Caskets such as this were probably used for the storage and safe keeping of jewellery and other small precious items.   4–1865

The Clare chasuble *c.* 1275 ▷
L. 115.6 cm W. 66 cm

Silver-gilt and silver thread and coloured silks in underside couching, split stitch and laid and couched work on satin. The vestment has been severely cut down in the post-medieval period. A stole and maniple with a shield of arms at each end, which were associated with the chasuble in 1786 but have since disappeared, were perhaps made of fragments from the original vestment; the remains of a similar shield (probably arms of Lacy) can be seen on the back of the chasuble. The coats of arms suggest that the work was commissioned by or for Margaret Clare, wife of Edmund Plantagenet, Earl of Cornwall, nephew to Henry III. Her marriage to the Earl, in 1272, remained childless, and she was divorced in 1294.   673–1864

Apparels of albs (detail) 1320–40 *H. 50.8 cm W. 81.3 cm*

The panel depicts the Nativity, the Annunciation, and the Three Kings, which are embroidered on velvet with coloured silks and silver-gilt and silver thread in split stitch, underside couching, laid and couched work, and raised work. The coats of arms are those of Bardolf and another family. Like the Butler-Bowden Cope, this panel is typical of that phase of *Opus Anglicanum* in which plain velvet grounds came into use, the embroidery being worked on them through a piece of thin cloth on which the design was drawn and which was laid on the pile surface to facilitate stitching.   8128–1863

Diptych   First half of the fourteenth century   *H. 21.6 cm W. 16 cm*
The ivory Diptych is carved in deeply sunk relief, on the left wing with
the Virgin and Child, and on the right with Christ blessing. The hair,
the borders of the garments, and the rosettes on the inner margin are
gilded and there are very slight traces of colour. Although the group of
the Virgin and Child is composed on typical French lines, the massive
and monumental style which characterizes the carving is not found in
French work of this period. Other details, such as the long faces with
high rounded foreheads, seem peculiarly English in style.   A.545–1910

Tile   Early fourteenth century   *L. 36 cm W. 20 cm*
The designs on this tile from Tring Church are taken from a
vernacular version of the Apocryphal Infancy Gospels describing the
miraculous childhood of Christ. The tile is an example of the so-
called *sgraffiato* technique, better known in pottery and fresco
decoration. Other tiles from the set are in the British Museum.
   C.470–1927

The John of Thanet panel   1300–20   *H. 100 cm W. 41.5 cm*
Embroidered with silver-gilt and silver thread, coloured silks and
pearls, in underside couching and split stitch, on silk twill. The figure
of Christ is on a larger scale than any other example of English
medieval embroidery. He is depicted enthroned, holding the orb of the
world. Above the arch is the inscription JOHANNIS DE THANETO. John
Thanet was 'a Monk and Chaunter' of Canterbury Cathedral 'well-
vers'd in the Mathematicks; but especially skilled in Musick' who died
aged 92 in 1330. The panel was probably originally part of a Cope, and
the triangular void at the top of the design was originally covered by the
cope-hood.   T.337–1921

The Ramsey Abbey censer   Second quarter of the fourteenth century   *H. 27.3 cm Diam. 14 cm*
This censer, the only example in silver-gilt of English workmanship of this date, was discovered in 1850 during the draining of Whittlesea Mere, Huntingdonshire. An incense boat and some pewter plates which were found with the censer include decoration in the form of a ram rising from the waves. This device is clearly a rebus for the name Ramsey and seems to indicate that the whole find was once the property of the neighbouring Abbey of Ramsey, unless it be supposed that the pieces bearing the rebus were gifts to the Abbey of Peterborough from the two abbots named Ramsey, who presided over it in the mid-fourteenth and late fifteenth century respectively.   M.268–1923

The Butler-Bowden cope (detail)
Second quarter of the fourteenth century
H. 162.8 cm W. 349 cm
Embroidered in silk, silver and silver-gilt
thread in underside-couching, split stitch,
and laid and couched work, on velvet; the
orphreys and hood of the cope, which are not
visible in this illustration, are of similar
materials and workmanship, on linen. The
cope was originally enriched with seed
pearls, of which only a few remain. Various
biblical scenes and saints and apostles are
depicted, of which this detail illustrates St
James the Great. The cope was cut up to
form another vestment but has now been
reassembled in its original form on a re-
placement velvet backing. T.36–1955

The Syon cope First quarter of the
fourteenth century *H. 142 cm W. 292 cm*
Silk, silver, and silver-gilt thread in underside-couching, split stitch and laid and
couched work on linen; the orphreys and a
morse which is associated with the cope are
of similar materials in underside-couching,
cross and plait stitches. In the quatrefoils are
depicted various apostles and biblical subjects. The cope was originally made as a
chasuble, and fragments of quatrefoils containing four other Apostles which were muti-
lated during conversion, are to be seen at the
sides. The spaces between the quatrefoils
are occupied by angels, except for two
figures of a cleric bearing the inscription
DAVN: PERS: DE . . . [?], for whom, presumably, the vestment was made. The cope was
formerly in the possession of nuns from the
Bridgettine Foundation of Henry v at Syon,
Middlesex. 83–1864

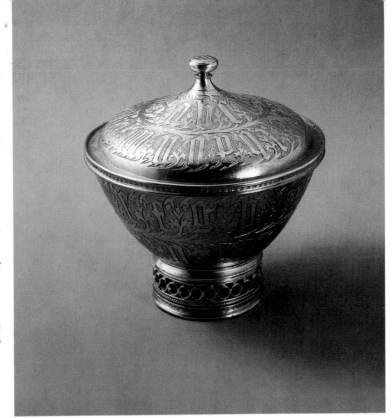

The Studley bowl Late fourteenth century *H. 14 cm Diam. 14.6 cm*
This covered bowl is the earliest piece of English domestic silversmith's work in the Museum. It was intended for porridge and similar foods, and was for a time the property of Studley Royal Church, near Ripon, Yorkshire. It is decorated with chased and engraved ornament, consisting, on each part, of a black-letter alphabet preceded by a cross and followed by various literal symbols and contractions such as were used in contemporary Latin manuscripts, all springing from a leafy wreath; on the knob of the cover is the letter 'a'.   M.1–1914

Stained glass window *c.* 1400
H. 354 cm W. 165 cm
This stained glass window is made up
from three lights showing St John the
Evangelist, the Prophet Zephaniah, and
St James the Less. It formed part of the
original glazing of Winchester College
Chapel put in by order of the founder,
William of Wykeham, about 1400. Between 1822 and 1828 the old glass was
replaced by modern copies in the process
of 'restoration'. It closely resembles the
slightly earlier glass still in the Chapel of
William of Wykeham's other foundation
at New College, Oxford, and is remarkable for the fine detail of the painting and
the silvery effect of the white glass beside
panes of soft, rich colour. The work was
done by the glazier Thomas of Oxford,
using sheet glass imported from Northern France. The elaborate style of the
canopies is superior to that found in any
English glass of the later fifteenth century.   4237–1855

Enamelled gold rosary *c.* 1500 Largest
bead *L. 2.8 cm Diam. 1.9 cm*
The single rounded bead bears four panels
engraved with the Adoration of the Magi,
and the remaining beads are each engraved
with two figure subjects, with titles round the
edge in black letter. Two of the beads are
inscribed in a cursive script and are of a later
date. This is the earliest English rosary to
have survived. When first acquired by the
Museum it was assembled in a different,
apparently haphazard form so far as the
saints were concerned, and two of the large
beads were attached as a pendant. The
present arrangement corresponds with at
least one example of a rosary illustrated on a
medieval brass.   M.30–1934

The Swinburne pyx *c.* 1320   *H. 2.8 cm*
Diam. 5.7 cm
A pyx is a small vessel, usually a round silver
box, in which the Sacrament is carried to the
sick. This example is made of parcel gilt and
was originally decorated with enamel, which
has since come off. The two subjects on the
cover of the pyx are copied from the arche-
type used for two manuscripts at Cambridge.
Interestingly, it is possible to connect genea-
logically the original owner of one of these
manuscripts, Alice de Reydon, *née* Reymes,
with ancestors of the Swinburnes of Pontop,
near Consett, to whom the pyx had belonged. The Museum purchased it from the
widow of the last remaining member of the
family.   M.15–1950

▽ **The Swansea altarpiece** Second half of the fifteenth century *H. 84 cm L. 213 cm* The altarpiece, which includes alabaster reliefs representing St John the Baptist, the Annunciation, the Nativity, the Holy Trinity, the Ascension, the Assumption, and St John in a framework of oak, was formerly in the collection of Lord Swansea at Singleton Abbey. Although a number of English alabaster altarpieces with the original wooden housing exist in France and Italy, this is the only one in Great Britain. The Museum has a large and comprehensive collection of English alabasters, many of which are on display. A.89–1919

Stained glass panels depicting cutting vines and harvesting corn   First half of the fifteenth century   *Diam. 20.3 cm*
These two panels are from a set of six in the Museum which depict the Labours of the Months. That showing a man cutting vines represents March and that depicting a man and woman reaping, August. Such subjects were popular for secular rather than church use at the time, and a number of sets are known, though most, like the Museum's, are incomplete. It has been suggested that the roundels may be Netherlandish, but the favour such series enjoyed in this country, the presence of one depicting Weeding (a subject which does not occur in contemporary continental manuscripts illustrating the months), and the character of the painting all point to an English origin. The roundels were formerly at Cassiobury Park, Hertford-shire.   C.123–126–1923

Alabaster relief of the Tree of Jesse   Early fifteenth century   *H. 53.5 cm W. 28 cm*
Jesse is depicted on his right side, while from his breast the Tree or vine issues upward, the tendrils enclosing figures of Kings, maternal ancestors of Christ, and prophets who foretold his coming. In the centre of the upper part of the panel are the Virgin and Child enthroned. In the fourteenth and fifteenth centuries alabaster quarries were opened in Derbyshire, Staffordshire, and Nottinghamshire and centres of carving sprang up also in Lincoln and York. The material was much easier to carve than stone or wood and found a wide range of applications for ecclesiastical purposes.   A.36–1954

Bust of Henry VII perhaps by Pietro Torrigiano (1472–1528)   First quarter of the sixteenth
century   *H. 91.4 cm W. 68.6 cm D. 35.6 cm*
The bust, which is made of painted and gilded terracotta, is life-size and shows the King late
in life. Its attribution to Torrigiano, which was first suggested in the eighteenth century, is
based not simply on comparison with that sculptor's known works, but also on the fact that the
bust bears a very strong resemblance to the figure on the bronze monument to Henry VII in
Westminster Abbey, which Torrigiano executed between 1511–17. The bust was formerly
associated with two others of Bishop Fisher and Henry VIII at Hatfield Peverell Priory, and
all three are said to have come from the Palace of Whitehall. It has also been conjectured that
they were commissioned by the Countess of Richmond, and that they were repaired by the
young John Flaxman in about 1769.   A.49–1935

Tudor (1485–1603)

Thomas Cromwell's fate, an earldom in April 1540 and a death sentence four months later, epitomizes the political and social uncertainty of Tudor England. New industries and fluctuating trade, coupled with outbursts of unrest at home and the successes and failures of an expansionist policy overseas, all led to a profound sense of instability. Yet the excitement, fragility, and tension which this created acted rather as a stimulant than a repressant to artists, writers, and craftsmen. It was, after all, the age which saw the supreme literary achievement of Shakespeare and the brilliant portraiture of Holbein and Hilliard.

Much of the story of Tudor decorative art has to do with the varying degrees by which it was influenced by classical canons of taste emanating from Italy and northern Europe. Interestingly, although Renaissance and other forms were freely adopted by craftsmen in this country, their work still retains an undeniably English quality. In architecture, for example, symmetry of plan and other classical concepts which were in common usage by the end of the century generally failed to impart a 'High Renaissance' quality. The effect of traditional elements asserted itself instead, even in houses such as Hardwick Hall, the design of which involved a great deal of classical thought.

The somewhat austere exterior of Hardwick, like that of many Tudor houses, contrasts strongly with the lavish interior with its elaborate plasterwork, panelling, painted decoration, and textile hangings. The design of these was based at first on naturalistic and geometric sources, such as had inspired medieval craftsmen, but these soon gave way to an increasing use of 'antique work'—the commoner Renaissance motifs—and strapwork and arabesque designs. The Museum's room from Sizergh Castle in Westmorland which was completed some time before 1582 reveals how widespread these designs became. The oak panelling is inlaid with arabesque patterns, now rather faded and discoloured with polish but clearly indicating their former splendour. The protruding porch is based on Flemish models and may be a little earlier in date.

In this and the adjoining gallery are displayed many examples of contemporary furniture: an oak bench dated 1562; an elmwood box with inlaid decoration in maple and other woods depicting flowers, birds, and figures resembling contemporary embroidery designs, which was probably used for storing small articles of clothing; a cupboard of typical form and decoration from the Moffat Collection; and a so-called 'Nonsuch' chest with elaborate inlay depicting buildings.

In the last of the Tudor galleries is that most famous of all beds, the Great Bed of Ware, and, next to it, examples of different tablewares including sets of beechwood roundels which were used as trenchers for the last course of a dinner, consisting of marzipan and other sweetmeats. A painted plaster frieze from Stodmarsh Court near Canterbury, with figures representing the planets after engravings by Virgil Solis of Nuremberg, dates from c.1600 and serves as a reminder both of the importance of Continental source books and the popularity of bright painted decoration at this time. A rather false impression is conveyed by the present appearance of most movable furniture of this date. Although painting was unpopular in the fifteenth and early sixteenth centuries, it did undergo a revival after 1530 or so, and remained fashionable until upholstery in textiles became general at the close of the century.

Much Tudor plate was acquired as a means of storing wealth and was consequently sold in times of need. Since its value was assessed by weight, many pieces were melted down so as to be remade in more fashionable forms, and as a result much has disappeared. The Museum's mounted Cologne stoneware and oriental jugs, and the Howard Grace cup of 1525–6 have probably survived because they contain relatively little precious metal. Other pieces like the Richard Chester steeple cup of 1625–6, the Mostyn salt, or the less pretentious snuffers with the arms and initials of Edward VI have probably survived because of their intrinsic value.

One gallery is largely given over to textiles. Whereas most of those discussed in Chapter 1 were made for ecclesiastical use, after the Reformation weavers and embroiderers applied themselves instead to the elaboration of their clothes and homes. Walls were hung with tapestries or embroidered or painted hangings; beds were equipped with lavish sets of curtains and valances; tables and cupboards laid with cloths and carpets; and wooden chairs and benches covered with loose cushions. While some of these textiles were woven, most were embroidered. Indeed, during the Elizabethan period the work of amateurs assumed for the first time an equal importance with that of professionals.

Most of the formal court costumes lavishly embroidered with metal thread and jewels have now vanished. Some idea of their splendour can be gained from the Museum's superb collection of contemporary miniatures by Hans Holbein, Nicholas Hilliard, and Isaac Oliver. To these has recently been added Rowland Lockey's miniature of Thomas More and his family of *c.* 1600. What is so appealing about these miniatures is not just their refreshing naturalism, but their insistence on individual character as reflected by external appearance. They foreshadow the greater freedom both of expression and emotional content which typifies not just miniature painting but all the arts during the next era.

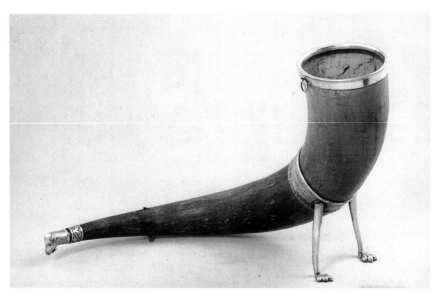

The Pusey horn   Mid fifteenth century
H. 25.4 cm W. 44.5 cm
Only five medieval drinking horns are known to have survived. Unlike earlier examples they are equipped with feet so that they could be set down, and the small end of the horn is finished with a head, sometimes that of a man or, as in this example, of a monster. The Museum's horn, which was mounted in the fifteenth century, is said to have been given by King Canut to William Pusey, together with the Manor of that name, as a reward for having saved him from a surprise attack by the Saxons, and an inscription on the silver band testifies to this.   M.220–1938

Monument to Sir Thomas Moyle (d. 1560) **and his wife Katherine** (d. after 1560)   About 1560   *H. 115.6 cm L. 217.2 cm W. 116.8 cm*
This monument is one of the most important of several acquired by the Museum from the ruined church of St Mary, Eastwell, Kent. Sir Thomas Moyle was the grandfather of Sir Moyle Finch and great-grandfather of Sir Heneage Finch. It was to Sir Heneage that Queen Elizabeth I is recorded to have presented the Armada Jewel (see p. 35). The stone of which the monument is constructed must have been formerly used in a building, since inside the tomb-chest are quatrefoil decoration, arch mouldings, and part of a window-transom. The church of St Mary at Eastwell had badly deteriorated by the end of the War, and in 1951 a gale blew down part of the nave roof. Every effort was made to find a home for the monuments, but without success, and during 1967–8 they were brought up to London and installed in the Museum.

A.187–1969

31

Close helmet   *c.* 1540   *H. 25.4 cm W. 28 cm*

This helmet was acquired by the Museum as part of a composite half-armour of mainly German provenance. The profile of the helmet is, however, unmistakably that of the Royal armourers' workshops established by Henry VIII within the precincts of the Royal Palace at Greenwich. The visor resembles in form that in the Genouilhac armour of 1527 in the Metropolitan Museum of Art, New York, but the slightly higher comb indicates a later date. There is a Greenwich helmet of similar form in Croydon Parish Church.   M.504–1927

Table desk   *c.* 1525   *H. 25 cm W. 40.6 cm D. 29 cm*

This highly ornate and important table desk, covered with painted and gilt leather, bears the heraldic badges of Henry VIII and Katherine of Aragon—the Portcullis, the Tudor Rose, the impaled Rose and Pomegranate, the Fleur-de-lis, the Castle (with cypher H. R.), and the Sheaf of Arrows. On the inner lid are painted the Royal Arms encircled by the garter, with boys blowing trumpets as supporters. On either side, standing beneath canopies, are figures of Mars in armour and Venus with Cupid, the design being executed with great spirit after woodcuts (*c.* 1510) by Hans Burgkmair, the celebrated German engraver. Such desks were introduced into England in the early Tudor period and used for the storage of scissors, penknives, and other small items.   W.29–1932

The Mostyn salt 1586–7. *H. 47 cm*
D. 18.4 cm
This is the most notable of the small group
of pieces of Elizabethan plate which the
Museum acquired from the ancient Welsh
family of Mostyn in 1886. From the Middle
Ages to the 1650s the great salt marked the
place of the host at the dining table, and the
present piece is a very fine example of one of
the standard designs of the second half of the
sixteenth century. The cylindrical body is
richly embossed with strapwork, cartouches,
masks, fruit, etc., whilst the cover is surmounted by a vase, which must have originally contained flowers. It bears the Goldsmith's mark 'T' in a pearled border and a
London hallmark for 1586–7.   146–1886

Glass attributed to Giacomo
Verzelini 1581 *H. 20.6 cm*
Giacomo Verzelini was the leader of a party
of nine Italian glass makers who settled in a
glass house in Crutched Friars in London in
1571. Born in Venice, Verzelini acquired the
royal privilege as sole producer of 'Venice
Glasses' in 1575, and kept it until his
retirement twenty-one years later. During
this time he not only established himself as
the foremost glass manufacturer in the country, but also established a rather less elaborate form of Venetian design which was to
dominate English glass design for the next
one hundred years.   C.523–1936

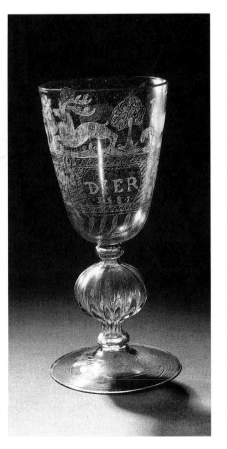

The Bradford table carpet (detail)   Late sixteenth century   *L. 396 cm W. 175 cm.*
Embroidery on linen canvas in tent stitch or varieties of cross stitch first came into prominence during the Elizabethan period and was much used for furnishing purposes. The subject-matter often reflected the Elizabethan's delight in gardens and the countryside, and motifs abstracted from these sources were frequently made into patterns of a formal type, such as the exuberant vine twined around a trellis in this table carpet. Typical country views with shepherds, hunting scenes, and anglers, such as form a border to the carpet, were also

Miniature portrait of Margaret Pemberton by Hans Holbein (1497?–1543)   *c.* 1536   *Diam. 5.2 cm*
The sitter can be identified by the coat of arms of her husband Robert Pemberton, which is painted on vellum on the back. The inscription in gold on the background indicates that she was twenty-three years old when the portrait was painted. Barely a dozen miniatures are now accepted as being by Holbein and it is generally agreed that this is the finest.   P.40–1935

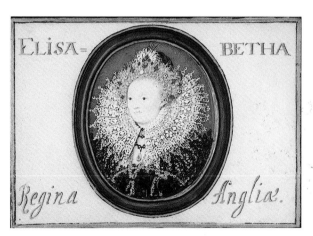

Miniature portrait of Queen Elizabeth I by Nicholas Hilliard (1547–1619)   *c.* 1588   *H. 4.4 cm*
This is the earliest portrait of Elizabeth I in the collection and belongs to a group of miniatures and large-scale portraits which all seem to derive from the same face-mask. In the Queen's hair is a crescent-moon-shaped jewel, the earliest allusion in miniatures to the cult of Elizabeth as the moon goddess, Diana or Cynthia, which was to become the dominant reference in miniatures at the close of the reign. The mount appears to be late seventeenth century.   P.23–1975

popular. Like oriental rugs, many embroidered carpets were considered too precious to risk damage on the floor at this time and were placed over tables instead. This carpet came from the collection of the Earl of Bradford.

T.134–1928

The Danny jewel Second half sixteenth century *L. (with chains) 8.9 cm W. 6 cm*
The jewel is in the form of a pendant and is made from a half section of a narwhal's tusk mounted in enamelled gold. At the top is a cavity which was probably intended for a charm. Narwhal's tusk, or 'unicorn's horn' as it was sometimes referred to, was itself considered a protection against bad luck and poisoning. A pendant pearl probably hung originally from the bottom. The jewel was formerly the property of the Campions of Danny, Sussex. A similar jewel is depicted in Zucchero's portrait of Robert Bristowe, purse-bearer to Queen Elizabeth I; and another made of 'golde' set with 'unicornes horne' is referred to in the will of Edward Lyttelton of Longford, Salop.

M.97–1917

The Armada jewel *c.* 1600 *H. 7 cm*
Enamelled gold set with diamonds and rubies. Under a convex glass on the front is a high-relief profile bust of Queen Elizabeth I, and the back forms a locket enclosing a miniature painting of the Queen dated 1580 by Nicholas Hilliard. This masterpiece of fine casting, the beauty of which is enhanced by its background of blue translucent enamel, appears to have been a gift of the Queen to Sir Thomas Heneage in reward of his services as Treasurer-at-War at the time of the Armada.

M.81–1935

35

**Miniature portrait of a lady called Frances, Countess of
Somerset** (1590–1632) by Isaac Oliver   (d. 1617)   *Diam. 13 cm*
Isaac Oliver was born in France but was brought to England while
still a child, and in 1606 became a British citizen. He received his
early training under Nicholas Hilliard, but amplified this with visits to
the Low Countries and to Venice. This miniature is typical of
Oliver's best work, in which he combines the ambitious ideas of scale
and complexity which he picked up on the Continent, with the
tradition of the portrait miniature he learned from Hilliard. It was
formerly in the possession of Horace Walpole, who inscribed a paper
label on the back of the frame with the name of the sitter.   P.12–1971

Bag and pincushion   First quarter seventeenth century   ▷
Bag 14 × 11.4 cm Pincushion 6.4 × 5.4 cm
Linen canvas embroidered with silver thread and silk in tent and
plaited Gobelin stitches, lined with green silk. Embroidery was a
popular art in the sixteenth and seventeenth centuries, many of the
patterns deriving from illuminated manuscripts, particularly that
involving coiled tendrils infilled with flowers, birds, animals, and
insects which appears on many examples of Elizabethan costume in
the Museum's collection. Bags with attached pincushions such as this
were hung at the waist.   316–1898

The Barbor jewel Second half sixteenth century *L. 6 cm W. 3.2 cm*
The jewel is made of enamelled gold, set with rubies and diamonds enclosing an onyx cameo of Queen Elizabeth I; and hung with a cluster of pearls. On the back is an enamelled oak tree. According to Fox's *Book of Martyrs*, William Barbor of London (d. 1586) 'for his firm adherence to the Protestant Religion was to suffer at the Stake . . . News came the Queen was dead, so that Popish party did not dare to put him to Death. In Remembrance of so Eminent a preservation . . . [he] had the effigies of Queen Elizabeth cut out upon stone; bequeathing the jewel to his elder Son, if he had a daughter and names her Elizabeth'.

889–1894

An unknown youth leaning against a tree by Nicholas Hilliard (1546–1619) *c.* 1588 *H. 13.4 cm W. 7 cm*
In this full-length portrait, the love-sick pose and the symbolisms of the thorn-bearing rose-tree are underlined by the Latin inscription at the top of the miniature, *Dat poenas laudata fides* ('My praised faith causes my sufferings'). The identity of the sitter and the cause of his melancholy are not recorded, but since Hilliard was a favourite of Elizabeth, it may depict a member of her intimate circle.

P.163–1910

Clock 1588 *H. 33 cm W. 16.7 cm*
This is the earliest known dated English clock. The case is of gilt brass and is inscribed 'Frauncoy Nowe fecit a London A°Din°
1588'. The engraved decoration is probably based on designs by Etienne de Laune and Abraham de Bruyn and is very similar to
that on the Magdalen Cup in the Manchester City Art Gallery, which bears the London Hallmark for 1573–4. The astronomical
dials which are shown separately indicate the date, the astrological indication, the phases and age of the moon, and the times of
high tide at London Bridge. The thirty hour, three chain movement, the hour and quarter bells, and the twenty-four hour
chapter ring are all of late seventeenth century date. Although Francis Nowe set up his workshops in London, he was born in
Brabant.

M.39–1959

The Vyvyan salt 1592–3   *H. 34 cm*
D. 40 cm

The Vyvyan Salt, so named from its having
been for over 250 years in the possession of
the Vyvyans of Trelowarren, Cornwall, is
among the most important pieces of English
sixteenth-century silversmiths' work in existence. The great attraction of the Salt lies in
the panels and small medallions of *verre
églomisé* (glass decorated at the back with foil
and colours) based on designs in Geoffrey
Whitney's *Choice of Emblems*, published in
1586; the medallions bear heads of Ninus,
Cyrus, Alexander, and Julius Caesar. It was
made by a goldsmith who used a mark
consisting of the letters WH and a flower,
the London Hallmark for 1592–3 is repeated on the body, the foot, and the
cover.   M.273–1925

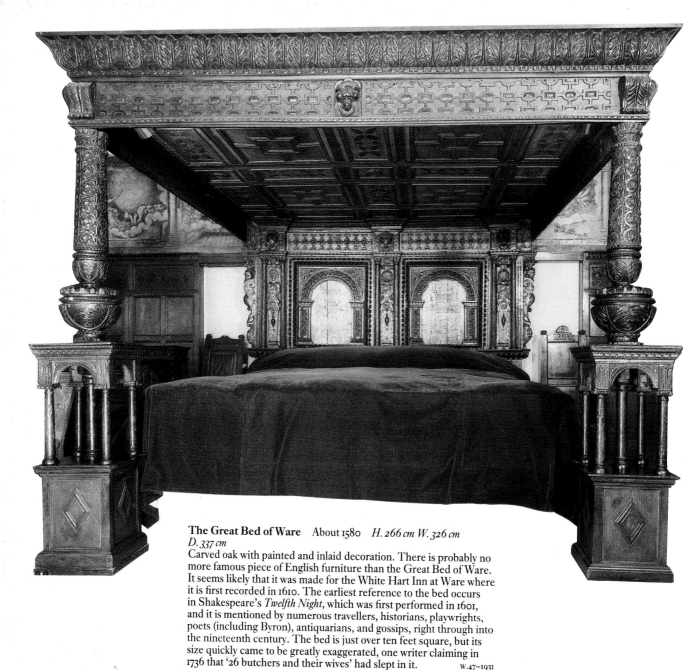

The Great Bed of Ware   About 1580   *H. 266 cm W. 326 cm D. 337 cm*
Carved oak with painted and inlaid decoration. There is probably no
more famous piece of English furniture than the Great Bed of Ware.
It seems likely that it was made for the White Hart Inn at Ware where
it is first recorded in 1610. The earliest reference to the bed occurs
in Shakespeare's *Twelfth Night*, which was first performed in 1601,
and it is mentioned by numerous travellers, historians, playwrights,
poets (including Byron), antiquarians, and gossips, right through into
the nineteenth century. The bed is just over ten feet square, but its
size quickly came to be greatly exaggerated, one writer claiming in
1736 that '26 butchers and their wives' had slept in it.   W.47–1931

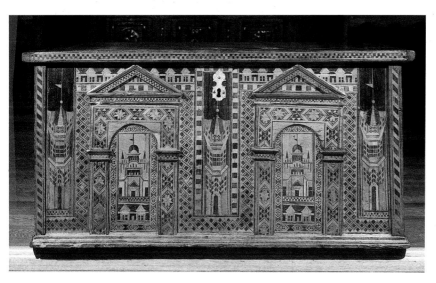

Coffer   Late sixteenth century
H. 58.4 cm W. 123 cm D. 58.4 cm
Oak with marquetry of bog and cherry-
wood. The name 'Nonsuch' or 'Nonesuch'
is often given to early inlaid chests of this type,
in which the design of the inlay is architectural in character and represents a quaint
building with castellations, high-pitched
roofs, cupolas and steeples set with vanes,
and flying flags. It probably derives from
Nonsuch or Nonesuch Palace, which was
built by Henry VIII at Ewell in Surrey, and
so-called as being without equal, although it
has also been suggested that the term may
derive from Nonsuch House on London
Bridge. In point of fact there is no reason to
suppose that either of these buildings is
represented rather than any other typical
Tudor or Elizabethan House.   342–1905

The Oxburgh hangings (detail)   *c.* 1570   *H. 84 cm W. 91 cm*
The Museum was very fortunate to acquire in 1955 thirty-nine panels embroidered by Mary, Queen of Scots and Elizabeth, Countess of Shrewsbury. This detail of the central panel of a hanging depicts feathers falling around an armillary sphere and is inscribed with a motto which translated means 'Sorrows pass but hope abides'. In the border are the arms of England, Scotland, France, and Spain and emblems copied from Claude Paradin *Devises Heroïques*, Lyon, 1557. The embroidery is in coloured silks and silver-gilt thread in cross, tent and long-armed cross stitches on canvas and is applied to green velvet.

T.33–1955

41

The Bostocke sampler 1598 *W. 35.6 cm L. 42.5 cm*
This sampler of linen embroidered in coloured silks, metal
thread, seed pearls, and black beads is the earliest dated
sampler so far recorded. It is called after Jane Bostocke, the
embroideress whose name appears one-third of the way down
with the alphabet. The stitches used include back, Algerian
eye, satin, arrowhead, chain, ladder, button hole, and detached button-hole fillings, couching in patterns, coral, speck-
ling, two-sided Italian cross, bullion, and French knots and
beadwork. It is possible that three small animals were
unpicked, or that the stitching has simply worn away. The
Museum's collection of textiles includes numerous samplers,
many of which can be seen in the Textile Study Rooms.

T.190–1960

Panel from a tapestry map by William Sheldon *c.* 1588
L. 126.4 cm W. 65.4 cm
This panel and another also in the Museum originally formed
part of the lower right-hand corner of a map of Oxfordshire
and Berkshire. Both pieces were formerly in the collection of
Horace Walpole and are recorded in the Strawberry Hill Sale
catalogue of 1842. There the figures depicted in the border of
this panel are described as Anthony and Cleopatra, but it is,
perhaps, more likely that they represent Temperance with
either Perseus or Mercury. William Sheldon was the first
person to establish Tapestry weaving on a commercial basis in
this country. A country gentleman of the Midlands who made
a fortune in the wool trade, he expressly stated in his will that
his aim was to provide work for the unemployed and to keep in
the country money that would otherwise be spent in buying
tapestries abroad. T.61–1954

Tapestry cushion-cover *c.* 1600
H. 45.7 cm W. 48.3 cm
This charming and simple cushion-cover, which depicts the Flight into Egypt, was also made in William Sheldon's workshop. The purity of colour and fine technique and sympathetic treatment of the animals and flowers are characteristic of the art of the period. William Sheldon's weavers under Richard Huckes, who died in 1621 aged 97, and his son Francis produced many magnificent works, and it must have been particularly upsetting for them when the official order for a set of tapestries to commemorate the Armada went to Holland. The workshops, which closed down in 1647, were situated at Barcheston in Warwickshire in a farm building which still survives. Another similar cushion-cover is also in the Museum's collection (T.85–1913). T.191–1926

Gamecock salt *c.* 1570–80 *H. 26.7 cm L. 14 cm W. 8.3 cm*
The salt is made from a Nautilus shell mounted in silver gilt. The head unscrews to form a caster and the lower part of the neck acts as a container, presumably for spices. The salt was held in a silver gilt container fitted into the shell. *Nautilus pompilus* was first caught for food, but by the sixteenth century the Chinese had begun to carve the shell. During the early seventeenth century, Amboyna, where many nautilus were caught, had become one of the trading posts of the Dutch East India Company, and shells were brought back to Europe. They were still considered very rare and precious, however, and were frequently mounted in gold and silver. The Museum's example bears no hallmarks but is typical Elizabethan work of the period 1570–80. M.13–1969

Earthenware dish depicting the Fall   1635   *Diam. 48.3 cm*

The last part of the fifteenth century and the early sixteenth century saw the rise in Italy of the manufacture of tin-enamelled pottery painted in bright colours, which is called maiolica. The pottery quickly spread throughout Europe and acquired distinct national schools of decoration. In the North the Netherlandish cities of Antwerp and Delft became the centres of manufacture specializing particularly in blue-and-white wares, and it was from there that the craft moved to England. The first centres of manufacture here were on the Thames at Lambeth, Southwark, and Bermondsey. The earliest dated piece is a dish of 1601 in the London Museum. This is very much in the Dutch style, whereas the Museum's dish, which is dated 1635, is similar to another in the British Museum and represents a less-accomplished and characteristically English version of this style. Such big dishes, archaistically named 'chargers', were used primarily to decorate sideboards or chimney pieces. Later their manufacture also spread to Bristol and Liverpool. Many were decorated with blue stripes around their rims in imitation of Delft plates, hence the description 'blue dash chargers'.

C.26–1931

Jacobean (1603–1715)

Just as the arts of the Elizabethan age had been marked by a growing awareness of the Italian and northern European Renaissance, so the dominant theme of the Jacobean period was the influence upon it of other cultures. Initially, however, there was little indication of impending change. James I, Jacobus, after whom the era is named, did bring with him a Scottish court, but this had little impact on the simple, essentially domestic community of the Tudor age. Solid, useful pieces of furniture such as long tables, press cupboards, and settles; silver influenced by German sheets of designs; lead glazed earthenware; and tent-stitch embroidery on canvas continued to be popular.

By the second quarter of the century, increasing wealth from foreign trade began to show itself, particularly by the large number of houses which were either rebuilt or remodelled. These, following the example set by Inigo Jones at Queen's House, had more and smaller rooms than their Tudor counterparts, and consequently required different furnishings. For example, although some large pieces of plate continued to be made for decorative purposes, the great salt and elaborate cups gave way to smaller, more personal items, and silver became more popular than gold. Similarly, in ceramics the large tin glazed earthenware or Delftware dishes were intended for display, whilst smaller pieces were made for daily use.

Stylistically the arts of the Low Countries and of France became more influential at this time, stimulated not just by Charles I's marriage to Henrietta Maria of France, but also by his encouragement of Rubens, Van Dyck, and many other distinguished foreign artists who came to work in Britain. Charles also acquired many important works of art from abroad, the best known of which are undoubtedly the famous cartoons by Raphael depicting the Acts of the Apostles, now on loan to the Museum from Her Majesty The Queen. The influence of the cartoons, as the design of the interior of Ham House indicates, was considerable.

Foreign influence was further encouraged after the Restoration in 1660. Charles II and his supporters had spent much of their exile in France and Holland, and as a consequence their taste had shifted away from the Italianism of Inigo Jones. Hugh May's 'Dutch' Eltham Lodge, and William Talman's Chatsworth, influenced by Versailles, both set new architectural standards, out of which the great Baroque buildings such as Castle Howard and Blenheim by Vanbrugh and his contemporaries later evolved. At the same time Wren was introducing Baroque features derived from Continental sources in his London churches, the rebuilding of many of which was made necessary by the Great Fire of 1666.

In the applied arts these sympathies were reflected not just by changes of style and form, but also by the introduction of new materials and techniques. For example, walnut was first extensively used for furniture during the reign of Charles II, when veneering was introduced and caning and gilding were practised for the first time. The naturalistic designs found in marquetry cabinets and other pieces of furniture, like the carvings of Grinling Gibbons, reflect the influence of contemporary Dutch still life painting. One important new piece of furniture introduced at this time is illustrated by the bookcase with glazed doors, which is seen to be very similar to those in the Pepys Library at Magdalene College, Cambridge.

A silver dressing-table set chased with scenes copied from Chinese prints serves as a reminder that the Dutch East India Company was responsible for introducing many Oriental objects to the West. Porcelain was particularly popular. Some pieces had reached this country in the sixteenth century, but it was not until after 1618 that they were imported in any quantity. Some large pieces were mounted in silver for decorative purposes in continuance of the earlier tradition, but many smaller wares, particularly bowls and dishes, were used especially for the drinking of tea. Like coffee 'black as soote, and tasting not much unlike it', as one contemporary writer remarked, tea seems to have been introduced here during the Restoration. The fine earthenwares of Dwight and the Elers Brothers based on these Oriental pieces represent the first serious attempts to imitate porcelain in this country. Another facet of Oriental influence was the vogue for lacquered screens and panels, frequently mounted as doors and fronts to cabinets, which resulted in the establishment of an English school of lacquering. Several japanned cabinets mounted on elaborate carved and sometimes silvered stands are shown in the Primary Galleries.

The dominant theme of the closing decades of the Stuart era was the influence of the large influx of Huguenot craftsmen who settled in this country. Not only were many industries revitalized as a result, like that of silk weaving at Spitalfields, but Huguenot styles gradually replaced the Dutch designs and were consequently largely responsible for the appearance of what is now called the 'Queen Anne Style'. Most influential of the designers was probably Daniel Marot, who followed William of Orange to this country in 1694 and was employed by the King at Hampton Court. His sheets of printed designs published in 1702 and 1712 were widely copied and adapted by British craftsmen. Other Huguenot craftsmen, like the silversmiths Paul Platel, and Paul de Lamerie, who settled in London with his parents in 1691, introduced radically new forms based to a large extent on the earlier ornament of Du Cerceau, Jean Berain, and Jean le Pautre, which were to prove particularly influential in the Georgian era.

The Betley window (detail) *c. 1621 H. 67.3 cm W. 39.4 cm*
This panel of painted glass depicting Morris dancers and figures from the Robin Hood games celebrating a 'Mery May' derives its name from Betley Old Hall in Staffordshire, where it first came to light in a room bearing the date 1621. Although the figures of the six dancers, one of which is illustrated here, and the musician are based on a print by Israhel Van Meckenham of about 1460–70, the clothes they wear are typical of a period some 30 or 40 years later. But enamel colours in which the pictures are painted were not in use until the mid sixteenth century, and it is likely that the panel was executed in about 1621, the date when Betley Old Hall seems to have been built.   C.248–1976

The Calverley toilet service   1683–4   *Mirror H. 57.2 cm W. 37.5 cm*
Although Renaissance inventories show that ladies already possessed a number of silver toilet utensils, the manufacture of whole sets does not seem to have begun before the Restoration. When such services ceased to be appreciated, they were generally broken up and dispersed so that there are now very few surviving sets which are nearly complete. The Museum's set, which was once the property of the Calverley family of Yorkshire, includes only a dozen pieces, whereas a set in the Farrer Collection includes twenty-eight pieces.   240–to 240m–1879

Mermaid ewer and basin   1610–11.   *Ewer H. 31.1 cm L. 21 cm. Basin H. 43.8 cm W. 45.3 cm D. 9.5 cm*
The ewer and basin had no provenance until 1928, when it was illustrated in a short article in *Old Furniture*. Escutcheons on the chest of the mermaid and in the centre of the scallop-shaped basin are engraved with the armorials of Sir Thomas Wilson (*c.* 1560–1619), author and Italian scholar, who was a protegé of the Cecils, and prosecutor of Sir Walter Raleigh. Ewers and basins were used by diners to wash their hands before a meal. Although originally introduced before the popularization of forks made eating with the fingers unnecessary, they continued to be made until the early eighteenth century.   M.10 and a–1974

Watch *c.* 1640–50 *H. 11.7 cm W. 9.3 cm*
This watch was made by Edward East, who held the appointment of watchmaker to Charles I and has been described as the most famous maker of his time. He was one of the original assistants of the Clockmaker's Company, named in its Charter of Incorporation in 1632, and became Master of the Company in 1645 and again in 1652. The existence of a number of watches bearing the name 'Edwardus East Londini', or similar, which are stylistically of dates in the third quarter of the century, has led to the supposition that there may have been a father and son of the same name.   M.64–1952

Tapestry depicting Hero and Leander First half of the seventeenth century *H. 426.7 cm L. 548.6 cm*
Hero is represented mourning over the dead body of Leander. This tapestry is one of a set of six representing the history of Hero and Leander which were made at the tapestry workshops inaugurated at Mortlake by James I in 1619. The cartoons for the series were designed by Francis Clein, a native of Mecklenburg and former court-painter of Christian IV of Denmark, who was artistic director of the factory until his death in 1658. In the bottom right hand corner is the mark of Sir Francis Crane, who was appointed first Director of the factory and remained so until 1636. The factory was closed down in 1703. Other Mortlake sets of Hero and Leander woven after the same designs are in the Swedish Royal Collection at Stockholm and at Hardwick Hall.   T.370–1910

Carpet (detail) 1672 *H. 348 cm × 233.7 cm*

The Museum possesses two remarkable English seventeenth-century carpets, both of which bear dates. The earlier (710–1904) is inscribed 'Feare God and Keepe His Commandements Made in the Yeare 1603', and the later, of which this is a detail, bears a shield containing the arms of Molyneux and Rigby and the date 1672. Both are made with woollen piles and Turkish knots. Although attempts were made to introduce the craft of carpet-knotting into this country at least as early as 1579, when it was proposed to bring over some Persian carpet weavers, the commercial production of carpets did not get under way here until the eighteenth century. Previously, knotted textiles, sometime called turkey work, tended to be made on a small scale for chair backs and seats, etc., rather than as carpets.

T.132–1924

Embroidered miniature of Charles I *c.* 1640–50 *H. 10.2 cm*
W. 11 cm
A number of small needlework portraits of Charles I such as this are
known. They show skill of such a high order that it has been
suggested that they are not the work of amateurs but of one particular
atelier, and that they were probably made as gifts for the King himself
or his friends, or for persons who wished to have memorial portraits
of the King after his execution. They fall into two or three groups,
and are copied from portraits by Van Dyck or his imitators.   812–1891

Charles I by Hubert Le Sueur (1595?–1650) 1631
H. 87.6 cm
Hubert Le Sueur was born in France but came to England
sometime before 1626. A considerable number of busts of
Charles I have been attributed to him, but the Museum's bust
is the earliest signed and dated example recorded. It is very
close in style and modelling to a number of bronzes, and since
Le Sueur was better known for his work in that medium it has
been suggested that this marble bust may have been a copy by
some carver employed in his workshop. The rather stiff
posture of the sitter and richly fashioned armour are characteristic of Le Sueur, whose most famous work is the bronze
equestrian statue of Charles I at Charing Cross.   A.35–1910.

Goblet by George Ravenscroft (1618–81)
H. 16.5 cm
George Ravenscroft, a shipowner, merchant, and amateur chemist, was employed by the London Glass Company in 1673 to produce a substitute for Venetian crystal glass from materials available in this country. After a series of experiments mainly designed to remove 'crisseling', he discovered in 1675 that the addition of lead oxide provided a fine-quality clean glass. Ravenscroft's experiments and glass were made in glasshouses he built on or near the site of the Savoy and at Henley-on-Thames.   C.530–1936

The Moody salt 1664   *H. 19 cm*
W. 19.7 cm
Although known as the Moody salt and pricked with the initials AVM, it was not originally made for that family but came into their possession in about 1730 through Ursula Sadleir, the last representative of the Sadleirs of Apsley Guise. The salt is made of silver, chased and repoussé, and bears a London hallmark. Stylistically it is typical of the simpler types of salt which were popular for some fifty years or so after the death of Charles I. Most were circular, square, or octagonal, with a waist and cavity on top. The scrolled brackets which form perhaps the most characteristic feature of the group were to support a dish of fruit, as is clearly seen in many Dutch pictures.   M.347–1912

Panelled room from Clifford's Inn 1686–8
This room of oak panelling with applied carvings in cedar is an
excellent example of the way in which the pure Palladian classicism of
Inigo Jones was domesticated by English architects of the late
seventeenth century. Above the overmantle is a shield bearing the
arms of Penhallow quartering Penwarin, which refer to the marriage
in the reign of Henry VII of John Penhallow with Mary, daughter and
co-heiress of Vivian Penwarin. The room was reconstructed for their
descendant John Penhallow, who in 1674 was admitted to the Society
of Clifford's Inn, an organization which leased rooms in their
property, originally an Inn of Chancery, to suitable tenants. After the
rebuilding of the original Court in 1686, John Penhallow had his new
rooms redecorated, and he moved into them in 1688.   1029–1903

Lime wood cravat Late seventeenth century   *H. 24 cm W. 21 cm*
This remarkable lime wood cravat, carved by Grinling Gibbons
(1648–1721) in imitation Venetian point lace, was formerly in the
possession of Horace Walpole and hung in his house at Strawberry
Hill. On 11 May 1769, Walpole described to George Montague how
at a frolic of several days before he had received a number of
distinguished foreign guests wearing the cravat and a pair of James I's
embroidered gloves, and how 'the French servants stared and firmly
believed that this was the dress of an English country gentleman.'
When Walpole's collection was dispersed in 1842 the cravat was
purchased by Miss (Baroness) Burdett-Coutts and remained in her
house in London until her death in 1906.   w.181–1928

Abigail Pett bedhangings (detail) Late seventeenth century
The Tudor and early Stuart vogue for tent stitch cushion-covers, bed valances, and table-carpets worked in crewels (i.e. worsteds) was succeeded, probably at some date in the reign of Charles I, by that for sets of bed-curtains, embroidered mainly in the new long and short stitch, with details in stem and other stitches, and French knots. The ground material is uniformly a twill, with linen warp and cotton weft, the average loom-width being nineteen inches. The set consisted of two wide curtains at the foot of the bed made from five breadths, two on either side made from two-and-a-half or three breadths; three narrow valances, and three 'bases'. Most sets are anonymous, but this particular one bears an embroidered inscription indicating that it was made by Abigail Pett, an amateur embroideress.   T.13–1929

Upholstered chair *c.* 1660 *H. 94 cm*
W. 52 cm D. 50.8 cm
The chair is made of turned walnut with upholstered back and seat covered in tent stitch embroidery on a linen canvas ground. The embroidery, which displays the arms of Hill of Spaxton Yarde and Poundsford, Somerset, impaling Gurdon of Assington Hall, Suffolk, and Letton of Norfolk, dates from 1641–55. That the chair is of a slightly later date than this is indicated by the barley sugar turning of the legs. The coloured crewel fringe is original. This type of chair appears very frequently in illustrations of interiors between the late sixteenth century and about 1670. Surprisingly, however, comparatively few now survive. The reason for this lies in the fact that the chairs were so simple, and it was found easier to discard them once their textile covers became worn rather than to have them re-upholstered. The turning and elaborate embroidery on the present example probably account for its having been preserved. Chairs such as this are commonly called 'farthingale chairs', or in seventeenth century inventories 'chaises à demoiselle', because they were most frequently used by women who found them convenient when wearing voluminous skirts held out by padded farthingales.   W.124–1937

53

'Lord and Lady Clapham' 1695–1700 *H. 54.6 cm*
These painted wooden dolls dressed in contemporary clothes of
the late seventeenth century are the largest and earliest fully-
dressed dolls known. The delicately painted eyes and eyebrows,
scarlet lips, and well-rouged cheeks are in a remarkable state of
preservation. The dolls were known in the previous owner's
family as Lord and Lady Clapham since their ancestors owned
property there. Particularly noteworthy among the dolls accessories are her very rare black silk mask with glass bead in the
mouth, and his hat, which bears the trade label of 'T. Bourdillon.
Hosier and Hatter to his Majesty'. The armchairs in caned
beechwood and elmwood are contemporary with the dolls.

т.846 and 847–1974

Fulham stoneware figure of Lydia Dwight *c.* 1674
H. 28.6 cm
This figure of a little girl represents Lydia Dwight, who died on 3
March 1674. Born in 1667, she was the daughter of John Dwight,
a notary public of the Restoration period and a man of scientific
interests who devoted himself, amongst other things, to experiments in making new kinds of pottery. Imitating and refining the
German types of stoneware, he sought also to discover the secret
of Chinese porcelain. To facilitate his experiments, Dwight set up
a pottery which still exists at Fulham, where he produced not only
useful wares but also a number of beautiful busts and statuettes
anticipating in a remarkable manner eighteenth-century porcelain
figures.

1054–1871

Boy playing the bagpipes by Caius Gabriel Cibber (1630–1700) *c.* 1680–90. *H. 112 cm*

This Portland stone group was probably made for Archibald, First Duke of Argyll. It was at Whitton Park, the 3rd Duke's home before coming to London, where it was first in Long Acre and then in Tottenham Court Road until 1835. Later still it figured in the Stowe sale of 1848 and was subsequently at Snitterfield, Warwickshire and Welcombe, Stratford-on-Avon. The group has been associated with Defoe's 'Blind Piper', whose experiences in the plague cart are described in the *Journal of the Plague,* but there are, it seems, no grounds for this. Cibber was born in Denmark and worked in Italy before coming to England. His best-known works in this country are probably the monument to Thomas Sackville (d. 1677) at Withyam in Sussex, and 'Melancholy' and 'Raving Madness', the two figures, recently aquired by the Museum, which he carved for the portico of Bethlem Hospital in *c.* 1680. Although Cibber married Jane Colley, the daughter of William Colley of Glaston, Rutland, who brought him a dowry of £6,000, he was, nevertheless, always in financial difficulties. Indeed, he was arrested for debt and confined in the King's Bench at the time he was cutting reliefs on the Monument in London (1673–5), but was allowed out from the prison to continue his work and forced to return there every night. A.3–1930

Stoneware teapot Late seventeenth century *H. 8.9 cm*
In 1693 John Dwight of Fulham brought a lawsuit for infringement of his 1684 patent for making red stoneware against the brothers John Philip and David Elers, who had come to England from Holland in about 1686. As a result John Philip Elers moved to Staffordshire, where he continued to make red stoneware until 1698. The crisp precision of this delicate teapot is very reminiscent of silver shapes, and since the brothers Elers had been silversmiths before becoming potters, it is almost certainly by them rather than Dwight. The decoration in the Chinoiserie manner is parallelled in many contemporary English productions of this date.   C.4–1932

Clock by Jeremie Gregory active from 1652, d. 1685) 1685 *H. 66 cm W. 35.6 cm D. 24 cm*

The monogram on the clock is a later addition and can be interpreted as 'GEO: REX: D:G:A:' for 'George by the grace of God the King of England'. It seems probable that the clock was in the Royal Collection during the reign of George I (1714–27). The case and mounts are exceptional for their architectural character and complexity. The gilt bronze group of Cupid on a Dolphin which forms the finial is a refined version of a model which exists in several examples, one being in the Museum. They can be attributed to Francesco Fanelli, who is known to have worked in London between 1635 and 1642. It may be supposed that his workshop survived the Civil War and was the source of the finial and the other mounts on the clock. Gregory, the clock maker, was Master of the Clockmakers' Company in 1665 and 1676. He also became a Goldsmith in 1668.

w.35–1976

◁
Staffordshire slipware dish *c. 1675 Diam. 43.8 cm*
The English slipware tradition involving decoration in a mixture of clay and water trailed on in lines and dots in the manner of sugar-icing, or combed and feathered as on marbled paper, can be traced back to the Middle Ages. The finest wares were made in North Staffordshire in the district now known as 'the Potteries'. This large dish belongs to a series, signed by the potter Thomas Toft, some of which have dates between 1671 and 1677. The mermaid with her comb is treated in a boldly simplified manner characteristic of the age, and the dish, like others bearing royal portraits and devices, was evidently intended as a show piece for occasions of family ceremony.

299–1869

Duke and Duchess of Lauderdale by Sir
Peter Lely   (1618–80)   *H. 137.2 cm
W. 162.6 cm*
Lady Dysart, whose father William Murray
had acquired Ham House in 1637, formed a
relationship with the Earl of Lauderdale
some time around the middle of the century,
and after the death of their respective
spouses, they married. Lely's oil portrait,
which hangs at Ham House, clearly depicts
the acute, politically minded, and rapacious
aspects of the Countess's character, whereas
her husband, whose ability and ambition had
first attracted her, is shown only a few years
before his death in 1682 when he was well
past the zenith of his powers. The Lauder-
dales were among Lely's greatest patrons.
HH262–1948

**The north drawing-room at Ham
House**   *c.* 1637
Accounts for this room record that the
plaster frieze and ceiling were made for
£35.4s, the wainscoting for £5.10s, and the
doors for £12 the pair, including door cases.
The tapestries, depicting the seasons, can be
dated between 1699 and 1719 and were
woven by ex-Mortlake weavers. The chairs
with their original upholstery were almost
certainly in the room in the 1660s. The
twisted columns flanking the fireplace are
copied directly from one of the Raphael
cartoons, which adds strength to the supposition that the room may have been designed
by Francis Clein (see p. 48), who had used
the cartoons at Mortlake.

The Melville bed *c. 1697   H. 462 cm   W. 243 cm   L. 274 cm*
This great bed made of pine and covered with silk damask and velvet is one of the few to have survived intact and in good condition from the last years of the seventeenth century. It belongs to the category of 'State Beds' which were designed, not necessarily for warmth or comfort, but to display the authority and wealth of their owner in a formal setting. The bed was commissioned by George, fourth Baron Melville and First Earl of Melville for the house at Monomail, renamed Melville, which he began in 1692. The design is probably based on those by Daniel Marot, some of which were published in his *Nouveaux Livres d'Apartements* in 1702, and the bed may have been made in London by the French immigrant craftsman François Lapierre.

W.35-1949

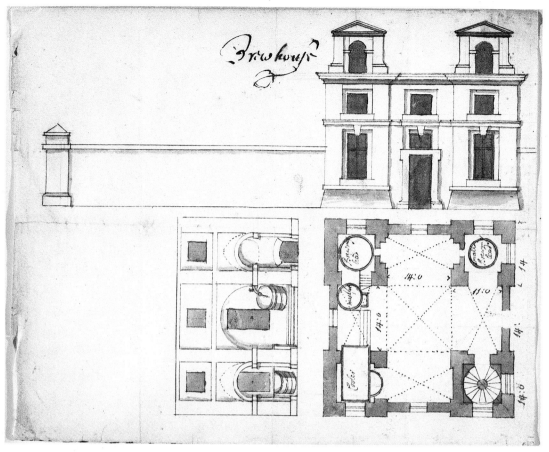

The brewhouse at Castle Howard   *c.* 1700   *H. 21 cm W. 27 cm*
This drawing is one of forty-eight connected with the names of Wren, Hawksmoor, Vanbrugh, and their associates, previously owned by the Marquess of Bute, which the Museum acquired in 1951. They constitute part of a group which probably belonged to Christopher Wren junior and was sold in 1749 after his death. Castle Howard was designed by Sir John Vanbrugh (1664–1726) and Nicholas Hawksmoor (1661–1736) and built from 1699 for Lord Carlisle. In the design for the brewhouse as executed the towers project much further forward from the rest of the building and do not diminish in the attic storey as depicted here.   E.429–1951

Sketch for a recumbent effigy by William Stanton (1630–1705)   *c.* 1683   *L. 35.6 cm W. 12 cm*
This figure was originally thought to be a sketch for the monument of Isobel Shirburne at Mitton in Yorkshire by William Stanton the elder, but has since been unquestionably identified with the figure of Lady Rebecca Atkins (d. 1711) and her family, from the monument to Sir Richard Atkins (d. 1689) in St Paul's Church, Clapham by the same artist. Stanton's father and uncle were also sculptors, though their work is generally considered inferior. William Stanton is recorded to have completed at least thirty monuments in various churches throughout the country, including three in Westminster Abbey.   A.1–1929

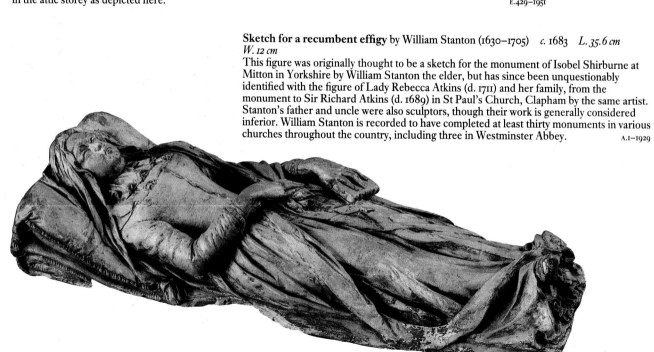

Queen Mary II probably by John Nost the elder (d. 1729) *c.* 1695
H. 59.7 cm
This painted terracotta statuette is probably the model for the statue
of Queen Mary by John Nost that was placed on the Royal Exchange
in 1695 after her death in December 1694. A companion statue of
William III was erected at the same time, the model for which is also
in the Museum (A.35–1939). Both statues vanished after the fire
which destroyed the Exchange in 1838. Nost was born on the
Continent but came to England and set up a workshop in the
Haymarket, where he employed many assistants. Vertue records that
he 'became a master of reputation and left behind him a good
fortune'.
                                                                A.208–1946

Wallpaper   Late seventeenth early eighteenth century   *H. 195 cm*
W. 60 cm
This detail of a strip of wallpaper made up from six separate pieces
came from Orde House, Berwick-on-Tweed, Northumberland. It is
printed from wood blocks and colour stencils and has been varnished.
The parakeets and Chinoiserie figures are evidence of the popularity
of Oriental subjects at this time brought about as a result of the
importation of Chinese and other goods by the Dutch East India
Companies.   E.5311–1958

Georgian and Regency (1715–1837)

The story of the arts in the eighteenth century is no longer one of Church and Court patronage, but one in which most of the important commissions came from the aristocracy and the middle classes. Furthermore, it is one of changes in style dictated to a certain extent by the tastes of these patrons. Thus, although the Baroque architecture of Wren, Vanbrugh, and others was already being criticized in the first decades of the century, it was Colen Campbell's *Vitruvius Britannicus*, which began publication in 1715, and more particularly Lord Burlington's employment of William Kent to design Chiswick House, which founded the Palladian style here in the mid 1720s.

Chiswick, in keeping with other Palladian houses, has an austere and dignified façade which contrasts strongly with its rich internal decorations. As the console table in Gallery 58 and other pieces make clear, part of this richness resulted from the retention of many Baroque forms within the new vocabulary of Palladianism. To a certain extent it was out of the flowing scrolls and curves of the Baroque and in reaction to the intrusion of classical formality in interiors that the Rococo style of the mid-century, with its delight in the fanciful and capricious, emerged. Chinese and Gothic forms, as well as the characteristic ornament derived from shell work—called *rocaille* in France where the style originated—were readily used by designers at this time.

No designer in Britain understood the Rococo idiom more fully, perhaps, than the furniture maker Matthias Lock, whose pattern books published in the 1740s were so influential. The mirror and side-table from the tapestry room at Hinton House in Somerset of *c.* 1745 which are displayed with Lock's original design in gallery 5 are splendid examples of his exceptional skill both as draughtsman and carver. Two other important contemporaneous furniture designers were John Linnell and his father William. The Chinese bed from Badminton House of *c.* 1755 which is now attributed to William, having being thought for many years to be the work of Chippendale, is perhaps the best-known piece of Rococo furniture in the Museum's collections. Among other interesting Rococo objects are the tapestry made at Soho in Gallery 58; the important group of ceramic Chinese musicians made at Chelsea in Gallery 123, which serves to remind us that it was at this time that Nicholas Sprimont introduced the art of making porcelain to Britain; and the pair of candlesticks by George Michael Moser, which illustrate the marked tendency towards assymetry exhibited during the Rococo period.

By the 1760s there were already signs of a return to more disciplined forms of ornament and decoration, and the greater study of the antiquities of Italy and Greece which were being undertaken by ever increasing numbers of Grand Tourists led inevitably to a concern with Neo-classicism. The discoveries made at Herculaneum and Pompeii; the architectural fragments and classical furniture in the Vatican Museum and the decoration of the Vatican itself; and classical monuments such as the Temple of the Winds and the Choragic monument of Lysikrates all provided models for new forms of ornament. Furthermore, the publication of several large volumes of engravings ensured that these sources were available to craftsmen and designers throughout the country.

Eighteenth-century Neo-classicism is usually referred to as the 'Adam' style after the architect Robert Adam, who was so widely patronized in the second half of the century. Osterley Park, the ceiling from David Garrick's villa at Hampton of 1770, the set of bookcases from Croome Court of *c.* 1763, and the panels from Northumberland House of *c.* 1773–4 constitute an impressive body of work by

Vertumnus and Pomona by Laurent Delvaux (1696–1778)   *c.* 1725
H. 129.5 cm
This group illustrating Ovid's story of the wooing of Pomona by Vertumnus, a nature god who had the gift of transforming himself into any shape, was made while Delvaux was working in partnership with Peter Scheemakers. Along with a companion group of Apollo and Venus it was almost certainly made for Canons, the house which James Bridges, Duke of Chandos, built at Edgware. After the demolition of Canons in the mid-eighteenth century, the groups passed to Stowe where they remained until 1921. Delvaux was born in Flanders but came to England in 1721 with Scheemakers to work in Westminster Abbey with Denis Plumier on the tomb of John Sheffield, Duke of Buckingham. In 1728 he went to Rome, but returned to England in 1733 and remained here for a short time before returning to Flanders. Delvaux's treatment of drapery and the soft, rounded forms of his modelling are more Baroque than those of his contemporary Scheemakers.   A.1–1949

Adam in the Museum and testify to his skill in manipulating a wide repertory of decorative and architectural motifs largely culled from Roman sources. Perhaps the most widely known of all Neo-classical objects are the 'basaltes' and 'jasperware' of Josiah Wedgwood, the master potter whose endeavours from 1754 were largely responsible for the successful expansion of the Staffordshire pottery industry. Amongst pieces of particular note by him are copies of the Portland Vase, and many portrait medallions designed by John Flaxman, whose sculpture is shown in the English Sculpture Court. Flaxman also designed for other manufacturers, such as Rundell and Bridge, whose silver is displayed in room 121.

Towards the end of the eighteenth century and throughout the Regency era Neo-classicism became increasingly concerned with accurate imitation and adaptation of antique models so as to ensure a firm basis for a universal criterion of good taste. This led to the rejection of Adam's simplicity and refinement in favour of more correct details and of greater opulence and exuberance of form. Supports for furniture in the form of animals, particularly lions, copied from articles found at Pompeii, for example, appear on several pieces of furniture in room 122, where a chair with a strongly curving arc-back and 'scimitar' legs which derives its form from fifth-century Greek vase paintings is also displayed. One of the most influential publications of the period was *Household Furniture and Decoration* (1807) by the wealthy connoisseur Thomas Hope, and the Museum is fortunate to have acquired several objects from his houses in Duchess Street, London and The Deepdene in Surrey. An Egyptian clock in gallery 121, which closely relates to one illustrated by Hope, is a reminder that Napoleon's Egyptian campaign in the early century added a further repertoire of archaic forms to the designer's stock in trade. But these sources were not English, and as the Industrial Revolution swept the country to world prominence, such considerations, as we shall see in the next chapter, became increasingly important.

Long case clock   *c.* 1725   *H. 266 cm W. 61 cm*
The clock is made of pinewood, japanned, with silvered finials and brackets, and the dial spandrels are filled with scrollwork ornaments of chased and gilt brass. The latter is inscribed with 'Markwick Londini' for James Markwick the younger.

W.49–1935

The Walpole salver   1728–9   *49 cm square*
This silver salver, which was probably engraved by William Hogarth (1697–1764), bears the maker's mark of Paul de Lamerie (1688–1751) and a London hallmark for 1728–9.   M.9–1956

64

George Frederick Handel (1685–1759) by Louis-
François Roubiliac (1705?–62) 1738 *H. 135 cm*
This famous marble statue of Handel playing Apol-
lo's lyre was commissioned by the impressario
Jonathon Tyers whose bust, also by Roubiliac, is in
the Museum, and placed in the Pleasure Gardens at
Vauxhall in 1738. It remained there until about 1814
when it was removed by one of Tyers' descendants,
and in 1854 it was acquired by the Sacred Harmonic
Society. From about 1900, until its purchase by the
Museum in 1965, the statue belonged to Novello and
Company, the music publishers. The pedestal dates
from the nineteenth century.   A.3–1965

**Model for the monument in Westminster Abbey
to Sir Isaac Newton** *c.* 1730 *H. 35.6 cm*
L. 52.7 cm W. 23 cm
The monument to Sir Isaac Newton in Westminster
Abbey, and a similar one to the first Earl Stanhope,
occupy a commanding position against the organ
screen, facing the nave. As the screen was altered in
the nineteenth century, the effect of the two
monuments, which were designed by William Kent
(1685–1748) and executed by John Michael
Rysbrack (1694–1770) is now a good deal
diminished. The terracotta model for the figure of
Newton is in detail very close to the finished marble
and must represent the final stage of the sculptor's
conception.   A.1–1938

Figure of a Heavy Dragoon *c. 1760   H. 19.9 cm L. 11.7 cm*
A very similar Staffordshire, Astbury type, group in the British
Museum of a Light Dragoon must date from after 1755, when light
troops were added to some dragoon regiments, and it is on this
evidence that the dating of this figure is based.   C.124–1938

Pew group   *c. 1740   H. 16 cm W. 17.3 cm*
It has been suggested that the famous Staffordshire pew
groups of which this is an example may all be the work of
Aaron Wood, who was born in 1717 and was apprenticed
in 1731 to Dr Thomas Wedgwood.   C.6–1975

Settee seat cover *c. 1730   W. 138.4 cm D. 52.3 cm*
Canvas, embroidered with wool and silk in tent and cross stitches with details in padded satin, overcast and cross stitches. The two
scenes which fill the centre of the cover are taken from illustrations by William Kent to Gay's *Fables*, first published in 1727.   T.473–1970

Cabinet on stand   *c. 1715*   *Cabinet H. 104 cm W. 91.4 cm D. 58.4 cm Stand H. 89 cm W. 122 cm D. 61 cm*
The cabinet is composed of four Japanese black lacquer panels set in an English aventurine lacquer framing. The stand of carved softwood covered with gilded gesso corresponds in design with a side-table by James Moore at Hampton Court Palace, except that the table bears the crowned cypher of George I at the central point of the apron in place of the cockleshell on the Museum's piece.
Believed to have been part of the furnishings of George II's bedchamber, the cabinet was obtained as a perquisite of office by the 4th Earl of Rockford, first Lord of the Bedchamber and Groom of the Stole.   W.30–1958

Gilt console table designed by William Kent (1685–1748)   *c.* 1730   *H. 89 cm W. 70 cm D. 45.7 cm*
This table, one of a pair, the other of which is now in 'The Great Chamber' at Chatsworth, was designed by Kent in about 1727 to 1732 for Lord Burlington's villa at Chiswick. The two tables probably stood in the Gallery, flanking its Palladian window. The design, etched by Vardy, is Plate 40 in *Some Designs of Mr Inigo Jones and Mr William Kent*, published in 1744. Although many of the houses designed by Kent contain furniture attributed to him, documented pieces are extremely rare; the Museum's table bears two labels on its back, the one printed with the words 'Dining-room' and the other with the ink inscription 'Devonshire No 26', and as a similar label is on a side-table still at Chatsworth, its Chiswick provenance is secure. The table is among Kent's earliest experiments in furniture design, combining revived Palladian and Baroque motifs.

W.14–1971

William Augustus, Duke of Cumberland
by Sir Henry Cheere (1703–81) 1746–7
Height including pedestal 66 cm
Sir Henry Cheere was probably of Huguenot extraction and was apprenticed to the mason-sculptor, Robert Hartshorne. From 1729–33 he worked in partnership with Peter Scheemakers's brother Henry, and thereafter he worked on his own, obtaining numerous commissions for statues and busts, particularly from Oxford University. This particular bust was for many years catalogued as by an anonymous sculptor. The recent discovery of an identical lead bust belonging to Lord Brownlow, with contemporary documentation, however, now enables a positive attribution to be made. Henry Cheere also executed a lead equestrian statue of the Duke for Cavendish Square. A.12–1947

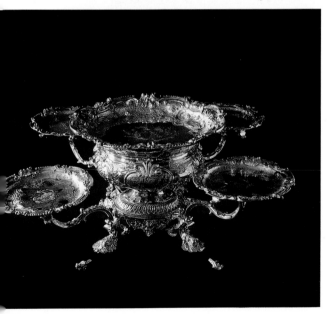

The Newdigate centrepiece by Paul de Lamerie (1688–1751) 1743–4 *H. 23 cm W. 52 cm*
When the épergne began to come into use in about 1725, it succeeded to the place of honour on the dinner table once occupied by the great salt. The present example, which bears the London hallmark for 1743–4, was made by Paul de Lamerie at his shop in Gerrard Street, Soho, and the richness and fine finish of its decoration are typical of the work with which his name is usually associated. M.149–1919

Centrepiece in the form of a tureen and cover by Nicholas Sprimont (*c.* 1716–71) 1747 *H. 46.4 cm W. 67.3 cm*
The base of this silver centrepiece, which bears a London hallmark for 1747 and the maker's mark of Nicholas Sprimont, is supported in part by the cast and marbled armorials of John, 2nd Earl of Ashburnham (1724–1812) and those of his wife. There are microscopic traces of a different patterning at the edges of the cartouches, which indicate that the piece was not commissioned by Ashburnham but by another patron, also an Earl, whose arms were erased. M.46–1971

69

Mantua and petticoat *c.* 1740
This mantua and petticoat of crimson ribbed
silk are embroidered with more than ten
pounds of solid silver wire in a Baroque
version of the oriental tree of life. A contemporary ink inscription below the embroidery
on the underside of the train reads 'Rec'd of
Mme Leconte by Me Magd Giles'. A
Madame Leconte is listed as an embroideress in the accounts of Princesse
Augusta in 1747, so that this dress was
almost certainly intended for court use. It is
the earliest signed dress in the world.

T.227 to B–1970

Bureau *c.* 1745   *H. 89 cm W. 157.5 cm*
D. 72.4 cm
The terms 'Library Table', and 'Bureau
Dressing Table' have been applied to pieces
such as this, which were intended to be
positioned in rooms, in pairs, back-to-back.
The quality of workmanship helps to rank
this piece among a small group of sumptuously produced furniture now attributed to
the Exeter and London maker John Chan-
non. The top drawer, which extends across
the whole piece, is a writing drawer, and is
supported on the corner trusses when pulled
out.   W.4–1956

Printed cotton   1769   *L. 236 cm W. 190.5 cm*

Printed in a mixture of linen and cotton yarn from engraved copper plates, and overprinted from woodblocks. Both this scene and another depicting a shooting party, which is printed on the same piece of material, are signed R. JONES & CO. indicating that they were made by Robert Jones, who established an extensive calico-printing works at Old Ford on the right bank of the River Lea some time before 1761. Until he sold the firm in September 1780 Robert Jones and his artists produced some of the finest copper-plate chintzes ever made. Indeed, although printed cottons of this type are often called 'Toiles de Jouy' after the famous factory near Paris, cotton printing had flourished in England for many years previously. Engraved copper plates were used for printing cotton in England at least as early as 1757, whereas they did not come into use at Jouy until 1770 when they were proclaimed as a great discovery!   T.140–1934

Pair of candlesticks   1740–5
H. 36.8 cm
In 1977 the Museum acquired two pairs of
unmarked silver candlesticks, each pair with
figures representing Apollo and Daphne.
The figure of Daphne resembles very closely
a drawing for a candlestick in the Museum
(E.4885–1968) signed by George Michael
Moser, R.A. (1706–83), the Swiss born
chaser and enameller who arrived in England *c.* 1721 and was to become a pioneer of
the Rococo style here.   M.329–1977

Chair   *c.* 1754
This ebonized beechwood chair is one of a
set of eight from Horace Walpole's Great
Parlour at Strawberry Hill, Twickenham. In
July 1754 Walpole planned the design of
some chairs, the backs of which were taller
than usual and were based on Gothic
window frames. Richard Bentley was employed to prepare the design and they were
made by William Hallet, who charged
£3.15.0 for each one in September 1755.
The set was sold at the Strawberry Hill sale
of 1842. Four chairs from the set are now in
the Lewis Walpole Library at Farmington,
Connecticut and two others in Bunratty
Castle, Ireland. This chair was formerly the
property of David and Lady Pamela
Hicks.   W.29–1979

Chelsea porcelain group of Chinese musicians *c.* 1755 *H. 35.6 cm*
This porcelain group, which is marked with a red anchor and painted in enamel colours and gilt, can probably be identified as the 'large group of Chinese figures playing on music' which was lot 82 in the catalogue of the sale held by the Chelsea proprietors on 8 April 1756. Another example of the group is in the Untermeyer Collection in the Metropolitan Museum of Art in New York. The group was probably modelled by the Flemish artist Joseph Willems, who was responsible for so many of the figure groups introduced at Chelsea between 1749, or slightly earlier, and 1766.

C.40–1974

Design for a mausoleum for Frederick, Prince of Wales (1751–2) by
William Chambers (1723–96) *H. 32.4 cm W. 48.3 cm*
William Chambers' work at Kew commenced in September 1757 when he was
first commissioned by Augusta, Dowager Princess of Wales. During the course
of the next six years some twenty-five buildings and objects were erected there
to his designs, but now only five survive, of which the Orangery and the Pagoda
are perhaps the best known. This design was never executed.
                                                                                              3339

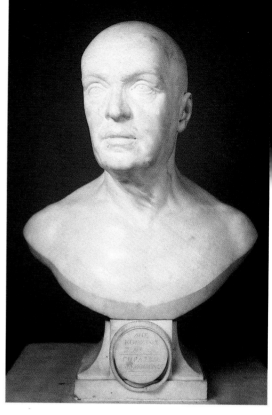

Dr Antonio Cocchi (1695–1758) by Joseph Wilton
(1722–1803) 1755 *H. 62.6 cm*
The bust was executed in the last year of Wilton's
residence in Italy. Cocchi was a celebrated Italian physi-
cian and scholar, who was an intimate friend of Horace
Mann, the British envoy in Florence. The unusual un-
draped form is evidence of Wilton's close study of Antique
busts.   A.9–1966

Commode attributed to Pierre Langlois *c.* 1760 *H. 86.4 cm W. 132.7 cm
D. 59.1 cm*
Surprisingly little is known of Langlois, a French cabinet maker who had set up
business in London by 1759 and who produced during the 1760s a considerable
quantity of very high quality furniture. This commode is attributed to him on
the basis of its similarity to two documented commodes at Woburn Abbey and
the Metropolitan Museum of Art, New York.   w.8–1967

Glass decanter enamelled by William Beilby (1740–1819)   1762   *H. 23.5 cm*
The glass is painted in enamel colours and gilt and is signed 'Beilby Junr. Pinxit & Invt. NCastle'. The date 1762 has been added in diamond point. The coat of arms is that of Sir Edward Blackett, who was M.P. for Northumberland from 1768 to 1774.

C.620–1936

Urn and stand   1767–78   *H. 53.3 cm*
W. 33 cm
Large, frequently silver, vessels such as this were used from the 1760s for preparing and serving tea. This example bears the mark of Thomas Whipham and Charles Wright, who were in partnership from 1757 to 1776. Thomas Whipham was elected Warden of the Goldsmith's Company in 1772.   M.4–1918

Riding habit   Mid-eighteenth century
This red cloth riding habit consists of a coat, waistcoat, and skirt. The buttons are covered with silver gimp and spangles, and floral embroidery, also in silver thread, gimp and spangles, is worked chiefly in satin stitch from the buttons and round the holes.

269 to 269C–1890

Armchair   1765   *H. 106.7 cm W. 77.5 cm D. 77.5 cm*
This gilded beechwood chair is known to have been made by Chippendale to Robert Adam's designs for the 'Salon' of Sir Lawrence Dundas's house at 19 Arlington Street, London. Contemporary records indicate that it was one of eight chairs for which he charged £160 in July 1765.   W.1–1937

Part of the glass drawing room from Northumberland House 1773–4
This room was designed by Robert Adam (1728–92) for Hugh
(Smithson) Percy, 1st Duke of Northumberland, for his house near
Trafalgar Square in London in 1773–4. The glass panels are backed
with gilt metal foil to simulate the richness of porphyry and the
overlay of Neo-classical motives are made of gilt metal, wood, and
composition. The round and oval paintings were probably carried out
by Giovanni Battista Cipriani, who is recorded as executing decorative painting at Northumberland House during this period.   w.3-1955

Charlotte Walpole, Countess of Dysart by Sir Joshua Reynolds
(1723–92)   c. 1775   *H. 237.5 cm W. 146.1 cm*
The picture hangs in the great Hall at Ham House. When Lord
Dysart died in 1727 he was succeeded by his grandson Lionel, the
4th Earl, who married Charlotte, the illegitimate daughter of Sir
Edward Walpole, within a week of first meeting her. Charlotte died in
1789. Reynolds was one of the most esteemed portrait painters of his
day; the flattering allusions to the Old Masters and to Antique
sculpture which he cultivated in the poses of his figures appealed to
the educated eye of the late eighteenth century.   HH229–1948

The Kimbolton cabinet   c. 1771   *H. 188.6 cm W. 177.8 cm*
This cabinet was designed by Robert Adam for the Duchess of
Manchester, wife of the 4th Duke. It is mounted in ormolu, the
wooden surface being of satinwood inlaid in darker wood with
foliated arabesques and other classical motives, and faced with land
and seascapes in coloured marbles (*pietre dure*) and the pilasters with
strips of this material framed in brass. On the back of one of the
panels is scratched the name of the maker 'Baccio Cappelli Fecit
Anno 1709 Firenza', indicating that they were probably bought in
Florence and sent home as curios.   w.43–1949

The Duet by Arthur Devis (1711–87)   1749   *H. 115.6 cm W. 103.5 cm*
This oil painting with its great charm, cool delicate colour, and high finish is typical of Devis' small portraits and conversation pieces. Most of his patrons were solidly middle class and are usually portrayed in their gardens or parks, or, as here, in a sparse but carefully detailed interior, as if they had been assembled rather than grouped before the painter. His brother Anthony was a minor painter of landscapes and his son Arthur William a painter and draughtsman in the service of the East India Company.

P.31–1955

Vauxhall Gardens by Thomas Rowlandson (1756–1827) *c.* 1784
H. 48.3 cm W. 74.9 cm
Rowlandson started as a painter of serious subjects but quickly
turned to cartoons. The Vauxhall Pleasure Gardens were opened in
1732 by Jonathon Tyers as a place of evening entertainment for the
summer months on a site across the Thames from the Tate Gallery.
Before their closure in the nineteenth century they provided anecdote
and incident galore in the novels, diaries, and letters of the time.
Many of the spectators depicted by Rowlandson have been identified.
They include Boswell, Dr Johnson, and Oliver Goldsmith, who are
seated beneath the box.   P.13–1967

Creamware teapot *c.* 1775   *H. 11.4 cm*
Cream-coloured earthenware was first made by Enoch Booth of
Tunstall, and improved in 1765 by Wedgwood, who called his pottery
'Queen's ware'. This teapot was made at Leeds, one of several
potteries where Wedgwood's techniques were copied. The demise of
creamware was occasioned by the development of bone china in the
early nineteenth century.   C.99–1911

Dessert stand by Paul Storr (1771–1844)   1810–11
H. 33 cm W. 21.6 cm
Paul Storr is best known for the pieces of presentation plate so much
in demand as gifts to victorious generals and admirals during the
Napoleonic Wars, and for many no less successful but smaller
domestic pieces which he produced when working for Rundell and
Bridge from 1811–19, and in partnership with John Mortimer and
others from 1822. He retired in 1839. Two further versions of this
dessert stand formed part of the first Duke of Wellington's
Ambassador Service now at Apsley House.   M.40 A & B–1970

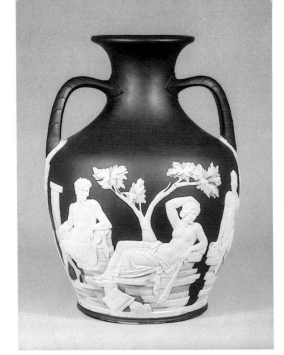

Facsimile copy of the Portland vase 1790–5 *H. 25 cm*
Diam. 18.4 cm
Wedgwood is recorded to have made between forty and fifty jasperware copies of the Portland vase (now in the British Museum), of
which only twenty or so are known to survive. This copy is said to
have been considered by Wedgwood himself as the most perfect of
them all.   Circ.732–1956

Henrietta, wife of the first Earl of Yarborough (d. 1813) by
Joseph Nollekens (1737–1823)   1810   *H. 64.8 cm*
Nollekens' able and lifelike busts ensured him a position in sculpture
almost equal to that of Reynolds in painting, and he died leaving a
fortune of some £200,000. He was, however, a very miserly man and
not liked by his pupils. One, J. T. Smith, ruthlessly delineated the
unpleasant aspects of his character in his biography *Nollekens and His
Times* and another, Joseph Bonomi, described him as 'that silly old
fool'.   A.120–1929

St Michael overcoming Satan by John Flaxman (1755–1826)
1822   *H. 90 cm W. 38 cm*
This plaster is the sketch model for the marble group which Flaxman
made for the 3rd Earl of Egremont between 1819 and 1826 and
which is now at Petworth House. The full-size model for the group is
on loan to the Museum from University College, London. It is one of
the sculptor's last works, and has links with Mannerist sculpture:
Benvenuto Cellini's 'Perseus', for example, which Flaxman had
studied in Italy.   312–1898

Pier table *c.* 1800 *H. 91.4 cm W. 183 cm
D. 48 cm*
This table of giltwood with bronze medallions was designed for the banker, patron,
and collector Thomas Hope (1769–1831)
for the 'Flaxman Room' at his house in
Duchess Street, where it formed part of the
elaborate setting for Flaxman's sculptoral
group, *Cephalus and Aurora.* Hope described
the table in his *Household Furniture and
Interior Decoration* of 1807 as follows:
'Females emblematic of the four horae as
parts of the day support its rail, the frieze of
which contains medallions of the deities of
night and sleep.' Such themes are representative of Hope's belief in the principle of
symbolic and narrative ornament. The
marble bust of 1790 is by Anne Seymour
Damer (1749–1828) and represents Mrs
Freeman as Isis.   W.19–1976

Bookcase 1806 *H. 176.5 cm W. 112 cm
D. 52 cm*
The bookcase is made of pollard Yew inlaid
with ebony, and the mounts are of bronze
and ormolu. It was supplied in 1806 by the
firm of Marsh and Tatham of Mount Street,
London for the Prince of Wales at Carlton
House, and bears the inventory mark of
George IV. A contemporary bill indicates
that this was one of four similar pieces which
Marsh and Tatham made for the sum of
£680. Thomas Tatham was the brother of
Charles Heathcote Tatham, and since the
latter's name appears on some of the firm's
bills dated 1806 it is possible that the
bookcase may be to his designs. A writing
desk made from fragments of furniture from
Carlton House in 1835, with end panels
bearing the same design as on the doors of
the Museum's bookcase, is at Windsor.

 W.102–1978

Night lamp *c.* 1820   *H. 22.4 cm* ▷

The burner is contained within a porcelain turret-shaped stand in two parts with battlemented top. The piece was acquired as an example of a 'food warmer' of 'Nant-Garw' paste, but subsequently a drawing of the shape was discovered in one of the pattern books belonging to Messers Minton of Stoke on Trent, where it is described as a 'night lamp'.   C.601 to E–1935

Cup and saucer *c.* 1810   *Cup H. 7.2 cm Diam. 6.6 cm, Saucer Diam. 13.6 cm*

The decoration is painted in red enamel and gilded. A cup and saucer with this pattern in the Museum at Tunstall, where they were made, is ascribed on traditional grounds to William Adams, the potter who trained under Wedgwood, and much of whose subsequent work was equal to that of his master in quality. Apart from painted wares, Adams also produced transfer printed pieces, and cream and jasper wares.   11 & a–1904

Cabinet *c.* 1815   *H. 113 cm W. 173 cm D. 56.5 cm*

The recent discovery of an album of tracings, which once belonged to the cabinetmaker George Bullock, in the Birmingham Museum and Art Gallery, has enabled this cabinet to be positively attributed to his workshop. Bullock started his career in Liverpool but moved to London in 1813. Apart from his cabinet making and upholstery work, he is also known to have been a sculptor and marble mason. Bullock's influence appears to have been extensive, for apart from his London and Liverpool commissions he also carried out work in Scotland for several wealthy clients, including Sir Walter Scott. The decoration along the bottom edge of the Museum's cabinet is very similar to that on two dwarf cabinets at Blair Castle, where he worked for the 4th Duke of Atholl.   W.32–1979

Satan arousing the Rebel Angels by William Blake (1757–1827)   1808   *H. 51.4 cm W. 39 cm*
This pen and water-colour painting is one of a series of illustrations which Blake made to John Milton's *Paradise Lost*. It illustrates the passage 'Awake! arise, or be for ever fallen' in which the fallen Satan summons the rebel angels to conference. Blake was concerned with illustrations for Milton's epic for more than fifteen years from 1801. This illustration is part of a series commissioned in 1808 by Thomas Butts.

The drawing shows Blake's linear, flatly-coloured style, which is typical of his work in the early years of the century, when he abandoned pictorial traditions in favour of a two-dimensional display of emblematic figures. Later his pictures were more highly finished and he applied the pigment in a broken technique to achieve an almost jewel-like finish.   6856 (FA 697)

Necklace Second quarter nineteenth century   *L. 59.7 cm*
From about 1820 a fashion for naturalism pervaded all the applied
arts. At first confined to somewhat stylized designs, by the middle of
the century craftsmen attempted to reproduce natural forms as
accurately as possible. In jewellery the illusion of reality was made
more complete by mounting stones in the form of flowers on
'tremblers' so that they would shake at the slightest movement. This
necklace is made of gold of two colours set with seed pearls.

M.133–1951

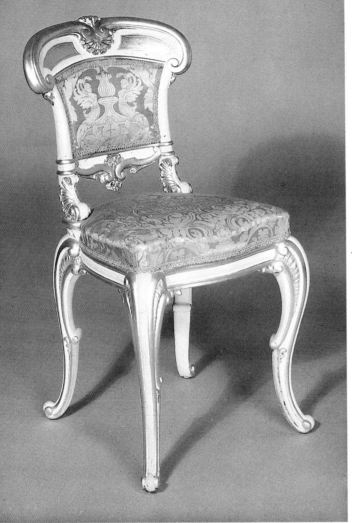

Chair designed by Philip Hardwick (1792–1870)   1834
H. 81 cm W. 42 cm D. 40.6 cm
This carved, painted, and gilded beech chair was designed by
Hardwick for the Court Drawing Room at the Goldsmith's Hall and
made by W. & C. Wilkinson. Most of the suite of which it formed part
was destroyed during the Second World War when the hall was
bombed. This chair was salvaged, however, along with three others
which are still in the possession of the Company. Until his health
broke down in 1843, Hardwick maintained an extensive architectural
practice in London, and in 1854 received the Royal Gold Medal of
the Royal Institute of British Architects. The commission to design
the Goldsmith's Hall, which was carried out between 1829 and 1835,
included other furnishings besides this chair, and among the pieces
to his designs which survive are a fine set of mahogany dining chairs
in the 'Grecian' style.   W.1–1964

Bashaw by Matthew Cotes Wyatt (1777–1862)   1834
H. 149.4 cm including base
In 1831 Lord Dudley and Ward commissioned Wyatt to execute a
sculpted portrait of his favourite Newfoundland dog, Bashaw, which
was to be placed in his house in Park Lane. The dog was sent to
London from Himley Hall and 'sat' to Wyatt some fifty times. Lord
Dudley died in 1833, before the marble had been completed, and in
the following year a dispute about the commission and the price
(£5,000) arose between Wyatt and the Executors. The argument was
never settled, Bashaw remaining in the possession of the sculptor till
his death in 1862. Wyatt showed the sculpture at the Great
Exhibition of 1851 with the title 'The Faithful Friend of Man
Trampling Underfoot his most Insidious Enemy'. It is made of
coloured marbles with eyes of topaz and sardonyx. The snake is of
bronze with ruby eyes.   A.4–1960

Porcelain plate made at New Hall
c. 1810   Diam. 20.6 cm
After the failure of the Longton Hall factory
in 1760 no porcelain was, as far as is known,
made in Staffordshire until 1782, when a
group of potters who had acquired
Champion's patent for making hard paste
porcelain in the previous year, set up at
Tunstall and later at New Hall, Shelton.
Naïve, colourful, almost peasant designs
such as appear on this plate are characteristic
of the pottery in the early nineteenth century,
and represent a genuine alternative to the
more formal patterns used by factories tied
to classical fashions.   C.1285–1924

Silk gauze scarf or stole (detail)   Early
nineteenth century   *L. 225.6 cm W. 47.6 cm*
In the eighteenth century a large number of
Huguenots fleeing from persecution in their
own country settled in Spitalfields, where
they re-vitalized the silk weaving industry.
The Museum's collections include many
important silks and water-colour designs
from this period by Anna Maria Garthwaite
and others. In the nineteenth century the
industry suffered from French competition,
a shortage of raw silk, and a lack of organization and good design. Attempts were made to
remedy this situation, but the industry never
achieved its former prominence.   T.291–1965

Caernarvon Castle by Peter De Wint (1784–1849) *H. 30.5 cm W. 52 cm*
As a result of wise purchases and generous gifts and bequests, the Museum possesses a very rich and varied collection of the work of Peter de Wint, which is further strengthened by a permanent loan from the National Gallery. Although of Dutch descent, Peter de Wint was born in England. He won little reputation in his own day, although Constable realized his talent and occasionally purchased his work.

589–1892

East Cowes Castle, the Seat of J. Nash Esq.; the regatta starting for their moorings by Joseph Mallord William Turner (1775–1851) *c. 1828 H. 91.4 cm W. 128.3 cm*
This oil painting, and a companion picture now in the Indianapolis Museum of Art, Indiana, were the direct result of a visit which Turner paid to the architect John Nash, who owned East Cowes Castle on the Isle of Wight, between July and September 1827. Nash set aside a special room in the castle for Turner's use.

FA 210

Stonehenge by John Constable   *c. 1835   H. 38 cm W. 59.7 cm*
Although Constable did not draw expressly as a preliminary to painting, this water-colour, which he exhibited at
the Royal Academy in 1836, was made in the previous year from a sketch of 1820. Into it he introduced the
rainbow which had fascinated him for more than twenty years as a symbol and embodiment of colour. Two
sketches for the water-colour are also in the Museum's collection.   1629–1888

Salisbury Cathedral from the Bishop's grounds by John Constable (1776–1837)   1820–3
H. 87.6 cm W. 111.8 cm
This painting, in oil on canvas, was commissioned in 1820 by Constable's friend John Fisher, Bishop of
Salisbury, who is depicted in the foreground with his wife. Constable was asked to alter the clouds and
was continually pressed to complete the picture.   FA.33

In a Shoreham garden by Samuel Palmer (1805–81)   *c.* 1829   *H. 28. cm W. 22.2 cm*
For some five years in the 1820's Palmer settled at Shoreham, in Kent, and here, amid surroundings of great pastoral luxuriance, he drew and painted many of the works from which his present-day fame chiefly derives. This water-colour sums up with great intensity Palmer's mystical feeling for exuberant nature in full bloom. Shortly before painting it, he had written of nature as 'sprinkled and showered with a thousand pretty eyes, and buds, and spires, and blossoms gemm'd with dew' and as containing 'rolling volumes and piled mountains of light'. The picture was purchased by the Museum from the artist's son in 1926.   P.32–1926

Victorian and Edwardian (1837–1910)

We have seen how earlier styles and the influence of exotic cultures have affected British art at various times since the sixteenth century. To suggest, therefore, that this was a uniquely Victorian process as has so often been done is not entirely accurate. What the Victorians did which was genuinely new was attempt to explain the nature and development of different styles in a logical and systematic manner. They hoped to deduce 'principles' from their historicist studies, and once the principles which motivated the ancients were understood they could be applied by artists, architects, and designers to put Victorian products on the same footing as those of the Greeks and the Goths. Thus, in surveying the somewhat bewildering collection of objects laid out in the Museum's Victorian and Edwardian primary galleries, one must not look simply for borrowed forms but for a genuine and original 'Victorian' style.

One of the first to write of such principles was the architect and designer Augustus Welby Northmore Pugin. His succinct advocacy of the Gothic style in various publications and his success in rebuilding the Houses of Parliament with Charles Barry after the disastrous fire of 1834 ensured a popularity for Gothic throughout the century. The Museum possesses several important pieces by him, including the large cabinet designed for J. G. Crace which was shown in the Great Exhibition of 1851, a desk from the Palace of Westminster, and various pieces of jewellery.

Interest in Gothic forms and decoration naturally led to a concern for medieval painted architecture and furniture. Most famous, perhaps, of the designers and architects who pursued this course was William Burges, whose best-known work is undoubtedly his rebuilding of Cardiff Castle and Castel Coch for the Marquess of Bute, between 1865 and 1875. The bed, wash-stand, and painted cabinet which he made for his own Tower House in Melbury Road, London show well his particular form of almost jocular medievalism. Among other important pieces of painted furniture are the large cabinet designed by Richard Norman Shaw and shown at the International Exhibition of 1862, and King René's Honeymoon cabinet designed by the architect John Pollard Seddon for his own use.

Another development of Gothic was the Arts and Crafts Movement championed by William Morris from the early 1860s. Morris devoted most of his life to the improvement of what he considered to be the debased standards of mid-Victorian mass production—a result of machine manufacture and the disappearance of hand craftsmanship. Although involved in the production of furniture and other three-dimensional objects, Morris's particular contribution to design was in the field of flat pattern making. Numerous books, wallpapers, printed and woven textiles, carpets, embroideries, and tapestries in the Museum's collections testify to the immense fertility and ingenuity of his imagination. He studied the different processes of manufacture in great detail not simply to facilitate production at the various workshops he set up but so as to ensure that his designs were appropriate to them. Morris's influence was so profound and far-reaching that few late nineteenth-century designers were unaffected by it. The Cotswold School, the name given to the various designers and cabinet makers including Ernest Gimson and Sidney Barnsley, who set up workshops in Gloucestershire, are perhaps the best known. Several examples of their elegant furniture and metalwork are on display; and particularly splendid is the cabinet made by Peter Waals, the experienced Dutch cabinet maker, who joined the School in 1901.

Contemporary with these developments in Gothic design and the crafts were those involving industrial manufacture. Morris's worries about the standards of design had, in fact, been voiced thirty years earlier by the Select Committee responsible for the foundation of the Schools of Design and the Museum. Sir Henry Cole himself set up Summerley's Art Manufactures to produce everyday articles designed by well-known painters and sculptors so as to 'promote public taste'. Most critics at this time were concerned about objects like the papier mâché tray (p.98), the ornamentation of which they did not consider appropriate. They held that patterns should be flat and disciplined and should not reproduce naturalistic forms faithfully.

The employment of designers in industry was not, of course, new, but it was undoubtedly given impetus by these developments. Most manufacturers requiring flat patterns turned at some time or another to architects and designers, and the number of tiles, wallpapers, carpets, and textiles in the Museum's collections which can be attributed to particular artists is prodigious. In the case of three-dimensional designs, those of Christopher Dresser for pottery and metalwork and Alfred Stevens for ironwork are outstanding.

By the 1890s a self-consciously 'new' decorative style was evolved, offering a lighter and more fanciful alternative to the rather academic and sombre 'aesthetic' taste of the 1870s and 1880s. Called Art Nouveau after a shop opened in Paris in 1895, it is characterized by limply swaying and curving forms, frequently stylized and naturalistic, and including female figures with long, flowing hair. Although many shallow relief and flat pattern designs in the Museum's collections, such as that by Archibald Knox for Liberty and Company, testify to the acceptance of the new style here, its more extreme forms were not as popular as on the continent. Similarly the work of Charles Rennie Mackintosh and the Glasgow School with its combinations of straight lines and gentle curves, frequently owing something to Celtic patterns, did not win the acceptance in Britain one might have expected. The furniture by the architect Charles Voysey typifies the more restrained forms favoured by English designers.

The Road to Capel Currig by John Sell Cotman (1782–1842) *H. 33.15 cm W. 43.8 cm*
John Sell Cotman was born in Norwich and spent the greater part of his working life there. Consequently, he is naturally associated with the Norwich School which flourished during the first decades of the nineteenth century. His true affinities, however, were much more with the new Romantic style of water-colour landscape typified by Girtin and the younger Turner, which he had studied at the house of the great patron, Dr Munro, in London. The rugged scenery of Wales, like that of Yorkshire, where he also travelled to paint, were consequently better fitted to his interests than the flat landscapes of East Anglia.   AL6860

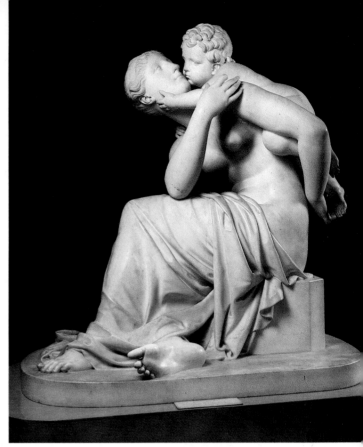

Maternal Affection by Edward Hodges Baily (1788–1867)
1837 *H. 94 cm L. 90 cm*
Although signed and dated 1837 Baily first conceived this group in
the early 1820s. He exhibited a plaster of it in 1823, and apparently
executed a marble in the following year. According to an entry in the
Art Union of 1847, this marble failed to sell and Baily eventually let
it go cheaply to Mr Neeld M.P. Since the Museum's group once
formed part of the Neeld Collection, and Baily did exhibit a group
under this title in 1837, the *Art Union*'s account, however, is not
wholly credible. A.33–1964

Pandora by John Gibson (1790–1866) *c.* 1856 *H. 172.7 cm*
Pandora was originally commissioned by the Duke of Wellington, but
Gibson did not carry out the work as the Duke had requested and he
declined to accept it. Gibson sold the figure instead to Lady Marion
Alford, of whom he remarked 'a lady of true knowledge in the arts,
and who had watched the progress of the statue with much interest in
Rome. . . . Lady Marion had become converted to polychromy, and I
therefore coloured the Pandora'. The Museum's uncoloured statue
is one of two marble copies which Gibson made. A.3–1922

Tiara First half of nineteenth century *Diam. 19 cm*
The tiara, which is made of gold set with diamonds and pearls, is
composed of three parts. The large and small blossoms, made up of
numerous four-petalled flowers, possibly meant to represent a
hydrangea, date from about 1820. The two large sprays of oak leaves
with eight Baroque pearls as acorns date from about 1840, and the
single small blossom of conventionalized designs, set with large
diamonds, dates from the mid-nineteenth century. M.117–1951

Cabinet bookcase designed by Augustus Welby Northmore Pugin (1812–52) *c.* 1851 *H.243 cm L.326 cm D.66 cm*
This carved oak cabinet bookcase which was made by J. G. Crace was shown in the Medieval Court at the Great Exhibition of 1851. Although the design resembles two bookcases illustrated in Pugin's *Gothic Furniture*, published in 1835, it is closer in style to a drawing in the Museum by Pugin dated 1849. Another drawing of the same date for fittings for Crace's showroom in Wigmore Street, which incorporates an 'IC' monogram like that on the shields in this bookcase, may indicate that Crace intended to include this piece in his showroom after the exhibition. Other drawings for this bookcase are also in the Department of Prints and Drawings, Paintings and Photographs. The glass panes are a modern addition.   25–1852

Marriage jewellery designed by Augustus Welby Northmore Pugin (1812–52) 1847–8
These pieces are part of a set of jewellery which Pugin designed in anticipation of his marriage to Helen Lumsden. Already twice widowed, Pugin had proposed to Helen in November 1847. She was prevented from marrying by her family, however, and Pugin gave the jewellery instead to Jane Knill, whom he married in August 1848. The pieces were made by John Hardman and Company of Birmingham, whose account and day books record the precise dates of manufacture and cost.   M.10, 20 and 21–1962

Manchester Town Hall by Alfred Waterhouse (1830–1905)   *c.* 1868   *H. 78.7 cm   W. 63.5 cm*
This is one of nineteen drawings which Waterhouse submitted in competition for the Town Hall in February 1868. Although he was placed fourth for 'architectural excellence', his designs were given first place for 'arrangment of plan and construction' and for 'economy and likelihood of being executed for the stipulated sum (£250,000)'. Furthermore, his design was said to be the best for 'natural light and ventilation' and he was declared the winner. The great hall, with its early English Gothic detailing and hammer beam roof, is decorated with wall paintings depicting scenes from Manchester history, which were carried out by Ford Madox Brown between 1876 and 1888.
D.1882–1908

Cabinet designed by William Burges
(1827–81) 1858 *H. 213.4 cm W. 140 cm
D. 38 cm*
This cabinet of painted and gilt wood was
designed by Burges for H. G. Yatman and
made by Harland and Fisher. The panels
were painted by E. J. Poynter (1836–1919)
and depict the story of Cadmus, the cutting
of cuneiform letters, Dante and Caxton, and
the heads of History, Poetry, Anaxagoras,
and Pericles. The lower part of the cabinet
draws out as a writing desk with two cupboards on either side. The gable roof and
finials are derived from cupboards in Noyon
and Bayeux cathedrals, and the dormers in
the roof act as a calendar. The cabinet was
exhibited in the International Exhibition of
1862. Apart from his furniture and metalwork designs, William Burges is best known
for his architectural work, particularly Cardiff Castle and Castell Coch which he
restored for Lord Bute. His own Tower
House can be seen in Melbury Road,
London.   Circ.217–1961

Decanter designed by William Burges
(1827–81) 1865 *H. 28 cm Diam. 17.8 cm*
The decanter is made up from a glass bottle
mounted in chased and parcel gilt silver set
with amethysts, opals, and other semi-
precious stones and Greek and Roman
coins. It is inscribed round the neck with the
name of James Nicholson for whom Burges
designed it, and the date 1865, and it bears
the maker's mark of Richard A. Green.
Burges had made two other very similar
decanters for his own use out of the profits
of his publications.   Circ.857–1956

Table designed by George Edmund Street
(1824–81) *c. 1854 H. 66 cm D. 98 cm*
This is one of a number of tables designed
by Street for the students' bedrooms at
Cuddesdon College. Although Street was
much involved with the firm of Holland
through his two wives Maraquita Proctor,
who died in 1874, and Jessie Mary Anne
Holland, who he married in 1876, it seems
more likely that this table was made on site at
Cuddesdon by local joiners. In style it is
similar to the later productions of the Arts
and Crafts Movement, and this is significant
because Philip Webb who designed furniture
for Morris and Company was working in
Street's office at the time of the Cuddesdon
commission.   w.88–1975

Model for the Albert Memorial *c. 1863*
H. 203 cm W. 71 cm D. 71 cm
After the death of the Prince Consort on 14
December 1861, seven architects were invited to submit designs for a national memorial in Kensington Gardens, and those prepared by Gilbert Scott, later Sir Gilbert
Scott, were selected. In November 1863
discussions were held with Scott to settle the
design, and shortly afterwards the working
drawings were prepared and this large plaster model made so that Queen Victoria could
see better what was proposed and could
consider the detail. The model was made by
Farmer and Brindley of Westminster Bridge
Road and all the decorative sculpture modelled by H. H. Armstead. After being kept at
Buckingham Palace for several years, where
it proved 'extremely valuable for reference',
Queen Victoria consented to the model
being displayed in the Paris Exhibition of
1867 and on its return to London it was sent
to the Museum.   A.13–1973

Vase designed by Alfred Stevens (1817–75)   1864
H. 43 cm W. 23 cm
Among the advocates of the Renaissance, as opposed to
the Gothic revival of the last century, the most important was undoubtedly the sculptor Alfred Stevens.
This vase is one of several which were made to his
designs by Minton, Hollins & Co.   184–1864

Model for the Wellington monument in St Paul's Cathedral by
Alfred Stevens (1817–1875)   1857   *H. 197 cm W. 70 cm L. 98 cm*
The Wellington monument is probably Alfred Stevens' best-known
work. The story of its conception in 1857 when Stevens was at first
placed joint fifth in an international competition and its completion in
1912, after Steven's death, is one of the most scandalous, tragic, and
intriguing in English Art. Stevens' slow rate of working was at the
heart of the problem. The heroic figure groups of Truth and
Falsehood, and Valour and Cowardice had a great influence on the
succeeding generation of British sculptors.   44–1878

Hot air stove designed by Alfred Stevens (1817–75)
1850   *H. 127 cm W. 67 cm D. 91 cm*
Alfred Stevens prepared several designs for metalwork for the
Sheffield manufacturer Henry Hoole between 1850 and 1857. This
stove was one of a number of objects he designed specially for the
firm's stand at the Great Exhibition and which won for them a
Council Medal. Stevens' sympathy with metal and the casting
method, particularly with the sculptured qualities which could be
achieved, gained for the firm a reputation for fine products second to
none in the mid-nineteenth century.   4030–1853

Parlourmaid's tray   *c.* 1865   *L. 62 cm*
W. 45.7 cm
The tray, which is made of papier mâché, with
inlay of ormer and other shell is shaped for
carrying in front of a maid or waiter, the outer
rim convex and scalloped, and the inner
slightly concave and plain. Useful and decorative articles made of papier mâché have been
produced all over the world from early in the
Christian era and are still being made today.
Interestingly, the term, although French, was
probably first used in this country in the
seventeenth century. Perhaps the best-known
manufacturers are the Birmingham firm of
Jennens and Bettridge. It was their patent of
1847 for applying steam to papier mâché
panels to make them pliable which enabled
machines to be made for pressing and mould-
ing items such as this.   w.8–1959

Jacquard woven picture   1862   *H. 17.8 cm W. 10.2 cm*
The picture was woven by the Coventry firm of J. and J. Cash, now famous for the
manufacture of woven name tapes, for the International Exhibition held in
London in 1862. As a result of the Cobden Treaty in 1860, import duties were
removed from foreign ribbons which flooded the British market. Weavers in
Coventry, which was the centre of ribbon weaving in Britain, were forced to
abandon the manufacture of dress and furnishing ribbons for which there was no
longer a market, and many turned their looms instead to making pictures such as
this. In spite of this expedient, however, hundreds of firms were shut down. J. & J.
Cash and Thomas Stevens, famous for his Stevengraph pictures, were among the
few to survive.   T.90–1957

Room from The Grove, Harbourne, Birmingham 1877

This panelled 'boudoir' or ante-room designed by the Birmingham architect John Henry Chamberlain (1831–83) for William Kenrick (1831–1919) forms one of the most outstanding features in the Victorian Primary Galleries. Since it was originally used as the main entrance to the drawing room and was, consequently, kept free of furniture, Chamberlain was able to use more lavish decoration than elsewhere in the house. The resulting synthesis of Gothic forms combined with extreme naturalism, and here and there a hint of Japanese, particularly in the floral panels, owes as much to the teachings of Owen Jones as to those of Ruskin. The panelling, which is of sycamore and oak with inlay of walnut and other woods, was given to the Museum by the Kenrick family and Birmingham City Council when the house was demolished in 1963.

W.4–1964

Group of furniture by the Pre-Raphaelites *c.* 1860
The large oak cabinet against the wall on the right was designed by the architect John Pollard Seddon (1827–1906) as a desk and receptacle for his drawings and instruments. The painted panels on the front were contributed by his friends William Morris and Ford Madox Brown. In front of it stands an oak table designed in about 1860 by Philip Webb (1831–1915), architect of William Morris's Red House at Bexley Heath, and behind it against the wall on the left is a wardrobe which Webb also designed. This has painted panels by Edward Burne-Jones (1833–78) depicting scenes from Chaucer's 'Prioress's Tale', and was presented to William and Janey Morris as a wedding present.
Wardrobe: Ashmolean Loan.
Table: W.45–1926. Cabinet: W.10–1927

Page from a book of verse by William Morris (1834–96) 1870 *H. 27.9 cm W. 20.3 cm*
This book, which includes a selection of Morris's poetry expressing the fear and anguish of love, was given to Georgina Burne-Jones. The delicate watercolours are by Edward Burne-Jones, Fairfax Murray, and George Wardle, some to Morris's own designs.
L.131–1953

Stained glass designed by William Morris (1834–96) 1872–4 *H. 71 cm W. 43 cm*
This is one panel from a set of three depicting minstrels, which with a similar set depicting poets were given to the Museum by Morris's daughter May. The set was many times adapted, by the addition of wings, as Minstrel Angels for church windows.
C.677–1923

Tapestry 'Angeli Laudantes' 1894 *H. 240.7 cm W. 204.5 cm*
This wool and silk tapestry on a cotton warp was made at William Morris's Merton Abbey works. The figures are taken from Sir Edward Burne-Jones's cartoon for the stained glass window which Morris & Co made for Salisbury Cathedral in 1879. The border and background were designed by John Henry Dearle who was director of the Merton Abbey tapestry works. Further copies of the tapestry were woven in 1898 and 1902, and in 1905 enlarged versions were made both of 'Angeli Laudantes' and a companion tapestry, 'Angeli Ministrantes', for Eton College Chapel. The Merton Abbey workshops by the River Wandle in Surrey were set up in 1881 when Morris & Co's premises at 26 Queen Square in Bloomsbury became too small. They continued to be used until 1940 when, rather than lower its standards because of the wartime conditions, the firm went into voluntary liquidation.

153–1898

Photograph of Isambard Kingdom Brunel (1806–59) by Robert Howlett (d. 1858)   November 1857   *H. 28 cm W. 23 cm*
This albumen print, of the engineer Brunel standing in front of the chains of one of the checking drums of his mammoth steamship the 'Great Eastern', is generally regarded to be one of the greatest masterpieces of 'environmental portraiture'. Although Howlett's short career was spent in the shadow of Joseph Cundall, one of the founders of The Photographic Club, which became the Royal Photographic Society in 1894, his series of 'Crimean Braves' photographed in 1856 by Royal Command established his importance as a photographer. In 1857 he took the photographs on which W. P. Frith based his famous painting of Derby Day.   246–1979

Evening dress _c._ 1894

This dress of midnight blue velvet trimmed with black jet and sequins was made in the United States of America by Stern Brothers of West 23rd Street, New York. It is included here both as an example of an evening dress of which the Museum has a large collection, but also because American dress and decorative art, of which there are also many examples in the collections of the Museum, do not fit rationally into the other volumes in this series. The necklace of silver and white pastes is English, _c._ 1840. T.272 and A–1972

Harlequin and Columbine Mid nineteenth century _H. 33 cm W. 25.4 cm_

This print from the _Graphic_ forms part of the enormous holding of theatre material given to the Museum by Mrs Gabrielle Enthoven in 1925. Along with many subsequent donations, it forms the basis of the Theatre Museum. At present the Museum's collections are housed in the Victoria and Albert Museum, but when the new Theatre Museum is completed in Covent Garden in the near future they will be moved there.

Soup tureen and ladle designed by Christopher Dresser (1834–1904) 1880 _H. 21.6 cm Diam. 23.5 cm L. of ladle 35 cm_

The electro-plated tureen and ladle are marked 'H & H 2123' and bear a registration mark for 28 July 1880. Dresser worked for the London and Birmingham silversmiths J. W. Hukin and J. T. Heath from about April 1878 for approximately three years, although the firm went on producing some of the designs until well into the present century. Dresser, a pupil of the Government Schools of Design, was much inspired by Owen Jones (1809–74), whose enthusiasm for scientific progress and belief in nature as an inspiration for design particularly appealed to him. M.26–1972

A Halt in the Desert by John Frederick Lewis (1805–76)   1885   *H. 36.8 cm W. 49.8 cm*
Lewis was born into an artistic family, both his father and his uncle being artists. As a boy he studied animals with
Landseer and many of his early exhibited works were of animal subjects. His predeliction for the Orient was
apparently first stimulated by a visit to Granada between 1832–4. This inspired him to go to Cairo in 1841 where he
lived for ten years. Many of his later paintings, such as this, were worked up from notes and sketches made during this
time.

FA 532

Design for an exhibition building by Owen Jones (1809–74)   *c. 1860*   *H. 37.5 cm W. 72 cm*
Surprisingly little is known about Owen Jones, who was one of the most important architectural theorists of the last century. Almost all his
buildings and decorative schemes have either been demolished or altered beyond recognition. This water-colour depicts one of three designs
he prepared for a permanent industrial exhibition hall, winter garden, and pleasure park at St Cloud, near Paris, which was not built. The
documentation of his involvement with the project is sparse and difficult to follow, but it is known that he was associated with Sir Joseph
Paxton in the inception, and that the scheme grew out of their joint involvement with the Crystal Palace in Hyde Park and later at
Sydenham.

D.946–1886

Sideboard designed by Edward William Godwin (1833–86) *c.* 1867 *H. 180.3 cm W. 259 cm D. 56 cm*
This sideboard of ebonized wood with silver plated fittings and inset panels of paper stamped in imitation of embossed leather was made to Godwin's designs by William Watt. Godwin was born in Bristol but moved to London in 1862. He was married for a time to the actress Ellen Terry, and was friendly with James McNeill Whistler, for whom he designed his most famous building, The White House in Tite Street, London, now demolished. The design of The White House, like this sideboard, reflects Godwin's great interest in Japanese art.   Circ.38–1953

Vase and cover in the form of an owl by the Martin Brothers 1899 *H. 26 cm Diam. 20 cm*
The Martin Brothers' pottery, active for more than three decades at Southall from 1877, was the joint enterprise of four talented brothers. Birds such as this were first made in the 1880s there by Robert Wallace Martin (1843–1923), who had a life-long love of humorous and grotesque ornament, inspired by stone carvings he carried out when working on the Houses of Parliament.   C.491 and A–1919

Group of pottery by William Frend de Morgan (1839–1917) *c.* 1890 *Largest H. 23.8 cm*
The son of a mathematician and professor of philosophy, De Morgan was born in London and studied at the Royal Academy Schools. Ceramics were his main interest, however, and at various potteries in Fulham, Chelsea, and elsewhere he specialized in the production of wares such as these, which are obviously influenced by Near Eastern ornament. These pieces date from his Fulham period.   C.421–1919, C.4–1905, 859–1905, Circ.193–1919

▷

Cabinet on stand 1902 *H. 188 cm W. 119 cm D. 48 cm*
This walnut and ebony cabinet with gilt gesso panels was designed by Ernest Gimson (1864–1919) and made at Daneway House, Sapperton in Gloucestershire, where he had set up workshops with Sidney Barnsley in 1902. Gimson himself executed the gesso panels but the remainder of the piece was made by Peter Waals, a Dutchman who before joining Gimson and Barnsley had had considerable experience of cabinet making on the Continent. The cabinet is illustrated as the frontispiece to *The Furniture and Joinery of Peter Waals* published by the Alcuin Press in 1930, and appears to have been one of the earliest pieces he made here. A design by Gimson for a similar cabinet, dated 1901, is in Cheltenham Museum and Art Gallery. This cabinet is remarkable for its radically innovatory form and proportions which anticipate developments in the 1920s. W.27–1977

Silver casket designed by Archibald Knox (1864–1933) for Liberty and Co. 1903 *H. 11.4 cm W. 21.8 cm D. 13.3 cm*
Archibald Knox was a native of the Isle of Man and began to work for Liberty's as a designer of silver, jewellery, and pewter in 1901 or 1902. He taught at the Kingston and Guildford Schools of Art and was also a water-colour artist and book illustrator. Many of his designs are in the Department of Prints and Drawings. This box is mounted with opals and bears a Birmingham hallmark for 1903–04, and the maker's mark of Liberty & Co. (Cymric) Ltd. M.15–1970

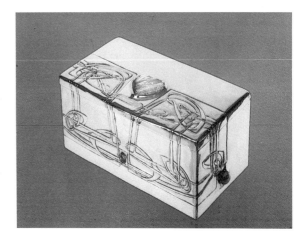

Queen Victoria by Sir Thomas Brock
(1847–1922)   1902   *H. 54.6 cm W. 38.7 cm
D. 25.4 cm*
After Queen Victoria's death in January 1901
a committee was appointed to consider what
form the National Memorial to her should
take. Several architects were invited to
submit designs for the replanning of the Mall
and the ground in front of Buckingham
Palace, and one sculptor, Thomas Brock, to
submit designs for a sculptural monument to
form the centre-piece of this scheme. Brock
was almost certainly chosen because he had
executed more statues and busts of the
Queen than any other living sculptor. This
bronze was cast by Singer of Frome, now
Morris Singer, from a model of his proposal
which was approved by King Edward in June
1902. A bronze cast from an earlier model
showing the complete monument with the
Queen surrounded by groups depicting
those virtues for which she was renowned is
also in the Museum. In execution few altera-
tions were made to this scheme and it was
unveiled on 16 May 1911, when Brock was
knighted.   A.8–1977

Printed cotton   1902   *H. 86.4 cm
W. 61.6 cm*
This is one of a number of samples of
furnishing textiles which were taken from
ledgers in the possession of the firm of F.
Steiner and Company Limited of Accrington
at the time of its liquidation in 1957. The
design, which is a typical example of the
kinds of 'art nouveau' patterns which were
mass produced on textiles and wall papers at
this time, was registered at the Patent Office,
and consequently its date is known
precisely.   T.128–1957

Writing desk and chair designed by Charles Francis Annesley Voysey (1857–1941) 1896 and 1909 *Desk H. 168 cm W. 84 cm D. (open) 87 cm, Chair H. 140 cm W. 64 cm*
The chair is made of oak, and is upholstered in leather. It is one of a set of twelve which Voysey designed in about 1909 for the offices of the Essex and Suffolk Equitable Insurance Company, Capel House, New Bond Street. A water-colour drawing in the Museum (E.711–1969) shows eight of the chairs arranged in the Company's board room with other furniture also designed by Voysey. The oak writing desk with copper hinges was designed for W. Ward Higgs Esq., and made by W. H. Tingey in about 1896. w.6–1953, Circ.517–1954

Hanging by Godfrey Blount (1859–1937) 1896 *H. 211 cm W. 180 cm*
The hanging, which was only recently acquired by the Museum, is made of variously coloured handwoven linens applied onto a natural coloured linen background. Godfrey Blount, who was educated at Winchester and Pembroke College, Cambridge, later studied art under Hubert Herkomer and at the Slade under Legros. His interests turned away from painting, however, and in 1896 he set up the Haslemere Peasant Industries, where this hanging was made, for weaving, embroidery, simple furniture, and other crafts. Later still he founded the Peasant Arts Society. T.173–1978

Chair and fireplace designed by Charles Rennie Mackintosh (1868–1928) c. 1900 *Chair H. 137 cm W. 49.5 cm D. 47 cm, Fireplace H. 152 cm W. 142 cm*
The chair was made for the Glasgow School of Art, Mackintosh's most famous building, and was exhibited at the Vienna Secession exhibition of 1900. The firegrate was made for the Willow Tea Rooms, also in Glasgow, in about 1904. The combination of straight and curved lines in Mackintosh's work provided a real alternative for British craftsmen to the more swirling and contorted forms of continental art nouveau, but was not as influential as might have been expected. Circ.130–1958, Circ.244–1963

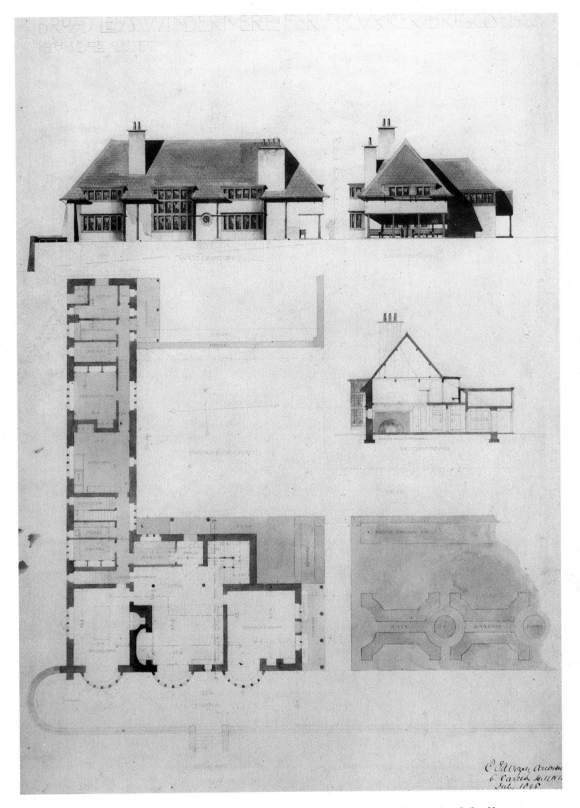

Design for Broadleys, Cartmel, Lancashire by Charles Francis Annesley Voysey (1857–1941) 1898 *H. 73.7 cm W. 52 cm*

Broadleys was one of several houses which Voysey designed for the Windermere area in 1898. All have steeply pitched roofs and wide eaves, and an austere severity which may reflect the harsh climate and barren landscape in which they were set. All Voysey's designs, unlike those of many of his contemporaries and predecessors, were structurally simple and relatively inexpensive to build. Contemporary accounts of a drawing of Broadleys which Voysey showed at the Royal Academy in 1899 notice that his style of draughtsmanship in pencil with 'whitey green' washes was something 'which Mr Voysey has invented'. It certainly marked a very distinct break with High Victorian architectural drawings and soon became the accepted mode among many of his contemporaries.   E.252–1913

THE ECONOMIST BUILDING

SCALE 1/16
E 6047
2 9 SEP
3 DEC 1960
2 4 MAR 1961

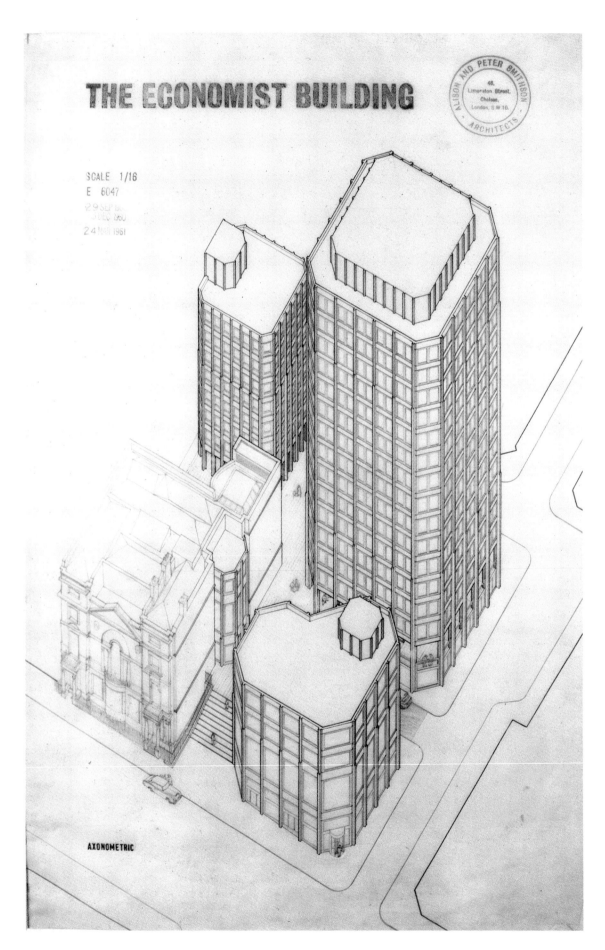

AXONOMETRIC

The Twentieth Century (1910–the present)

Much of this chapter is concerned with the post-First World War period and its concern with industrial design rather than individual handcrafted objects. Before considering that, however, it is necessary to look briefly at the work of Roger Fry, the artist who was so passionately concerned to encourage the arts in Britain in the early years of the century. It was Fry who organized the exhibition in 1910 of 'Manet and the Post Impressionists' which so stimulated British artists, and resulted in Eric Gill, Wyndham Lewis, Stanley Spencer, Duncan Grant, and others showing alongside Picasso, Braque, and Matisse in a second exhibition in 1912.

Fry's importance in the field of the decorative arts lies in his founding of the Omega Workshops in 1913, a studio where objects of everyday use were designed and decorated with bold patterns in Post-Impressionist colours. Many objects made in the workshops are now shown in the twentieth-century study collections: wooden candlesticks painted by Duncan Grant; an embroidered footstool designed by Fry and worked by Mrs Bartle Grant; a marquetry tray depicting Wrestlers designed by Henri Gaudier Brzeska; and a ceramic stove with tiles painted by Duncan Grant and Vanessa Bell. Among post-War objects made in the workshops is a wooden frame with embroidered panels by Mary Hogarth after designs by Wyndham Tryon of c. 1923. In the context of most other pieces of furniture in the Museum they appear somewhat amateur and rather exaggeratedly brash, but they do, nevertheless, possess a strength both physical and artistic, and an originality which contrasts strongly with the often excessively attenuated, structurally weak forms of Art Nouveau.

Roger Fry's concern with public standards of taste and the spirit of working together which the First World War encouraged both contributed to a generally felt desire to improve standards of design in British industry after 1918. The Design and Industries Association and 'Fitness for Purpose' grew up out of the Arts and Crafts movement with its emphasis on work by individuals and its belief in the rural tradition. The result of this, in the early 1920s at least, was to encourage the production of objects of simple form such as could be made by existing machinery from traditional materials. The best-known examples in the Museum's collections, perhaps, are the pieces of furniture by Sir Ambrose Heal, whose shop in Tottenham Court Road did so much to foster good design at this time, and those by Gordon Russell.

But while the members of the D.I.A. were concerned with pursuing this somewhat nationalistic course, new and exciting innovations were being made on the Continent, particularly in Scandinavia and at the Bauhaus in Germany. International Modernism, with its emphasis on structural and formal rationalism and its concern with new materials, made its first strong impact here with the exhibition of modern French and English furniture which Serge Chermayeff organized at Waring and Gillows in 1928. Some British artists were already familiar with the idiom, most notably the Irish designer Eileen Gray, whose superb lacquer screen was made as early as 1923. But she had lived in Paris for many years: to those resident in Britain Chermayeff's clear statement of what constituted honest twentieth-century design was a revelation. Numerous V & A objects were shown in the recent 'Thirties' exhibition organized by the Arts Council, and many are now on display in the twentieth-century study collections. They include a chromed steel standard lamp by the architect Oliver Hill of 1934; a pair of glass stands and a mirrored screen designed by Syrie Maugham, Somerset Maugham's wife, in 1935; laminated wooden furniture designed by

Economist centre by Peter and Alison Smithson c. 1960 H. 73 cm W. 44.8 cm
In 1959 The Economist newspaper arranged a limited competition for designs for a new building to house its offices, a bank, and some residential accommodation. Later, the site was enlarged when it agreed with the proprietors of Boodles that new Club premises would be included in the scheme too. The competition was won by the Smithsons, whose design was much praised, particularly for its sympathetic treatment of the difficult site. By designing three quite separate blocks and keeping the smallest on a line with St James Street, the centre is made to harmonize very successfully with the surrounding buildings. The project was completed in 1965.
Circ.376–1974

Marcel Breuer for Isokon, the firm set up in 1931 to put into production the design concepts of Wells Coates and Jack Pritchard; a dining table and chairs designed by Eric Ravilious in 1936; tubular steel chairs by P.E.L. Ltd; carpets by Marion Dorn and Betty Joel; pottery by Keith Murray and Susie Cooper; the extraordinarily original furniture designed by Denham Maclaren as early as 1931; and best known of all, perhaps, the entrance foyer of the Strand Palace Hotel designed by Oliver Bernhard between 1929 and 1930.

Just as the D.I.A. and Modernism had grown out of the First World War, so the Council of Industrial Design and utility grew out of the Second. The Utility Furniture committee was set up soon after November 1942 and the Council in December two years later. Gordon Russell was very influential on both. But after the gloomy War years utility was not popular. Designers and public alike felt the need for something lighter and more frivolous, and two important exhibitions, 'Britain Can Make It', held in the Victoria and Albert Museum in 1946, and the Festival of Britain in 1951 provided exactly the opportunity that was required to indulge this taste. Both had very far-reaching effects on British design, not only because so many designers participated in staging them, frequently without any of the usual shackles imposed by anxious manufacturers, but also because they involved larger numbers of the public than had been reached since the Great Exhibition a century before.

The Museum's recent 'A Tonic to the Nation' exhibition documented the Festival of Britain and its influence fully, and included many objects from the collections: Robert Gooden's silver tea service made for the Royal Pavilion at Brighton; formica with designs derived from molecular structures by the Festival Pattern Group; and furniture designed by Ernest Race and Lesley Dunn, to name but a few. These objects, like Robert Heritage's 'Hamilton' sideboard designed for Archie Shine Ltd., and Robin Day's work for Hille later in the decade, have an undeniably 50s character, 'not exactly stark but not exactly cosy' as one writer has put it. By the mid 1960s such generalizations were quite impossible, for design quite suddenly veered in several directions at once as Op and Pop and other styles quickly succeeded each other. Even the concept of permanence was brought into question as products were deliberately designed to be disposable. Terence Conran's Habitat shops had perhaps the most widespread influence, particularly on middle-class interiors, with their promotion of 'basic' objects owing as much to rustic cultures as to those of 'advanced' society.

In the 1970s the dominant theme may well prove to have been the revival of the crafts. Certainly John Makepeace's column of drawers, Roger Doyle's clock, Jacqueline Poncelet's bowls, Archie Brennan's tapestry, and Rupert Williamson's chair are all elegant witnesses of a move away from industrialism. Like Habitat's involvement with scrubbed pine and peasant weaves this is appropriate, for the applied arts have always reflected developments in technology, and in the 1970s scientists developed for the first time alternative technology as seriously as its conventional counterpart.

North Wind stone sculpture by (Arthur) Eric (Rowton) Gill (1882–1940) *c.* 1928 *H. 25.4 cm L. 69 cm D. 11.4 cm*
Although most famous, perhaps, for his calligraphic and other printed work, Eric Gill also carried out many sculptural commissions. The best known are probably the Stations of the Cross which he carved between 1913–18 for Westminster Cathedral, decorative sculpture for the exterior of Broadcasting House, of which North Wind was a part, and similar work for the League of Nations Building in Geneva in 1936. His sculpture is characterized by the same crispness and flatness so evident in his typographic work. Although he was made a Royal Designer for Industry in 1936, throughout his life Gill was much involved with hand as opposed to industrial production. After conversion to Roman Catholicism in 1913, he took part in the formation of the Guild of St Joseph and St Dominic, a semi-religious community of craftsmen; in 1920 he was a founder member of the society of Wood Engravers; and in 1928 he set up his own printing press at Speen in Buckinghamshire. A.10–1942

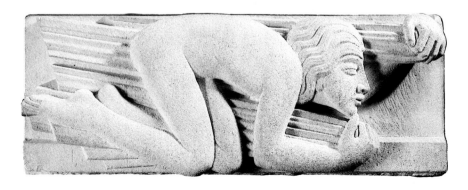

Book illustration by Edmund Dulac
(1882–1953)   1911   *H. 31.8 cm W. 25.4 cm*
Edmund Dulac was born in Toulouse. After
two years of training for a legal profession he
gave this up and moved to Paris, where he
studied art at the Academie Julian. Already
an Anglophile and deeply interested in book
illustration, he emigrated to England in 1904
and became a British subject in 1912. This
pen and ink and water-colour drawing was
for an illustration of 'The Snow Queen' on
page 51 of *Stories from Hans Anderson*
published by Messrs Hodder and Stoughton
in 1911; it depicts the sentence '"It is gold,
it is gold!" they cried.'   E.392–1948

The Eclipse of the Sunflower by Paul
Nash (1889–1946)   1945   *H. 42 cm
W. 57 cm*
Paul Nash was educated at Chelsea Poly-
technic and the Slade, and held his first one
man exhibition at the Carfax Gallery in 1912.
He served in the First World War at the
front before being appointed an Official War
Artist in 1917. He was again appointed in the
Second World War, at the end of which this
picture was painted. It reveals both the poetic
and surreal aspects of his work. He had
earlier been rather stimulated by Surrealism
and exhibited with the Surrealists in their
Paris Exhibition of 1938. An oil version of
this picture is in the collection of the British
Council. Nash also did much work as a
designer and book illustrator, and both these
aspects of his work are well represented in
the Museum's collections.   P.19–1962

Writing table 1925 *H. 107.7 cm
W. 135 cm D. 52 cm*
Designed by (Sir) Edward Maufe, this writing table of gilded mahogany, camphor wood, and ebony, gessoed and faced with white gold, was made by W. Rowcliffe and shown at the Paris Exhibition of 1925. Although Maufe designed furniture and other appplied arts he is best known as an architect, his most famous commission being Guildford Cathedral, which he won in open competition in 1932.　　Circ.898–1968

Lacquer screen designed by Eileen Gray (1879–1976)   1923   *H. 207 cm*
Eileen Gray was born in County Wexford, Ireland but moved to London to study at the Slade in 1898. It was while she was there that she learned the technique of making oriental lacquer in the shop of D. Charles in Dean Street which she happened upon one day in her lunch break. In 1902 she moved to Paris and not long after met and began to work with Sugawara, a Japanese master of Lacquer. It was not surprising, therefore, that when in 1922 she opened a gallery in Paris called Jean Desert, lacquer objects such as this screen should have featured among the exhibits. Because of the time involved in their production, however, such objects were very expensive and few were made and sold.   W.40-1977

Wardrobe decorated by the Omega Workshops   1916   *H. 173 cm W. 157.5 cm D. 45 cm*
In 1913 Roger Fry (1886–1934) opened a communal artistic workshop with Duncan Grant and Vanessa Bell, which he called the Omega Workshops. Fry was intent on applying the decorative qualities of Post-Impressionist Art to works of domestic utility so as to elevate general taste. They were obliged to close in 1919, however, partly for financial reasons but also because the participants were artists and consequently lacked enthusiasm for their roles as decorators. This wardrobe is said to have been part of a suite of furniture designed by Fry for Madame Lala Vanderville.   Circ.272-1975

Design for Fisher's restaurant by
Raymond McGrath (1903–77)
1932   *H. 22.7 cm W. 35 cm*
Like Serge Chermayeff, Raymond
McGrath, who was born in Australia and
educated at Sydney University, came to
modern architecture by way of his interior
design work in the new style of the late
1920s. A chance meeting with Mansfield
Forbes, the Cambridge Univeristy don, resulted in the commission to remodel the
interior of 'Finella', Forbes' Regency House.
McGrath received much publicity for the
work, which he carried out in coloured
glasses and copper and green and pink paint,
and other commissions quickly followed,
including this restaurant in New Bond
Street, now demolished.   Circ.564–1974

Rug designed by Serge Chermayeff (b.
1900)   1930   *L. 152 cm W. 140 cm*
Chermayeff was born in the Caucasus, but
came to England in 1910 and remained here
until 1939 when he emigrated to the U.S.A.
During his time in this country he was a
director of Waring and Gillow's 'Modern Art
Studio' and a member of the influential Mars
Group with Eric Mendelsohn. For much of
this time he was also in private practise. It is
possible that this rug may have been made
for his own use. Certainly, very similar
carpets appear in illustrations of his house in
The Studio in 1930.   T.157–1938

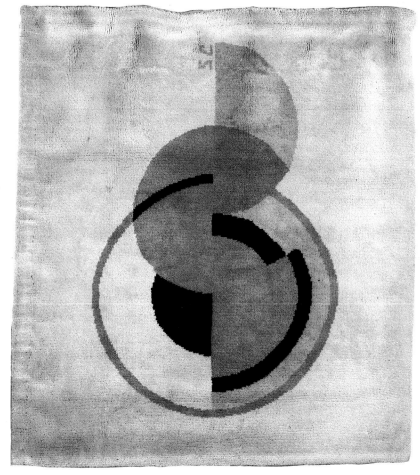

Pendant Brooch by George Hunt   *c.* 1935   *H. 8.9 cm W. 6.7 cm*
The brooch is made of gold and silver, decorated with ivory, enamel, mother of pearl, rubies, pearls, and tourmaline. It was shown at the Royal Academy in 1935 by George Hunt, the Birmingham jeweller and designer whose mark is stamped on the back. Egyptian influence has pervaded western art and design since before the Christian era. Napoleon's Egyptian campaign in the early nineteenth century and Howard Carter's opening of Tutenkhamen's tomb in 1924 have both been responsible for particular Egyptian fashions, however, which have affected the design of everything from clothes to biscuit tins.   M.41–1971

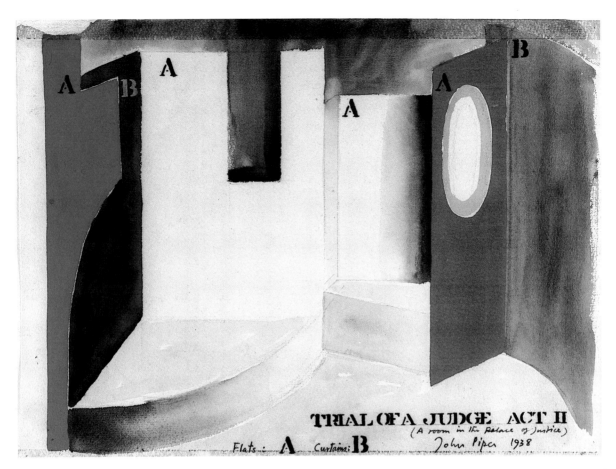

TRIAL OF A JUDGE ACT II
(A room in the Palace of Justice)
John Piper 1938
Flats: A Curtains: B

Design for a stage set by John Piper (b. 1903) *c.* 1938 *H. 23.5 cm W. 32 cm*
The design depicts a room in the Palace of Justice from Act II, Scene I of *Trial of a Judge, A Tragedy in Verse* by Stephen Spender. Piper, who studied at the Royal College of Art from 1928–9, is best known for his paintings and stained glass designs at Coventry and Liverpool Cathedrals. He has, however, designed various sets and costumes for the stage, particularly for Benjamin Britten's operas *Rape of Lucretia* in 1946, *Albert Herring* in 1947, and *Billy Budd* in 1951.   E.79–1967

Printed cotton by Marion Dorn (1899–1964) 1938 *H. 183 cm W. 127 cm*
Marion Dorn was born in San Francisco and came to England in the early twenties. She was eventually persuaded to move back to the U.S.A. in 1940 but in the intervening period she established a reputation here as one of the leading textile and carpet designers. After an exhibition of hand-knotted rugs in 1929 with E. McKnight Kauffer, she received numerous commissions for textiles and carpets for domestic interiors, hotels, and liners. This particular printed cotton entitled 'Exotique' was designed for Messrs Donald Bros.   Circ.282–1938

Farmyard tapestry by Edward Bawden (b. 1903)   1950   *H. 167.6 cm W. 134.6 cm*

Bawden studied at the Cambridge School of Art from 1919 and at the Design School of the Royal College of Art where Paul Nash was a tutor from 1922–5. Although known primarily as a mural painter and illustrator, he has also designed earthenware for Wedgwood, tile decorations for London Transport's Victoria Line, wallpapers on which he experimented with John Aldridge, and textiles for the Orient Steam Navigation Co. Ltd. The tapestry was woven by the Edinburgh Tapestry Company Ltd. in their Dovecote Studios at Corstorphine, and reflects Bawden's love of rural life in Essex. Contented cows, for example, such as appear in a group at the top, re-appear frequently in his mural and graphic work.

T.273–1978

Seated Mother and Child by Henry Moore
(b. 1898) 1975 *H. 50.4 cm W. 38.3 cm*
Henry Moore is the most eminent living
British sculptor. He was trained in Leeds,
where he met Barbara Hepworth, and in
London before travelling to Paris and Italy in
1925. His earliest major work was the
'North Wind' (1928) for London Transport,
and his international reputation dates from
1948 when he was awarded the sculpture
prize at the Venice Biennale. This print was
made to be issued as a gift with the 125
copies of the Deluxe edition of the catalogue
raisonné of Moore's graphic work published
in 1976. E.1422–1976

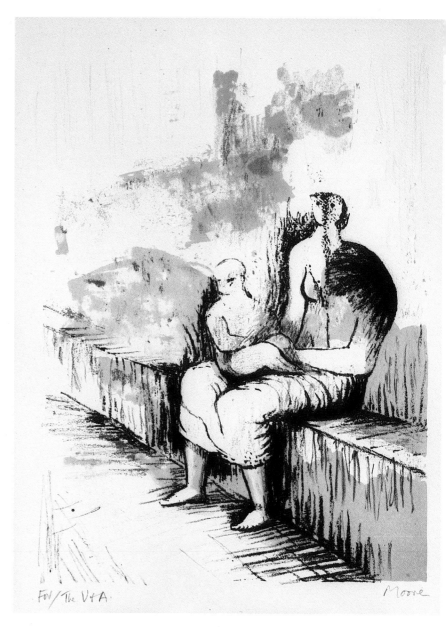

Nude girl, bronze by Frank Dobson (1888–1963)
H. 123 cm
Frank Dobson was the son of a Christmas card illustrator
and studied painting at the City and Guilds College,
Kennington. He took up sculpture after completing war
service in 1918 and was the only sculptor to exhibit in the
group X exhibition of 1920. Although best known for his
sculpture, he also designed and printed his own textiles
including batiks and lino blocks. Another example of his
sculpture is to be seen in the tiles he designed for
Goodhart-Rendel's Hays Wharf, on the Embankment.
A.32–1971

Dark Island, textile hanging by Archie Brennan 1971 *H. 172.7 cm W. 99 cm*
Archie Brennan trained at the Dovecot studios in Scotland before he went to art school and returned in 1963 to become a Director. It was there that he learnt the skills of tapestry weaving which have stood him in such good stead. Many of his tapestries take the form of visual jokes and would not succeed but for his great technical skill. Some of the effects he incorporates are the result of mistakes which he deliberately works into the designs, and it has been said of him that the 'risk-taking, real life quality' of weaving 'is the thing he really loves'.

Circ.331–1973

Stoneware vases by Bernard Leach (1887–1979) 1963 *Larger H. 28.6 cm D. 19 cm*
Bernard Leach, until his recent death, was the leading figure in the development of studio pottery in this country. He first discovered pottery when living in Japan between 1909 and 1920, and after returning to this country set up his own studio with Shoji Hamada at St Ives in Cornwall. From that time until he stopped pottery in 1972 as a result of failing eyesight, he held regular exhibitions of his work, taught and lectured frequently, particularly at Dartington Hall in Devon, and wrote numerous books. During the 50 years or so that he potted, Leach's style changed surprisingly little. The influence on him of Japan, and also of Korea which he visited on a second trip to Japan, is always apparent. It is interesting that his work has always been much respected by the Japanese, who in 1966 awarded him The Order of the Sacred Treasure, second class.

Circ.551–1963, 1192–1967

Chair by Rupert Williamson (b. 1945)
1976   *H. 96.5 cm W. 48.3 cm D. 50.8 cm*
The chair, which is of maple and rosewood with a
leather seat, was made by Rupert Williamson while
he was a student at the Royal College of Art. After
leaving the college, Williamson worked for a short
while in two reproduction and restoration busi-
nesses before setting up with the aid of a grant from
the Crafts Advisory Committee in his mother's
house at Milton Keynes. He admits to being
uncertain about the derivation of his ideas, stating
in an interview with *Harpers and Queen* in 1978:
'people always put me in the class of Art Deco, and
it's true that I did look to the Twenties, because I
never liked the Sixties international style and I
didn't like the Fifties stuff either. I don't like
William Morris much or the Bauhaus, which is
what the Sixties were all about. At college I was
more interested in Celtic work than anything. I like
clean pieces like Biedermeir; although I didn't
discover the existence of Biedermeier until two
years ago, they use woods like I use them.' At the
same time he admitted to being 'Really . . . a
sculptor, making functional things . . . what I want to
make is exclusive, decorative objects'.   w.18–1977

Bone China bowls by Jacqueline Poncelet
(b. 1947)   1972 and 1976
Larger H. 8.9 cm D. 13.3 cm
Jacqueline Poncelet, a student of the Royal
College of Art, made her first pieces in
stoneware. After finding that she was doing
more and more carving, however, she turned
to bone china quite naturally as a much more
responsive vehicle for this type of technique.
She casts all her pieces to begin with and
then proceeds to carve their surfaces, sometimes spending as long as two days whittling
away at a single piece. The later of these two
bowls was made in the St Pancras workshop
she set up with Glenys Barton, a fellow Royal
College student, who also works in bone
china.   Circ.256–1976, 255–1976

Design for a new casino at Monte Carlo 1970 *H. 64 cm W. 87 cm*
This is one of a number of drawings and collages which were submitted by Archigram Architects for the competition arranged by the 'Societé des Bains de Mer' at Monte Carlo for a new summer casino and club in 1970. Archigram, which consisted at the time of Peter Cook, Dennis Crompton, and Ron Herron, won the competition, but although building was begun it was not completed when the project fell through in 1973.

Circ.470–1974

Gouache study by Bridget Riley (b. 1931) 1969 *H. 62 cm W. 98 cm*
This is a study for the emulsion on canvas painting 'Byzantium' which Riley completed in 1969. The identity of each red stripe is shifted by the band it encloses, and the white stripes, which appear to expand as they move outwards, are suffused with a delicate colour spread from the adjacent reds. The painting developed from a green and magenta canvas closely related to the 'Chant' series completed in 1967.

Circ.663–1971

Man running towards a bit of blue by David Hockney (b. 1937) 1963 *H. 63.5 cm W. 52 cm*
This drawing was made at the time Hockney made his first excited visit to California and shows his early interest in painting water. Not only was the idea of depicting moving water in a very slow and careful manner appealing to him, but he was also impressed by the athleticism of young American men and painted at least one figure from photographs taken by the Athletic Model Guild, a group of Los Angeles photographers who specialized in studies of the male nude.

Circ.298–1963

Bowl by Michael Lloyd (b. 1950) 1975 *H. 5 cm W. 9 cm*
Michael Lloyd graduated from the Royal College of Art in 1976. He says of himself 'I never sit down to draw the shapes, I just raise the silver until I feel that I've arrived at the correct shape for the design then I paint it white all over and draw the design on in pencil. I look at it for a few days while I work something else, maybe sketching. Only then I go back and see if its really what I want it to be, design and bowl an integral whole. My mind works incredibly slowly, and raising and chasing silver proceeds at just that same pace. That's why I like it.' Lloyd has made his home on a canal long boat and admits a debt to William Morris and Art Nouveau metalwork, particularly the work of Gaudi and Omar Ramsden.

M.250–1977

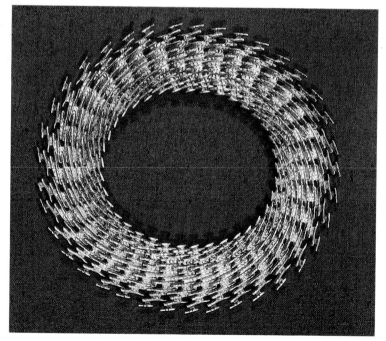

Collar 1968 *L. 36 cm*
The work of the London jeweller Anthony Hawkesley, who designed and made this silver gilt collar, played a prominent part in the revival of the crafts in the 1960s. In the 1970s this revival was, perhaps, the most significant development in the area of the applied arts and was reflected in the establishment of the Crafts Council in its own right instead of as a Committee of the Design Council.

M.25–1973

Dragon-fly clock by Roger Doyle (b. 1947) 1977 *Diam. 10 cm*
After leaving the Central School of Design, Roger Doyle served a five-year apprenticeship with Cartier Ltd. In 1969 he worked for Louis Osman on the crown used by Prince Charles for his investiture as Prince of Wales, and in the same year he set up his own workshop in London. This clock was specially designed for one of the series of Jubilee Masterpiece exhibitions organized in the Museum by Lady Casson in 1977.

M.126 & a–1978

Industrial pottery 1977
This pottery is from the 'Concept' range which Martin Hunt of the Royal College of Art and Colin Rawson designed for Hornsea Pottery in Yorkshire in 1977. It is made of vitramic stoneware, unglazed except on the interiors of all the receptacles, which are glazed. In style the design harks back to Art Deco which underwent a period of popularity at this time.

C.207 to K–1977

Column of drawers by John Makepeace (b. 1939)   1978   *H. 131 cm W. 51 cm*
John Makepiece first set up a furniture workshop at Banbury in Oxfordshire which flourished
and in 1977 he moved to larger premises at Parnham House, Beaminster, Dorset, where he
was also able to instigate a residential course for student craftsmen. 'We expect that at the end
of two years each student will have learnt all the basic skills and techniques of working with
wood, and will have built up his own clientele and begun to have developed an individual style
so that he is completely ready to set up and successfully run his own workshop.' Makepeace
understands well the business needs of the modern craftsman and has ensured that this is a
vital part of the course. This column of drawers, the depth of each drawer indicated by a
coloured band at its base, is one of a number of objects in different media which the Museum
has recently commissioned from contemporary craftsmen, in continuance, in point of fact, of
the traditions of the Museum when it was first founded. It represents a development on a
rather similar column of drawers which Makepeace showed at the Craftsman's Art exhibition
held in the Museum in 1973.   w.56–1978

126

The Prince Consort's Gallery, from a drawing by John Watkins *c.*1876–81

European Art
in the Victoria and Albert
Museum

Eltenberg reliquary Copper and bronze gilt on oak, champlevé enamel, ivory Rhenish Late 12th century *H. 54.6 cm*
This splendid reliquary illustrates the art of the 12th century Rhenish goldsmiths. In the form of a Byzantine church (a Greek cross surmounted by a dome), it is richly decorated with brilliantly coloured champlevé enamels, designed in a variety of floral, geometrical, and imbricated patterns. Round the drum of the dome are ivory figures of Christ and the Apostles, and in the niches below the figures of the Prophets and four scenes from the life of Christ. In the 19th century, the reliquary was the centre-piece of the collection of the Russian Prince Peter Soltykoff.

7650–1861

Introduction

At a meeting of the Museums Association of Great Britain in 1901 for a lecture on industrial art museums, a member of the audience remarked that it did not matter that the V&A's collections were mostly of European art, for, on the way to South Kensington, one could call in at Westminster Abbey to see English art.

Since 1901 the Museum's English art collections have been greatly strengthened, but it is true that in the early days the European decorative arts were its first concern. The reason for this must have been partly ideological. The Museum was created to help improve the design of British products, at a time when they were succumbing to foreign competition in world markets. If the Museum's collections were to offer a good example to British industry, it must have seemed right that they should display foreign rather than British traditions in decorative art. This bias accorded, in any case, with current taste in collecting, which had taken a new direction in the early nineteenth century, and which must be briefly considered before introducing the Museum's collections.

The reigning taste throughout Europe during the latter half of the eighteenth century had been for classical statuary. Well-born young men on the 'Grand Tour' had always made for Italy, where they bought Old Master paintings; under the influence of Winckelmann and other Neo-classical luminaries they now concentrated on Greek and Roman sculpture. English gentlemen were among the most eager collectors, and the British Museum was enriched by the fruits of their enterprise: by 1825 it was established as the national museum of antiquities.

In the early nineteenth century collectors rediscovered the arts of the Middle Ages and the Quattrocento, particularly their decorative arts. (The High Renaissance, which had never fallen out of favour, had overshadowed the Early Renaissance.) A sentimental partiality for the Middle Ages had already been promoted by a few enthusiasts, pioneers of the Romantic Movement, but they were interested mainly in literature and architecture. A serious interest in the art of the Middle Ages quickened when medieval artifacts were liberated onto the market by the French Revolution.

The great art accumulator of the Revolutionary era was Baron Vivant-Denon, Napoleon's cultural commissar. His collection (sale 1826) included fine medieval objects, though it also contained oddities such as the moustache of Henri IV and relics of the Inquisition. Even more influential as a collector of medieval art was Alexandre Lenoir, who rescued as many as he could of the art objects turned out of churches at the Revolution, and reconstructed them in Paris as a Musée des Monuments Français. Although he saved some stained glass and Limoges enamels, his museum consisted mostly of sculpture, and was dispersed at the Restoration. But he made his own collection of minor artifacts, which was sold in 1837.

In the early decades of the century, medieval church art could be picked up in Europe for almost nothing in the dusty shops that sold 'bric-à-brac' or 'curiosités': there were as yet few organized or well-informed dealers. Consequently, men of no great wealth were able to assemble excellent collections. Alexandre du Sommerard, like many another collector, worked in a dull daytime job (in the Audit Office), while devoting his leisure passionately to his hobby. Objects from his own and other collections are illustrated in the luscious plates of his *Arts au Moyen Age* (1838–46). In 1832 he installed his collection in a medieval house, the hôtel de Cluny, which was opened to the public and in 1843 was acquired as a museum by the French State.

Already in 1828 the Louvre had accepted the collection of Pierre Révoil, who had also started collecting in the very earliest years of the century. His friend Charles Sauvageot, a violinist at the Opéra and a customs official, was the very pattern of the obscure, obsessive collector who wins renown through his treasures. Applauded by Balzac in *Cousin Pons*, he received the Légion d'Honneur on giving his collection to the Louvre in 1856. Some of the more ambitious collectors also began to take an interest in medieval art. By this time, the ambition of a connoisseur was to make a systematic, representative collection rather than a capricious one. So Baron Pourtalès (catalogue 1842) augmented his Greek vases and Old Master paintings with medieval and Renaissance works; and later Louis Fould (sale 1860, fine catalogue by J. M. A. Chabouillet 1861) similarly added such works to his Egyptian, Greek, and Roman antiquities.

Others were specialists. Perhaps the most influential medieval and Renaissance collection was that of Debruge Dumenil, who began collecting furiously in 1830, taking advantage of the dispersal of some of the first-generation collections. After his death in 1838, his collection was systematically arranged and catalogued by his son-in-law, Jules Labarte; the introduction to the catalogue (1847) looks back at Debruge Dumenil's forerunners and provides a survey of the collection, which, in an enlarged translation (1855), became the standard text book on the subject in England. It conveniently displays for us what kind of objects the early collectors expected to assemble: ivory carvings, which provide a miniature history of sculpture from late Antiquity to the eighteenth century; small sculpture in stone and wood, especially German, from the late Gothic period; medieval bronze vessels and Renaissance bronze sculpture; medieval enamels, both cloisonné and champlevé, and the Renaissance enamels of Limoges; gold- and silversmiths' work, mostly church plate; lapidary's work on crystal, agate, and other semi-precious stones; jewellery; Hispano-Moresque and maiolica pottery; Venetian glass; armour; and furniture.

Upon the scene just described the V&A—in its early form as the Museum of Ornamental Art at Marlborough House—entered in 1852. Sale prices of medieval and Renaissance art were just beginning to rise, following the now established taste, but there was still time for the Museum's first curator, J. C. Robinson (who had studied in France, obviously to good effect), to begin to create a national museum of medieval and later art. In England there had been only one collector to match those of France already mentioned, the middle-class M.P., Ralph Bernal; at his thirty-five-day sale in 1855 (catalogue 1857), the V&A did not miss the chance to buy heavily, especially maiolica. The next year Robinson and his chief, Henry Cole, acted even more energetically in securing the entire collection of Jacques Soulages of Toulouse, which, like Bernal's, had been formed in the 1830s and '40s (catalogue by Robinson, 1856). In 1861 came the dispersal of the collection of the Russian Prince Peter Soltykoff, who had bought most of the Debruge Dumenil collection in 1848. The V&A and the British Museum dominated the sale room; the *Gazette des Beaux-Arts* lamented that the French museum curators were present, unarmed, at a battle where they could not fight, and pronounced that the V&A would soon, in its speciality, be the first museum in Europe. At this sale the Museum, now the South Kensington Museum, bought the Eltenberg Reliquary for £2,130.

Robinson was not content with keeping watch on the sale rooms for the 'drain of works of art from the continent of Europe to this country', but determined to 'tap these waters at their sources'. Every year, therefore, he spent some months in purchasing-tours abroad. His principal foreign triumph was the acquisition in 1860 of the Gigli-Campana sculpture collection, which laid the foundations of the V&A's incomparable holdings of Italian sculpture. Robinson was something of a dealer (which was why he bought so effectively) and became increasingly at odds with the Museum bureaucracy: he left the Museum in 1867. He had set it on its course with such momentum that ten years later the collector Edmond Bonnaffé ruefully remarked that 'what France invents, England makes perfect: du Sommerard invents the museum of decorative arts, and England founds South Kensington'.

It has to be admitted, though, that in the later decades of the century, the

Museum began to lose its ascendancy in the collecting world, and the German museums (many of them founded in direct imitation of South Kensington during the '60s and '70s) rose to prominence under the leadership of the great scholar-curator Wilhelm Bode of Berlin. The V&A's holdings do include works from many of the great later nineteenth-century collections: from the huge, diverse 'San Donato' collections of the Princes Demidoff (sales 1870, 1880); from Sir Andrew Fountaine's collection (sale 1873), which contained medieval and Renaissance works surprisingly acquired in the seventeenth century by an ancestor of the same name; from the 'Colworth' collection of Hollingworth Magniac (sale 1892); and from the Paris collection of Frederick Spitzer (sale 1893, grandiose catalogue 1890–2). Most of what the V&A obtained from these sources, however, came indirectly, through the great collection (formed with profits from Australian sheep-farming) of George Salting, bequeathed in 1910.

Salting's was one of the last comprehensive collections in the du Sommerard tradition. But it is interesting to note that the First World War dislodged a good deal of medieval and Renaissance art from European collections, such as the Guelph treasure formerly belonging to the royal house of Hanover, the Hohenzollern-Sigmaringen collection, and works sold off by the Soviet regime from the Hermitage (which included the situla once in the collection of Prince Basilewsky, now in the V&A). This fresh access of art works went to form a further series of private collections, which have been sold from time to time. In 1978, the Robert von Hirsch collection, reputedly the last of these, came up for sale; the prices were so high that the V&A was unable to purchase anything.

In the view of the mid-nineteenth-century collectors, the Renaissance extended through the seventeenth century. The use of 'Baroque' as an art-historical term began in 1888 with Wölfflin's book *Renaissance und Barock*; and 'Mannerism', a style intervening between these two, was detected only in the 1920s. So works which we would now describe as Baroque or Mannerist slipped into the great collections without much difficulty, especially if they could hang on to the coat-tails of great men. Much late maiolica passed as 'Raffaelle ware' because its designs were often copied from prints after Raphael; any Mannerist goldsmiths' work, northern or southern, might be ascribed to Cellini; small Baroque sculpture was often given to 'Fiammingo' (i.e. François Duquesnoy). Some kinds of objects which appealed to nineteenth-century taste, like Venetian fancy glass, German ivory tankards, and Palissy ware, enjoyed as high esteem then as they ever have.

Consequently the Museum acquired, even in its early days, some sixteenth- and seventeenth-century objects. But many of the most elaborate pieces of Mannerist and Baroque art had gone straight into the treasure cabinets of princes, for which they had been commissioned, and stayed there through the centuries, eventually ending up today in German public museums. When such objects, which were rich men's art in the first place, did find their way on to the market, they were usually bought by rich men, especially (and appropriately) the Rothschilds. From the 1820s these new merchant princes of Europe were acquiring such costly *objets d'art* as once graced the Green Vaults in Dresden or the Schatzkammer of Rudolph II in Prague. One of the surviving Rothschild collections came on the market in 1977 when the contents of Mentmore Towers, Buckinghamshire, were sold. From this sale the V&A was able to acquire both small, exotic objects and larger pieces of furniture, especially the richly decorated cabinets which so strikingly embody in miniature the princely treasure chambers.

During the many decades when Mannerist and Baroque art was out of favour, the V&A did acquire examples through the good offices of Dr Walter Hildburgh, an American collector who for forty years devoted himself to buying for the Museum in neglected fields. He worked closely with the staff of the Sculpture and Metalwork Departments, who became accustomed to his 'sturdy, rubicund figure, in its thick tweed suit and black overcoat, bustling along the galleries or rising behind a library desk to ask his invariable question, "Anything you want to see me about?"'. The collections of English eighteenth-century sculpture, of Spanish metalwork, and above all of English alabasters, are largely his creation; and many seventeenth- and eighteenth-century *objets d'art* in the European galleries were given by him. He served as an invaluable corrective to the Museum's own taste: when the curatorial staff baulked at spending the Museum's money on an interesting object they did not like, they spent Dr Hildburgh's instead.

Since the art of the seventeenth and eighteenth centuries survives in much greater quantity than that of the Middle Ages and Renaissance, it has been possible for the Museum to build up wide collections in less expensive areas, such as pottery, glass, and base metalwork. The curator's desire to have a little of everything has often been gratified by the readiness of modest, specialist collectors to donate objects that seem to 'fill a gap' in the collections.

Textiles have always attracted dedicated, specialist collectors, partly because they make a poor show on display. To be sure, this is not true of tapestries, and the return to esteem of Gothic tapestries is one of the more startling episodes in the history of taste: at the beginning of the nineteenth century they were being used as horse-blankets and tarpaulins, and at the end had become the most precious trophies of the first generation of American millionaires.

Decorative textiles have attracted a more archaeological interest: indeed, the very earliest of them were actually dug up. Coptic textiles, made in the fourth to twelfth centuries A.D., have survived only because they were used as grave-clothes in Egypt and the dry sand of the desert preserved them. Although some had been found as early as the seventeenth century, it was not until the 1880s that the hunt really began, chiefly at the instigation of museums. The V&A's collection consists largely of discoveries by the German archaeologist Robert Forrer, acquired in 1899. Many Byzantine fabrics have also been recovered from mortuary surroundings: used, because of their richness, to shroud relics, they have been later recognized in cathedral treasuries, where Gothic vestments also survived. For its early accessions of medieval textiles, the V&A was indebted to Canon Franz Bock of Aachen, who, catching Gothic revivalism from A. W. N. Pugin's example, rifled presbyteries throughout Northern Europe and assembled a huge collection of woven and embroidered textiles which was sold in 1864, part to the V&A and part to the Decorative Arts Museum in Vienna.

The appreciation of French eighteenth-century art has been subject to comparatively little fluctuation. The taste of the French court, especially of Mme de Pompadour and Mme du Barry, was for luxurious, expensive objects, which, by virtue of the cost of their manufacture and the prestige of their owners, took their place at once at the top of a high-priced connoisseurs' market. At the Revolution, the French royal household goods were deliberately sold off by the Directoire at low prices, but the effect on the market was, in the long run, beneficial, since a great deal of first-class furniture and decorative art was thus put into circulation. Much of it came to England, the Prince Regent being among the principal purchasers. When, in the early 1850s, Henry Cole and J. C. Robinson were setting up the Museum of Ornamental Art, they ransacked the Royal collections for loans of French eighteenth-century furniture and porcelain.

The early decades of the nineteenth century saw the lowest fortunes of the *dix-huitième* market, and even small collectors, like Balzac's Cousin Pons, could find bargains. But it had steadied again by the 1860s, just as the finest English collection, that of Lord Hertford, approached completion. On Hertford's death in 1870, it passed to his son Sir Richard Wallace, whose widow left the cream of it to the nation in 1894; it was opened to the public as the Wallace Collection in 1900. The first English collection of French eighteenth-century art to enter the public domain was, however, that of the tailor and army clothier, John Jones, bequeathed to the South Kensington Museum in 1882. It was then excitedly described by the *Art Journal* as 'the noblest donation ever made by a private individual to any country in the world's history', but it has been somewhat overshadowed since, not only by the Wallace Collection but also by Baron Ferdinand de Rothschild's collection at Waddesdon Manor, which was left to the

National Trust in 1956. In the very year in which the Jones Collection came to South Kensington, Rothschild was buying *dix-huitième* furniture at sky-high prices at the celebrated Hamilton Palace sale (where the Museum bought some Gothic and Renaissance objects), and he continued to dominate the market until his death in 1898. If the Jones Collection falls below these two collections in quality, it has the advantage that in the V&A it occupies a place in a broader collection that includes the art of other periods and countries.

Museum taste is usually antiquarian taste, so it might be expected that the South Kensington curators would have been little concerned with acquiring the decorative art of their own time, the latter half of the nineteenth century. This seems to have been true of Robinson, but Cole sustained the Museum's original purpose, to influence contemporary art, and examples of commendable contemporary art (i.e. art which revived historic styles) were acquired. The usual policy was to buy at international exhibitions, and in consequence the V&A's collection is weighted with pieces in which technical skill and historicist orthodoxy are taken to ostentatious lengths.

Nineteenth-century art was all too gladly disparaged or ignored by the generation of curators who led the Museum into the next century. Yet the Museum can claim in due course to have pioneered a revival of twentieth-century interest in Victorian decorative art. The exhibition of 'Victorian and Edwardian Decorative Arts' in 1952 was extremely influential, and although it dealt only with British art it stimulated European museums to study the nineteenth-century art of their own countries. Since there is no European monarch whose name can be used, like Queen Victoria's, to characterize an epoch, European art historians have adopted the useful term *Historismus* (historicism) to describe nineteenth-century decorative art: several important exhibitions with this title, held at decorative art museums in Vienna (1964–5), Berlin (1973), Prague (1975), and Hamburg (1977), show the growth of European studies in this field.

At the turn of the century English taste grew insular. At the Paris Exhibition of 1900, George Donaldson, Vice-President of the furniture jury, was impressed by the Art Nouveau furniture and decorative arts exhibited by firms from France and other European countries. Fearing that England had been left behind, he purchased a large selection of pieces and presented them to the V&A, a most valuable and timely gift. When exhibited in England, this 'New Art' was denounced by the English art establishment as corrupt, and the Museum seems to have lost its nerve. When the new Director, Sir Cecil Smith, produced his first report in 1911, he announced that the acquisition of contemporary art presented 'such grave difficulties that there is a disposition among the authorities of modern museums to exclude [it] altogether'. This, he implied, would be his policy, and although he did set up a 'British Institute of Industrial Art' to channel contemporary British art into the Museum, it must be admitted that the Museum paid little heed to the important design movements of early twentieth-century Europe. After the last War, the Museum's Circulation Department fostered an interest in contemporary art, especially Scandinavian design, and began to repair the omissions in the nineteenth- and twentieth-century collections. Since 1975, each of the curatorial Departments has had a special budget for post-1920 purchases, and contemporary design, now international in character, is regularly acquired.

This brief summary of the Museum's growth in relation to changing taste may help to explain why the European collections took the shape they did. But it may also suggest, through over-simplification, that Museum taste is unduly capricious. It should be remembered, however, that the V&A began at a time when systematic collecting was in vogue, when the collector's ideal was a 'complete series' of objects of every kind, showing the historical development of styles and techniques. The monotonous displays which tended to result from this method of collecting have now been changed, but the approach remains sound. It is still the curator's aim to collect widely and objectively, so as to form a 'representative collection' sufficient to demonstrate the history of art, rather than personal taste.

Basilewsky situla Ivory Ottonian (Milan) c.980 *H. 15.9 cm*
A *situla* is a ceremonial holy water bucket; this example has been
named after the collection in the Hermitage, Leningrad, from which
it came. It was made for the liturgical reception of the Holy Roman
Emperor Otto II at Milan in 980. Ritual was a chief characteristic of
the Ottonian era and something of the splendour of medieval
ceremony can be seen in the lively and rhythmic figures depicted; the
Repentance of Judas is almost in the form of a ceremonial dance, the
figures graceful symbols of power and energy. The *situla* is decorated
with scenes from the Passion and Resurrection of Christ;
architectural elements provide the setting and divide up the narrative,
although a harried-looking Apostle can be seen rushing from the
Divine Presence in one scene to appear in the next with Doubting
Thomas.   A.18–1933

Early Christian, Byzantine, Romanesque

The earliest objects collected by the V&A date from the first centuries of the Christian era. Perhaps, however, the Museum collections should begin earlier. Since the Roman Empire included much of what is now Europe, it might be argued that the earliest truly European art was Roman art. Furthermore, the style of Ancient Roman art (itself derived from Greek art) was prolonged into the early centuries A.D. and intermittently reproduced in later times: so it has been a fundamental influence on European art. Nonetheless, the V&A does not collect classical antiquities: that is the business of the British Museum. Since the principal shaping influence upon modern Europe was Christianity, it is appropriate that a collection of European art should start at the momentous period when Christianity conquered the western world. It is salutary to remember that styles in art, which are merely a historian's overlay upon an adventitious succession of things, do not necessarily correspond with the political, religious, or economic interpretations that the historian puts upon human affairs.

The Emperor Constantine gave Christians freedom of worship in 313 A.D., and Christian art, hardly more than a few symbols, came out of the catacombs. Pagan religion was not displaced at once: on the Symmachi panel (late fourth century) a maiden is still gravely absorbed in an instinctual rite, undisquieted by Christian scruple. Pagan motifs were adopted by Christian art: the Winged Victory turned into an angel.

In 330 A.D. Constantine moved his imperial capital from Rome to Byzantium (renamed Constantinople), a city on the threshold of Asia. This city, where Greek philosophy mingled with the new Christian faith to inspire incessant theological controversy, became the centre of a rich, severe art which persisted, with little alteration, for eleven centuries, although inhibited by Iconoclasm (the prohibition of religious images) from 720 to 842, checked by the sack of Constantinople in 1204, and brought to an end in 1453 when Constantinople fell to the Turks.

Although some surviving secular objects, such as the Veroli Casket, evoke the brilliant, luxurious life of the urban élite, Byzantine art was predominantly religious. Its church buildings were unspectacular (save for the prodigious Hagia Sophia) but their interiors were transfigured by mosaic decoration, the noblest of Byzantine art forms, which is now best seen not in Constantinople but in outposts of the Empire such as Ravenna, Venice, Rome, Daphni, and Saloniki. Of this resplendent art only the faintest echo can be caught in the V&A from a tiny (and late) portable mosaic. Byzantine art is peopled with tall, still figures, their bodies veiled under stiff robes, their facial expressions both withdrawn and demanding, and their eyes suggesting an inner life of spiritual or intellectual power. They shimmer in mosaics, and are seen also in ivory carvings: it is here that Byzantine sculpture must be studied, for there is little large-scale carving in stone, and hardly any carving in the round. Byzantine art tends to flatness; and its woven silks, using flat patterns derived from Persia, have at their best a grandeur perhaps never since attained in textiles.

In 800, while the Byzantine throne was occupied by Irene, the first woman Emperor, Pope Leo III, in Rome, crowned a rival Emperor: Charlemagne, the King of the Franks. Charlemagne consciously set out to create an imperial culture in his barbarian realm, calling in aid the examples of Byzantium and classical Rome, and the monastic culture of the North. Consequently the works of art of the 'Carolingian renaissance', and of the later 'Ottonian renaissance' promoted by the three successive Emperors Otto (962–1002), show a blending of Mediterranean and Northern styles. These must be distinguished (as with Byzantine art) in small-scale objects, notably ivories and illuminated manuscripts;

but since the art history of the period must now be pieced together from scanty evidence scattered through many museums, the discrimination of styles may safely be left to scholars. No museum has enough to demonstrate the whole story, but the V&A can provide—in the Lorsch Gospels, for instance—testimony to several important episodes.

The political stabilization of Europe, and the growth of international interests encouraged by Benedictine monasticism, led to a widespread and fairly coherent artistic revival in the later eleventh century, to which the label 'Romanesque' is given. This label is most pertinently used of architecture: for the first time for centuries great buildings rose which bore comparison with those of Rome. Mostly churches, these essentially blockish constructions achieved imposing effects by complex aggregation. Large-scale sculpture was revived upon these churches: this too was blockish, as if only with difficulty released from the stone. But its vehement expressiveness was all the more arresting, and was echoed in small-scale work. In ivories, manuscripts, and enamels urgent men appear, tense and crooked in posture, their draperies snagging on projecting knees, elbows, and bellies, their hands pointing or making logic-chopping gestures, their toes turning out or dancing along. The contrast with the remote, formal, veiled figures of Byzantine art is unmistakeable. An interest in the odd rather than the ideal is evinced in the frequent representation of grotesques and monsters, especially in what art historians dryly call 'inhabited scrolls'—thickets of vegetation in which struggling men and animals are entangled.

In the Romanesque period, metalwork—goldsmiths' work, champlevé enamel, bronze sculpture on doors, fonts, or lamps—took pride of place among the arts. Extraordinary vessels of precious metal were made to contain the relics of saints, which inspired growing veneration. To such an extent have Romanesque churches been altered, and so widely are their contents dispersed, that it is difficult, even at a great centre like Hildesheim, to imagine the united effect of architecture and the decorative arts. But the Eltenberg Reliquary, combining ivory carving, goldsmiths' work, and enamels in an architectural form, powerfully embodies this integration in miniature.

The triumphant cross Tapestry of wool and linen East Mediterranean area 5th or 6th century *38 × 61 cm*
Tapestry, a very ancient and widespread technique of pattern-weaving, was extensively practised in the Byzantine empire. Many examples have been found in Egyptian graves, where they served as wrappings for the dead. This fragment, which comes from the burial-grounds at Ahkmim in Upper Egypt, was probably part of a curtain originally intended to hang in a doorway or between columns, or perhaps at an altar. The jewelled cross symbolizing the Christian faith, with alpha and omega for the Almighty and birds representing the souls of the faithful, was framed in a wreath of flowers and borne aloft by a pair of winged victories or angels, crowned with jewelled diadems.   349–1887

Symmachi panel Ivory c.400 Italian (Rome) *H. 29 cm W. 12 cm*

This ivory panel forms half of a diptych; its companion piece is now in the Cluny Museum in Paris. Both panels are inscribed with family names, this one alluding to the 'Symmachi' and that in the Cluny to the 'Nichomachi'; the diptych probably commemorates an alliance, such as marriage, between the families. Its subject-matter suggests that these families were among the patrician Romans who tried to preserve their old cultural heritage in despite of Christianity, adopted as the State religion in 380. Here a statuesque and somewhat passive-looking priestess before an altar takes incense to sprinkle on the sacrificial fire. Her ivy wreath shows that she is of the cult of Bacchus and she stands beneath an oak tree, sacred to Jupiter. The boy holds up a wine jar and bowl of fruit. The style and subject matter look back to a classical prototype, a consciously archaic style to remind the beholder of the glorious past of ancient Rome. 212–1865

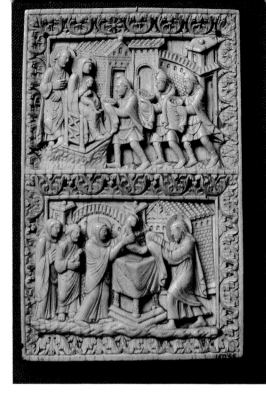

Adoration of the Magi and the Presentation
Ivory   Carolingian (Metz)   c.900   *H. 18.5 cm*
W. 11.5 cm
Charlemagne's artists, looking for models in Christian
antiquity, found inspiration in the architecure, painting,
and sculpture of early Christian Rome and
Constantinople. This ivory, a fine example of the best
work of the Metz school, illustrates the late Roman and
Byzantine influence in the stocky, vigorously modelled
figures, set against realistically-achieved backgrounds
of city walls.   150–1866

Lorsch Gospel cover   Ivory   Carolingian (Aachen)   c.810   *H. 35.1 cm*
W. 26.7 cm
These ivory plaques once formed part of the cover of a ninth-century manuscript of
the Gospels from Lorsch Abbey. The Virgin and Child are flanked by St John the
Baptist and, on the right, Zacharius, holding a censer and incense box. Above are two
flying angels holding a medallion containing Christ Blessing; below, the Nativity and
annunciation to the shepherds. The monumentality of the figures and their clinging
drapery hark back to sixth-century Byzantine prototypes.   138–1866

St John the Baptist and other saints   Ivory   Byzantine
12th century   *H. 23.5 cm W. 13.5 cm*
Probably part of a book cover, this relief has faint traces of colour and gilding. The end of the ninth century saw the dawn of the most brilliant period of Byzantine art, with an austere beauty and fineness of execution which can be seen in this ivory. In the centre is the bust of St John blessing. His features are delicately modelled, the eyes gazing intently, yet giving the impression of other-worldliness. Above him are Sts Philip and Stephen, below Andrew and Thomas.   215–1866

Virgin and Child   (*Hodegetria*)   Ivory   Byzantine
12th century   *H. 32.4 cm*
This statuette is the only free-standing Byzantine ivory to have survived (the head of the Child is a restoration). The Virgin is of the type called *Hodegetria* or 'she who points the way'; she either stands or sits, holding the Child on her left arm, her right hand placed over her breast, pointing to the Child as the 'Way of Salvation'. She gazes directly at the spectator, in a manner not unlike the saints in the ivory above. The delicate rendering of the features and naturalistic fall of drapery make this a supreme example of work done in the 11th and 12th centuries in the Byzantine Empire.   702–1884

◁
Veroli casket   Ivory   Byzantine   Late 10th or early 11th century   *H. 11.4 cm W. 40 cm*
The casket came from the Cathedral of Veroli, near Rome, but was probably a secular object, made to hold scent bottles or jewellery. It is decorated with scenes and figures from classical mythology, and numerous nymphs and centaurs disporting themselves. The stocky figures are derived from late Imperial Roman art but are extremely lively, creating a sense of constant movement within the episodes.
216–1865

A lion-slayer Woven silk, compound twill East Mediterranean area 8th–9th century. *H. 40 cm W. 32 cm*
Silkworm-culture and silk-weaving, Chinese monopolies in antiquity, later spread westwards to Sassanian and Byzantine territory. This textile was produced by an advanced silk industry, employing the drawloom to ensure automatic repetition and reversal of the pattern. The designer, trained in the Byzantine pictorial tradition, depicts a lion-slayer—probably Herakles or Samson—in a landscape setting suggested by a single flower, framed by segments of circles decorated with rose buds. Silks with this pattern were exported to various parts of western Europe in the Carolingian period; this example comes from the cathedral of Chur, in Switzerland. 7036–1860

Sion Gospel cover Beechwood, gold, enamels German 10th or 11th century *H. 25.4 cm*
The cover, made of beechwood overlaid with gold and enriched with cloisonné enamels and precious stones, was made for the Sion Gospels which date from about AD 1000. The outer border is probably of the same date as the Gospels but the Christ Enthroned and beautifully stamped work around it are of the twelfth century. Few of the large stones are original. 567–1893

Brooch Gold, enamel, and garnets Frankish 7th century
Diam. 47.5 cm
The Franks were the Germanic race which conquered Gaul in the 5th century, giving their name to the territory which ultimately became France. This life-size reproduction shows clearly the primitive filigree with which the gold plate of the brooch has been set. The four small rectangular stones are garnets. M.119–1939

Moses and the Brazen Serpent Champlevé enamel, gilt copper Mosan c.1160 *H. 102 cm W. 102 cm*
On this page are two examples of champlevé enamelling, one of the most important decorative arts of the Middle Ages. The copper base is engraved to form cavities which are filled with a vitreous substance; this is fused in a furnace, then ground and polished. The enamel is missing from this plaque, so that the chiselled cavities can clearly be seen. Moses, bearing his tablets, and Aaron stand on the left; on the right stand the Wounded (*Vulnerati*) Israelites, about to be cured of their snakebites by the Brazen Serpent, which Moses has raised on a pole. M.59–1952

Annunciation Mosaic Byzantine Early 14th century
H. 13.3 cm W. 8.3 cm
This mosaic belongs to the last phase of Byzantine art during the Paleologue Revival (1260–1450). Such small portable icons were made mainly for the court of the Orthodox emperors, which was luxurious and supported by nobles and intellectuals. It is composed of microscopic tesserae of gold, silver, lapis lazuli, and semi-precious stones, almost indiscernible as separate entities. The dramatic and psychological moment is brilliantly captured as the Angel moves, his drapery fluttering, and the Virgin turns away in fear. An exquisite example of Byzantine court art, where a new vividness and humanism are evident. 7231–1860

Nativity Champlevé enamel, gilt copper Limoges (?)
13th century *H. 11.7 cm, W. 12.7 cm*
A bewildered and despondent St Joseph is seated to the right of the scene of the Nativity. The Virgin's child-birth bed has the appearance of an altar with liturgical hangings, an iconographical motif common in the 12th and 13th centuries, and emphasized by the lamps hanging on either side of the altar-bed. Within each cavity in the base two colours of enamel are used, so as to produce a shaded effect. 6815–1860

Saints Stained glass French Mid-13th century *H. 52.1 cm*
W. 49.5 cm
This glass-painting is a work of art of the first quality in an unusually
fine state of repair. The subject is still in dispute: in the left panel is a
preaching sainted deacon, possibly St Stephen or St Lawrence; on
the right, the ordination of a sainted deacon who stands in obeisance,
receiving a copy of the gospels from the veiled hands (*velatis manibus*)
of an unseen bishop. The style is similar to that of the windows of St
Germain des Prés in Paris. The brilliant colours—ruby, sky blue,
forget-me-not blue, yellow, and greens—are skilfully juxtaposed to
create a vivid and harmonious balance.   C.1362–1924

Early Medieval and Gothic

The word 'Gothic' was at first applied insultingly to medieval architecture, for it means 'to do with the barbarian Goths', but it is now used without detraction to describe the building style based on the pointed arch and on two closely-related devices, the rib vault and flying buttress. These were new methods of dispersing stress in a building. Romanesque buildings were constructed chiefly of solid load-bearing walls, and large, splendid buildings were composed by piling together smaller units. In Gothic buildings where the new methods were used, loads could be supported on a series of separated props; space could flow more freely, and a building might be regarded as a logically articulated framework rather than as solid masses. The first great demonstration of the pointed-arch style in Europe was in the rebuilding of the abbey church of St Denis near Paris in 1140–4. Through the next century, in the great cathedrals of the Île-de-France (the area around Paris, which was the artistic capital of the Middle Ages) the Gothic style was developed with strict logical consistency and rhythmic beauty. Here the style was (as many consider) at its most refined and mature. From France it spread through Europe; once its linear, skeletal quality had become clear, it was open to all kinds of playful variation, and was easily applied to all the decorative arts.

The great Gothic churches, like their Romanesque predecessors, inspired rich sculptural decoration, especially upon their outside portals, where ranks of tall, thin, single figures, like human columns, seemed to grow out of their architectural setting. This sculpture cannot be studied in museums, any more than the architecture can. But Gothic figure sculpture soon advanced fully into the round, while decorative sculpture in an architectural setting took more ornamental shapes, usually derived from plant forms, which were, indeed, sometimes directly copied with astonishing realism: Gothic leafage is a subject in itself. In the high Gothic period (1250–1350) church-building was set going less by monastic initiative and more by civic pride, and private patrons commissioned more small sculpture, in the form of altarpieces and monuments both for churches and domestic chapels. The Blessed Virgin, attracting intensified devotion, was frequently represented. It is this type of sculpture that has tended to find its way into museums.

In Gothic sculpture the human body is still concealed under draperies, which often enough seem to have been treated by the sculptor as exercises in abstract form. Naked bodies were depicted only in circumstances of sin or death; none but that of the crucified Christ might be contemplated without shame, and His was beautiful because it was broken. The skeleton enters art only in the Middle Ages. Faces, however, were carved with sympathetic expressiveness, though few can be presumed to be real portraits.

Since the structural stresses of a Gothic building were concentrated at isolated points, its walls might be largely reduced to windows. These empty spaces were regulated stylistically by networks of stone tracery, and were filled with stained glass, one of the most important art forms of the Middle Ages. Although most stained glass is pictorial, its effect is chiefly of kaleidoscopic pattern; representational forms are composed of patches of glass (usually red and blue, until a new stain permitted golden tonalities in the fourteenth century) held in place by lead strips; only faces and details are drawn, boldly. In its architectural setting stained glass can, as it were, speak with tremendous harmonic resonance; but there, it can rarely be examined closely, whereas detached specimens may be scrutinized in a museum.

The objects of metal, ivory, wood, and fabric with which early Gothic churches were furnished were in the massive Romanesque style. But by 1250 Gothic tracery and arcading, with its crust of crockets and pinnacles, had been adopted in metalwork; reliquaries, monstrances, and censers were formed like miniature churches. Thereafter, such ornament, equally lively at any scale, was adopted in other media and spun out to the frailest delicacy. A purely linear style like this almost demanded to be drawn on paper. Some architectural drawings survive, evidence of the craftsmen's considerable new skill in geometry; and after the invention of engraving in the mid-fifteenth century, Gothic ornament began to circulate in prints. Already, however, from 1350, the whole of Europe was employing a common style, 'International Gothic'. In its tendency to elaboration this is often decried as dishonest—concealing architectural function or obscuring representational form in a riot of pattern; but its virtuosity often disarms criticism.

The Gothic style must have been shaped partly by technical discovery; but its aspiration towards lightness and height must also reflect an aesthetic impulse, and perhaps a religious one. There is no doubt that the imagery of Gothic church art embodied programmes of theological exposition; more than that, there is reason to believe that church buildings themselves, by their stupendous height, prismatic brilliance, and dizzying immateriality, were designed to evoke a sense of the transcendent. The Gothic style was, however, applicable equally to religious and secular uses. Although even the grandest castles evidently had little furniture, interior decoration (to judge from contemporary miniatures in illuminated manuscripts) was provided by splendid fabrics, especially tapestries, and spectacular displays of wealth in plate. Little of all this survives, but small luxury objects, such as combs and caskets, reflect in their decoration the ritual pastimes of courtly life and the literature of chivalry, such as the Arthurian legends. But Gothic art is essentially Christian art, and is still best appreciated in churches: displaced in a museum it seems diminished.

Censing angel   Brass   Franco-Flemish   c.1350   *H. 11.5 cm W. 4.5 cm*
Monumental brasses were introduced in Europe in the early 13th century. Less expensive monuments than their funerary counterparts, they were made of sheets of engraved brass set into stone slabs. The angel holds a censer in one hand and an incense-boat in the other. It probably originally formed part of a monumental brass, flanking a main figure.   M.15–1971

'December' tapestry   German (Alsace)   Mid-15th century   *H. 0.34 cm W. 2.73 cm*
Labours of the Months were one of the most popular secular motifs of the early Renaissance. This detail is from a long tapestry illustrating the occupations of the last six months of the year. Groups of figures are shown in a landscape with fruit trees and flowers. 'December' (*volrot* or 'full circle') is shown as two jolly medieval gentlemen quaffing ale and eating—apparently a *déjeuner sur l'herbe*—while acorns burgeon and flowers blossom, as though in perpetual spring. It is woven in brightly coloured wools and linen thread on linen warps.   6–1867

Chasuble Woven silk Italian Early 15th century *L. 148.4 cm*
The silk is brocaded with silver gilt thread in a design of golden camels bearing baskets of flowers, and wandering in a setting of flowers and foliage. It is among the most attractive examples of the use of naturalistic animal motifs, characteristic of International Gothic taste. The silk is one of a rare group, using silver-gilt thread on a silk core rather than the more usual gilt membrane. The shield on the upper left shows that it belonged to Sir Thomas Erpingham (c.1375–1428), a soldier, politician, and patron of the Church and arts. The embroidery is English.

T.256–1967

Hildesheim altar Porphyry and gilt metal North German Before 1132
H. 10.2 cm W. 16.4 cm
This portable altar is made of porphyry mounted in copper gilt, engraved and enriched with black lacquer. On the front is the Trinity, flanked by Sts Peter, Paul, Boniface, and Pancras, with Sts Simplicius and Faustinus in the roundels; each saint is identified by an inscription. Portable altars, usually decorated slabs of wood or stone, were used by missionaries and priests when travelling in areas where there were not necessarily churches with consecrated altars.   10–1873

Casket Ivory with metal mounts Hispano–Arabic Early 11th century
H. 27.3 cm W. 27 cm
In the Middle Ages, Cordoba was one of the great capitals of the world, rivalling Constantinople and Baghdad in wealth and beauty, its court renowned for luxury and pomp, and for its learning, poetry, and music. Ivory caskets such as this are the principal relics of the Umayyad dynasty's artistic patronage, probably made to house scent bottles and jewellery. A running scroll border interlaces round the medallions which contain figures seated eating, or playing music, eagles pouncing on animals, and other exotic beasts.   10–1866

Christ in benediction Silk embroidery Italian (Venice) c.1325 *H. 25.5 cm W. 23 cm*

Venice is one of the few places which combined the Far Eastern, Byzantine, Islamic, and Latin elements which are to be found in this extremely beautiful embroidered icon. The silk damask is embroidered with silk and silver-gilt thread in split-stitch and underside couching. The half-length figure of Christ holds a book inscribed EGO SUM LUX MUNDI ('I am the Light of the World'). The face of Christ is Byzantine in character, typical of eleventh to fifteenth-century Venice. T.92–1969

Drug jar (*albarello*) Pottery, painted in lustre and blue Hispano-Moresque (Manises) Mid-15th century *H. 39.4 cm*

8th-century Spain was the meeting-ground of two civilizations, Middle-eastern and European; Moorish armies invaded in AD 711, rendering it a province of the medieval Islamic Empire. Despite the reconquest of the 13th century, Moorish craftsmen continued to work in eastern styles—Moorish Malaga became widely known for pottery painted in the gold lustre technique. This drug jar is of typical Near-Eastern shape, decorated in a rhythmic pattern of foliage, with the badge of a hospital or religious order. 52–1907

Mirror case   Ivory   French   First half of 14th century
Diam. 13 cm
The theme of Courtly Love was a popular subject for poetry, song,
tapestry, and painting during the Middle Ages. Small domestic ivory
objects such as caskets, mirrors, and combs were often carved with
Courtly Love themes, real or allegorical. This mirror shows a scene of
an attack on the Castle of Love. The castle is held by four ladies who
are busy hurling flowers on the besieging knights below. From the
battlements, Cupid rains arrows on the combatants.   9–1872

Virgin and Child   Ivory   French (Paris)   Early 14th century
H. 35.6 cm
Statuettes of this kind are typical of the Gothic period and would
probably have been gilded and painted, often with bases of gold or
silver, enamelled and set with precious stones. The Virgin is
crowned, and the Child holds an apple, symbol of the Fall of Man,
and stretches out towards the branch of lilies, now broken away, the
symbol of her purity. The exaggerated sway of the composition is due
to the natural curve of the tusk from which it was carved.   4685–1858

St Martin and the beggar   Ivory   German   c.1310–20
H. 13.65 cm
Born in the fourth century, St Martin of Tours became a popular
medieval saint and symbol of charity. While a soldier at Amiens, he
gave his cloak to a beggar who revealed himself as Christ; Martin thus
became a convert to Christianity. In this ivory, St Martin is dressed as a
medieval knight. Both he and the beggar have the expressive faces
associated with German art of the Middle Ages, where realism is
expressed in a strong and vigorous style.   A.28–1939

Reichenau crosier   Silver and enamel
South German   1351   *H. 52.1 cm*
The technique of setting translucent
enamels on engraved silver became popular
in the fourteenth century. Here, plaques of
enamelled silver are set in a framework of
copper gilt with sculptural and architectural
details. According to the inscription, it was
made in 1351 for the Benedictine abbey of
Reichenau, on an island in Lake Constance.
The Abbot kneels before the Virgin and
Child in the crook, and the treasurer prays
on a bracket lower down.   7950–1862

Entombment of Christ   Tapestry
Arras   Early 15th century   *H. 112 cm*
W. 320 cm
This is the central part of the surviving
fragment of a tapestry showing three
continuous scenes divided by stylized rocks
and set against a background of sky and
foliage and a foreground of grass and
flowers. To the left of the Entombment is the
Deposition, to the right, the Resurrection. In
this scene, Christ's body lies on the lid of the
tomb before burial, surrounded by sorrowing
figures. The tapestry is woven in brightly
coloured wools and silks, and silver gilt
thread on a woollen warp.   T.1–1927

Burghley Nef by Pierre le Flamand   Nautilus shell mounted in silver, parcel gilt   French (Paris)   c.1527–8   *H. 35.3 cm*
The ornamental nef (ship) was used in France, Germany, Italy, and the Low Countries as a status symbol, marking the place of the host at table, just as the great salt did in England. This nef has a salt-cellar in the poop of the ship. The hull of the ship is dictated by the shape of the nautilus shell, but the upper part bears some relation to contemporary naval architecture. Invisible in this illustration but seated in front of the main mast are the tiny figures of Tristram and Iseult, playing chess. The ship is supported on the back of a siren. The nef was acquired from the Marquess of Exeter whose collection in Burghley House (Stamford) it had reached in 1844.   M.60–1959

Mazer Maple-root Anglo-French
15th century *H. 14 cm Diam. 20.3 cm*
This covered bowl was presumably a secular
object, perhaps a courtly present. It is
decorated with carvings of flowers and
foliage round the edge, and the inscriptions
are in pseudo-Nashki script and purely
ornamental. Under the cover is a scene of
Samson slaying the lion with the Latin
inscription 'And the spirit of the Lord
poured into Samson'; under the foot, the
somewhat ominous-sounding inscription
reads in French 'You must pay some day'.
221–1866

Merode Cup Silver gilt with enamelling   Flemish (or French)
Early 15th century   *H.17.8 cm*
This covered beaker, named after the ancient Belgian family to whom
it formerly belonged, is an extremely rare medieval survivor of the
difficult enamelling technique known as *émail de plique à jour*. The
backing is removed from translucent cloisonné enamel, so that it
gives the appearance of stained glass when light is seen through it,
and especially where the piercing takes the form of Gothic traceried
windows.   403–1872

Ewer Green porphyry mounted in silver gilt   Flemish
(Malines)   c.1488   *H. 15.2 cm*
This ewer bears the mark and rebus of Seger van Steynemolen
(1443–1508), a silversmith working at Malines, a town which in the
1480s was the favourite residence of Margaret of York, widow of
Charles the Bold. The spout and handle are in the form of somewhat
fishlike dragons with wings, the silver gilt a perfect foil for the green
porphyry. The ewer is believed to have come from the collection of
the Duchesse de Berry.   627–1868

Retable of St George by Marzal de Sas (?)
Tempera and gilt on pine   Spanish
(Valencia)   c.1410–20   *H. 660 cm*
W. 550 cm
This large retable has been attributed to
Marzal de Sas, a German painter working in
Valencia from 1393 until after 1410. Late
fourteenth-century Valencian painting was
influenced by Catalan painting, itself
influenced by Italian art; these elements can be
seen here along with distinct German
characteristics such as the very naturalistic and
expressive quality of the crowded, lively
scenes, and perhaps also what has been called
the 'Teutonic cast of features'. Important
attempts were being made to depict nature,
exemplified here in realistic depiction of
tortures and battles. The story of St George
and the Dragon tells of the dragon which
threatened the city of Silene. In order to pacify
it, the townspeople daily sacrificed a man,
child, or sheep, as in the scene to the left, told
with gruesome relish for realistic detail.
Detail: *St George & the Dragon.*
One of the three large central panels of the
altarpiece, this shows the International Gothic
style's predilection for courtly elegance and
surface decoration. The Princess wears the
sumptuously brocaded high-waisted *hopa* or
cassock, with extremely long sleeves, which
was fashionable at the time, and the scene is
set against a richly gilded background.

Christ on a donkey (*Palmesel*)   Painted limewood   South German   c.1510–20   *H. 147.2 cm*

This is a spectacular and charming example of a type of sculpture popular in the Rhineland and Alsace-Lorraine during the late Middle Ages. The statue was towed (the base has slots for wheels, now gone) through the streets in religious processions on Palm Sunday to commemorate Christ's entry into Jerusalem. The carving of the draperies dates the statue to the early 16th century. The figure is made in two sections, the upper part of Christ's body forming one, while His lower half and the ass's body forms the other. Christ's hand, feet, and the legs ears and tail of the ass, are in separate pieces. The Christ would have originally held a bridle in its left hand.

A.1030–1910

155

Devonshire Hunting Tapestry   Wool
Probably Arras   1425–30   *H. 406 cm*
W. 1021 cm
This is a detail from the 'Boar and Bear
Hunt', one of four large tapestries showing
scenes of hunting the otter, bear, boar, and
deer. These are among the finest and largest
surviving Gothic tapestries. They are hung
on the four sides of a gallery so that the
spectator finds himself surrounded by forests
with glimpses of fairy-tale castles, hilly
pastures, flowery bushes, caves, and
glittering streams. In this setting, the
elaborate hunt ritual takes place, an
important part of court etiquette, and in
subsidiary scenes knights and ladies pass the
time making courtly love, sewing, reading,
and in other courtly occupations.   T.204–1957

157

Pietà by the Master of Rimini Alabaster German (Rhineland) c.1430 *H. 38.4 cm*
In comparison with the popular alabaster carvings exported into Europe from England, German alabaster sculpture shows a more monumental and incisive style. This example is by an anonymous master named after a *Crucifixion* group commissioned about 1430 by the German community in Rimini (eastern Italy). He probably trained in the Netherlands and worked in the Rhineland and in north Italy. The realism of Christ's emaciated body is in strong contrast to the rounded features and voluminous draperies of the Virgin; thus the sense of pathos is intensified. This type of devotional image, called in German *Vesperbild* ('vesper image'), probably originated in the region of Franconia-Thuringia, spreading through Germany down to Italy, where it took the form of the *pietà*, notably in Michelangelo's marble sculpture in St Peter's, Rome. A.28–1960

Reliquary-coffer Gilt wood South
German 15th century *H. 61 cm L. 88.9 cm*
This reliquary-coffer from Konstanz is reputed to
have contained the relics of St Boniface. It is carved
with episodes from the Passion, Death, and
Resurrection of Christ, each scene full of action and
expressive gesture. On the side seen in the
illustration from bottom left to right are Christ's
entry into Jerusalem, the Last Supper and the
Agony in the Garden, the nailing of Christ to the
Cross, the Crucifixion, and the Entombment. The
reliquary has lost its corner pinnacles and the
cresting along its rooftop: it would originally have
had a more spiky, Gothic outline. 357–1854

Chasuble Embroidery Bohemian Late 14th
century *H. 96.5 cm W. 73 cm*
The mid-fifteenth century silk velvet is probably
Italian; the cross orphrey on which are depicted the
Crucifixion, Virgin and St John the Evangelist,
Angels, and Pelican are embroidered with silver gilt
and silver thread in couched work and coloured
silks. The Pelican, which traditionally pecks itself to
death for its young, is often seen in early Christian
iconography as the symbol of Christ's self-sacrifice.
It is in raised embroidery, as are Christ's head and
the chalices receiving His blood, and the nails.
1375–1864

159

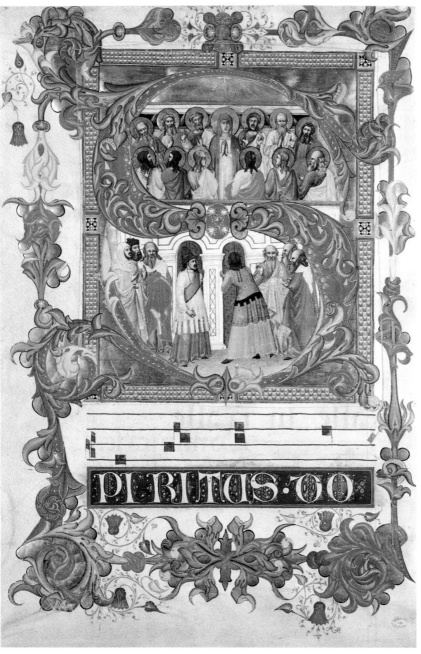

Illuminated initial 'S' by the Maestro delle
Canzoni   Vellum, gold leaf, and
watercolour   Italian (Florence)   c.1350
H. 14.6 cm
Little medieval wall-painting survives, and
many paintings on panel must have perished;
but a great deal of medieval painting on a
small-scale survives in prayer books, which
were, of course, written and decorated by hand
before the invention of printing in c.1450. In
these 'illuminated' manuscripts full-page
illustrations of Scriptural events appropriate to
the various religious services were provided,
and also decorative borders and (as here)
initial letters. This illuminated letter is
surrounded by an elaborate stylized floral
scroll border and contains two scenes—one of
the Virgin among the Apostles, the
Assumption, and the lower one of orientally-
dressed figures.   D.218–1906

Box   Painted and gilt wood   Italian
(Florence?)   c.1400   *H. 22.2 cm L. 61.6 cm*
This casket was probably given as a chivalric
gift by a knight to a lady as it bears on the top
the words ONESTA E BELA (honourable and
beautiful). Lively scenes of hunting, jousting,
and courtly life cover the lid and sides,
executed in raised gesso and painted in gilt
against a blue background. The lettering is in a
rounded form of Gothic script developed in
Italy (compare the lettering on the manuscript
above).   9–1890

Virgin and Child by Peregrinus   Tempera and gilding on
panel   Italian   Signed and dated 1328 (obviously a mistake
for 1428)   *H. 150 cm W. 61 cm*
This painter, close to Gentile da Fabriano in style, probably
worked in Umbria or the Marches in eastern Italy; although he
signed the panel, nothing is known of him. Executed about
seventy years later than the painting below, it shows the
transition from the Giottesque attempt to create solid,
monumental forms to the more decorative art of the
International Gothic style in which emphasis was laid on
surface ornament, use of expensive pigments, and a lyrical,
flowing line.   6559–1860

Coronation of the Virgin by Nardo di Cione
(active 1343–66)   Tempera on panel
Italian (Florence)   14th century   *H. 46.5 cm
W. 30.5 cm*   (Ionides Bequest)
The theme of the 'Coronation of the Virgin'
was a favourite among Giotto's followers;
there are innumerable extant 14th-century
Italian paintings in which it is treated almost
identically. Nardo was the brother of the more
famous Florentine painter, sculptor, and
architect Andrea Orcagna. The heavy figures
in their voluminous garments of pure bright
colours are typical of Nardo. The bird and
plant floor pattern is derived from
contemporary silks and appears often in works
of the Orcagna school.   CA.I–104

161

Cupboard interior   Intarsia in wood   Italian   c.1521–5
H. 110.5 cm W. 77.5 cm

Intarsia, an early form of marquetry, was used for the decoration of choir stalls and other furniture and panelling on doors and in rooms such as the *studioli* (studies) in the famous Ducal Palace in Urbino. This piece was executed by Fra Raffaele da Brescia to a design of Giovanni Battista da Imola, as part of the choir stalls of S. Michele in Bosco, Bologna. An extremely effective example of *trompe l'oeil*

composition, it shows the Renaissance preoccupation with linear perspective, and is an amusing rendering of what might be found in a sacristy cupboard: half-open doors reveal a tipped-over chalice, book fluttering open, a clock, and a crucifix. Designs were often supplied by important painters such as Paolo Uccello and Piero della Francesca, both known for their interest and experiments in mathematical perspective, Ghirlandaio, and Botticelli.   150–1878

The Renaissance

Whereas 'Gothic' is a term that is precisely used to denote certain stylistic features in medieval art, 'the Renaissance' is a much bigger idea. It describes a great process of cultural change, which, beginning in Italy about 1400 and developing over four centuries, transformed the philosophy, literature, politics, and science of Europe, and in many respects laid the foundations of our modern world. The metaphor of 'renaissance' or rebirth was, however, first used in 1550 by Giorgio Vasari (the father of European art history) to describe Italian art.

The clearest evidence of rebirth was the sudden appearance of men of artistic genius, first in early fifteenth-century Florence, and later in other cities. Why they appeared is in the end inexplicable, though reasons have been found in the political, economic, and intellectual conditions of the independent, mercantile city-states of Italy. In their works these artists brought to birth again (so it seemed) the art of classical Greece and Rome.

Three innovations should especially be noted. First, the 'Five Orders' of classical architecture were re-adopted, as the basis of a style enriched and codified by contemporary theorists. Since many Ancient Roman buildings survived in Italy and were put to continued use, the classical style could never have been forgotten there; and Gothic, consequently, did not influence Italian architecture deeply or for long. A second revelation was the naked human form, now disclosed, solid, and shapely (no longer abashed or ravaged), in sculpture emulating Greek or Roman originals. Painters, too, learned how to represent figures with a substantial physical presence. The third rediscovery was of a repertory of ornamental forms, first encountered in ancient buildings dug up in Rome, and therefore called 'grotesque' because of its apparent origin in grottoes or caves. While the Renaissance was the first culture consciously to base itself upon historical revivalism, it went far beyond mere imitation, and most of its lasting achievements were not derivative but the result of a new spirit of enquiry. The re-discovery of the past served the interests of a larger discovery: of man and the world.

The broad human sympathies of the Renaissance artists are immediately sensed in the V&A's great collection of Italian figure sculpture. Much of this is religious, and might seem, therefore, to offer little prospect of new discovery: and yet the numerous representations of the Virgin and Child manifest abundantly varied and winning shades of expression. The greatest works in the collection are the reliefs by Donatello, which, with his followers' similar works, are a discovery in technique, for these sculptors, as Pater said, 'seek their means of delineation among those last refinements of shadow, which are almost invisible...'.

The V&A possesses much architectural sculpture, which may help to suggest the original setting of smaller decorative art objects. Italian domestic interiors in palaces or big houses were spacious, uncluttered, dominated by doors and fireplaces, lit by modest windows (to keep out the heat), their walls and ceilings often decorated with frescoes. Such rooms demanded and received grand, weighty furniture. The grandest pieces were chests (*cassoni*), which at first had an architectural framework enclosing painted panels (often taken out in later centuries and hung as pictures) or *intarsia* decoration (used also on doors and walls); later they received a more sculptural treatment. Sideboards (*credenze*), beds, and tables could be constructed equally heavily. Even chairs took on ponderous forms, such as the *sgabello*, seemingly built from wedges of sculpture. Fabrics were an important part of interior decoration: the weavers of Italy excelled in opulently patterned silks and velvets, the splendour of which is today better understood from contemporary paintings than from the rather small specimens in museums. And large furniture supported smaller ceramics and metalwork.

Of Italian ceramics the most celebrated is maiolica: plates and vessels of earthenware, tin-glazed (a technique that reached Italy via Spain from the Middle East) so as to provide a white background for painted decoration in green, orange, and blue, the characteristic colours of the Italian landscape. Maiolica was made in a group of cities in North Central Italy, from the early fifteenth to the late sixteenth century. The earliest painted designs have the rough simplicity of folk art; later, complicated pictorial compositions were (rather tediously) copied from prints; the best maiolica designs are those that use (separately or combined) patterns such as grotesque ornament and simple likenesses of faces or landscapes, with respect for the contours of the vessels. On the tin glaze a brushstroke, once made, is indelible, so good maiolica painting has a quality of assured spontaneity. This quality, achieved above all in fresco painting, may be seen also in the enamelled decoration on glass vessels made in Venice, which was the centre of European glass production at this time.

From bronze figurines and plaquettes the Renaissance collector gained a peculiarly intimate understanding of sculpture. Some statuettes were scaled-down imitations of full-sized marble sculpture, but others, not least those which were to serve as inkwells, door-knockers, or candlesticks, offered opportunities for more original fantasy. Despite their small size, but by virtue of their weight, colour, and texture, bronze sculptures are remarkably commanding. Indeed, all the artifacts of the Italian Renaissance have strong, independent but concordant characters, which enable them to hold their own in a museum.

Ascension of Christ with the Giving of the keys to St Peter by Donatello (1386–1466)   Marble   Italian (Florence)   c.1430   *H. 40.6 cm W. 114.3 cm*
One of the earliest and most important acquisitions of Italian sculpture by the Museum, this low relief panel (*rilievo schiacciato*) remains one of its true masterpieces. Once owned by the Medici, it was probably carved in the late 1420s, when Donatello was pioneering the application of linear perspective to relief carving. Curiously, Donatello appears to have conflated two episodes recorded separately in the New Testament. The composition and monumental figures show the influence of Masaccio's fresco cycle in the Brancacci chapel in the Carmine, Florence.   7629–1861

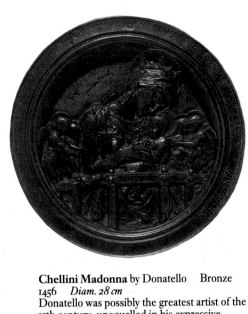

Chellini Madonna by Donatello   Bronze
1456   *Diam. 28 cm*
Donatello was possibly the greatest artist of the
15th century, unequalled in his expressive
range and technique. In this beautiful *tondo*,
the Madonna and Child are perceived as if
through a circular aperture, behind a
balustrade, and flanked by four putti (little
boys).   A.I–1976

Dr Giovanni Chellini by Antonio Rossellino   (1427–c.79)
Marble   Italian (Florence)   1456   *H. 51.1 cm*
This is one of the earliest and finest examples of the Renaissance
portrait bust, a *genre* which was revived from observation of antique
Roman practice at a time when Florentine statesmen and humanists
looked to Ciceronian Rome for models. Chellini, an eminent doctor,
was eighty-three at the time this bust was made, the year that he
received from Donatello, in lieu of a fee, the bronze *tondo* shown
opposite. The head is sensitively modelled, an individualized, rather
than an idealized, portrait of an elderly man.   7671–1861

The Virgin and the Laughing Child by Antonio Rossellino
Terracotta   c.1450   *H. 48.3 cm*
Rossellino was a leading 15th-century Florentine marble sculptor.
This terracotta statuette was probably a sketch-model, and much of
its spontaneity derives from its sketchlike character, especially in the
free handling of the drapery and hair. The relationship between
Mother and Child is rendered to convey great naturalness and
intimacy. For a long time the statuette was attributed to Leonardo da
Vinci, presumably on account of the mysterious smile of the
Virgin.   4495–1858

Month of May by Luca della Robbia (1400–82)   Glazed terracotta   Italian (Florence) c.1450   *Diam. 56.8 cm*
Luca was regarded by contemporaries as one of the great innovators of the early fifteenth century, along with Donatello, Ghiberti, and Masaccio. Early in his career, he pioneered the use of coloured glazes on terracotta sculpture, and the Museum has one of the best collections in the world of sculptures produced in his technique. This is from a series of twelve Labours of the Months, which came from the ceiling of the study of Piero 'the Gouty' de' Medici in the Palazzo Medici, Florence.

7636–1861

Altarpiece of the Adoration by Andrea della Robbia   (1435–1525)   Glazed polychrome terracotta   Italian (Florence)   c.1470
H. 223 cm W. 243 cm
Andrea was Luca's nephew and succeeded him in control of the family workshop. Unlike Luca, he worked only in modelled terracotta but introduced a wider range of colours into the glazes. The 'Adoration of the Magi' was a popular subject for paintings in 15th-century Florence; the Medici often commissioned works in which they had themselves portrayed as the Magi as, for example, in Botticelli's painting in the Uffizi. Here the composition is similar to Perugino's 1475 painting of the same subject in Perugia.   4412–1857

Vase Tin-glazed earthenware (maiolica) Italian (Deruta) c.1515 *H. 24.1 cm*
Maiolica, the tin-glazed terracotta of the Renaissance, is thought to derive its name from Majorca where traders trans-shipped the tin-glazed and lustred Hispano-Moresque pottery of Spain. By the late 15th century, the range of colours available included brilliant orange, yellow, green, and blue, with bold designs often inspired by artists of the day. This vase, from Deruta, near Perugia, bears symmetrical classical ornament composed of a palmette and leafy scrolls with flowers, the lower part painted with false gadroons.

1613–1855

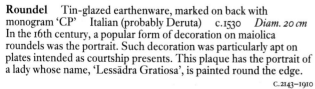

Roundel Tin-glazed earthenware, marked on back with monogram 'CP' Italian (probably Deruta) c.1530 *Diam. 20 cm*
In the 16th century, a popular form of decoration on maiolica roundels was the portrait. Such decoration was particularly apt on plates intended as courtship presents. This plaque has the portrait of a lady whose name, 'Lessādra Gratiosa', is painted round the edge.

C.2143–1910

Plate Tin-glazed earthenware (maiolica) Italian (Cafaggiolo) c.1510 *Diam. 23.5 cm*
In the 16th century, many new maiolica factories were set up, especially in Tuscany and the Duchy of Urbino, and the pictorial style was developed further. On this plate, a maiolica painter is shown at work, his pigment table at his side, and a finished plate and jug are on the ledge in the foreground. A delightful, but unlikely, 19th-century tradition has it that the two spectators were none other than Raphael and his mistress, la Fornarina.

1717–1855

Plate with the story of Phaedra and Hippolytus by Nicolò da Urbino (?) Tin-glazed earthenware (maiolica) Italian c.1525
Diam. 27.3 cm
Maiolica dishes were often decorated with episodes from classical authors or the Bible, adapted from engravings to cover the vessels almost entirely. Nicolò (formerly known as Pellipario, active c.1520–40) was the greatest exponent of this *istoriato* (story-telling) manner. Hippolytus (*right*) flees from Phaedra's passion. Theseus (*left*) pursues him, as (*above*) Hippolytus escapes in his chariot to his tragic death. The mottoes and coat of arms belong to Isabella d'Este (Marchioness of Mantua, d. 1539), one of the most famous and learned women of her day.   2229–1910

Ewer Blue glass, enamelled Italian (Venice) 15th century ▷
H. 20.3 cm
The art of enamelling on glass was brought to perfection in Syria in the 13th and 14th centuries. The Venetian glass houses became the most famous in Western Europe in the 15th century. The jug is rather crudely painted in dense, opaque enamels of red, blue, orange, and yellowish green, with the figures of tritons pursuing nereids among foliage.   273–1874

Goblet Green glass, enamelled and gilt Italian (Venice)
c.1480 *H. 17.1 cm*
Venetian glass vessels in the 15th century usually took comparatively simple forms, like the jug and goblet illustrated here. The goblet is decorated in fusible enamel colours with medallion heads of a man and woman in contemporary costume, a foliage design in gold leaf and blue and white enamel.   409–1854

Illuminated initial 'M' by Giuliano Amadei, from an illuminated manuscript of the elder Pliny, *Historia Naturalis*   Italian (Rome) c.1480   *Volume, H. 40cm W. 28.6 cm*
Pliny was a man of enormous industry and thirst for knowledge. His most important achievement, the *Historia Naturalis* in thirty-seven books, contains much fascinating and entertaining information about the civilization of his day; it evidently inspired the painter of this initial (which belongs to one of the books on Mineralogy) to depict three occupations of his own time, a fresco painter, an apprentice grinding colours, and a *cassone* painter.

AL.1504–1896

Triumph of Love by Apollonio di Giovanni   (1415–65)   Painted wood ceremonial *desco da parto*   Italian (Florence)   Mid–15th century   *Diam. 59.7 cm*
The *desco da parto* was a ceremonial tray used in Florence to bring food or sweetmeats to a woman after childbirth, often decorated with allegorical, mythological (as here), and New Testament stories.

144–1869

Chest (*cassone*)   Inlaid woods   Italian (Florence)   Early 16th century   *H. 86.4 cm W. 213.4 cm*
Cassoni like this usually came in pairs and were made for important weddings. They apparently stood in bedchambers and were used for storage. They were often decorated with painted scenes or, as in this case, marquetry of different woods.   5924–1859

Illuminated initial 'B' by Girolamo dai Libri (1475–1555)
Vellum, watercolour and gold leaf   Italian (Verona)   c.1550
H. 27.9 cm
The illuminated initial encloses a miniature of King David playing the lute with four companions. The rose, blue, and green scrollwork, typical of Girolamo's palette, is set against imitation mosaic in gold leaf.   E.1168–1921

Virgin and Child by Agostino di Duccio   (1418–81)   Grey marble
Italian (Florence)   Mid-15th century   *H. 55.9 cm W. 49.7 cm*
This is one of the most important examples of Italian sculpture in the
Museum. Agostino is one of the most easily recognized of Italian
Renaissance sculptors, owing to the linearity of his compositions and his
idiosyncratic facial types, influenced by Piero della Francesca. Best known
for his reliefs in the Tempio Malatestiano at Rimini, and on the façade of
San Bernardino in Perugia, he produced a number of independent panels
showing the Virgin and Child. The four-petalled rosettes round the border
of the niche and on the foreheads of the angels are a heraldic device of his
patron in Rimini, Sigismondo Malatesta. The pendant round Christ's neck
reproduces a Syracusan coin, while the ornamented vase at the right is
derived from sarcophagi at Ravenna; these motifs show the antiquarian
interests of Agostino and his patrons, characteristic of the Renaissance.

A.14–1926

Virgin and Child by Carlo Crivelli (active 1457–93)   Tempera on
panel   Italian (Venice)   Late 15th century   *H. 47 cm W. 34.5 cm*
This painting shows the Venetian love of exquisite ornamentation, rich
colour and gilding, and sumptuous accessories. The Virgin's mantle is
heavily decorated with gilt on raised gesso, and a pearl and ruby coronet
holds her veil in place. A swag of mulberries and apples hangs behind her;
the Child holds an apple, symbol of the Fall, and to the left of the crack in
the parapet is a carnation, to the right a violet, symbol of the Virgin. The
various fruits and flowers are symbolic as well as decorative; the leafless tree
on the right, with a vine climbing through it, refers to the crucified Christ.
The linearity of Crivelli's style is similar to Agostino's (see opposite); it is
elegant and refined, expressing delicately conventional, if somewhat vapid,
emotions.   492–1882

The Shouting Horseman by Andrea Briosco, called Il Riccio (active 1480 to c.1532)   Bronze   Italian (Padua)   c.1505–10   *H. 33.5 cm*
The classical art form of the bronze statuette was revived in Florence in the mid-15th century. The equestrian monument was derived from the great classical monument to Marcus Aurelius, and became an important Renaissance art form. Adapting the form to his own purposes, Riccio uses it to express an intense energy, fear, and bridled violence, imbuing i with psychological insight which is wholly original.   A.88–191

Satyr and Satyress by Andrea Riccio   △
Bronze   c.1510   Italian (Padua)
H. 23.2 cm
An extremely lustful satyr and satyress are the inhabitants of a new Arcadia presented by Riccio, peopled also by shepherds and goats. The fine modelling and chasing of the faces and torsoes show Riccio's training as a goldsmith; he was nicknamed 'Riccio' because of his curly hair.   A.8–1949

◁
Meleager by Pier Jacopo Alari Bonacolsi, called 'l'Antico' (c.1460–1528)   Bronze
Late 15th century   Italian (Mantua)
H. 30.8 cm
'L'Antico', working at the court of Mantua, produced elegant statuettes like this of Meleager, made of bronze, partially gilt, and inlaid with silver. It is a reduced version of a classical marble, now lost. Meleager bends to kill the Calydonian boar, but his expressively determined stance is somewhat obscured by the glittering decorative attractions of his trim curls and intricately pleated drapery.
A.27–1960

Allegory with youth leading a rearing horse by Agostino Busti, called Bambaia (1483–1548) Marble Italian (Milan) c.1515 *H. 41.3 cm W. 36.4 cm*
The original purpose of this relief (formerly thought to have been part of an unfinished monument to Gaston de Foix) remains uncertain, but the design is evidently allegorical. The inscription AUT NUMQUAM TENTES AUT PERFICE suggest that the relief may be interpreted as success won through perseverance—the youth who has succeeded in taming the horse he leads. Success is also indicated by the arms piled up against the broken trunk of a palm tree with a single flourishing branch. 7260–1860

St George and the Dragon Circle of the Gaggini Slate Italian (Genoa) Late 15th century *H. 79.4 cm W. 205.7 cm*
This relief in slate (*pietra nera di promontorio*) was a *sopra porta* or bas-relief placed over the outer doorway of a house, a typical feature of Genoese houses of the 14th and 15th centuries. St George on a rearing horse spears the dragon; to his right and left are men in classical armour. Behind, in the stylized rocky landscape is the princess praying, and to the right, the king and queen and their court. Below are a shepherd and his flock. 7255–1861
▽

174

Deposition by Jacopo Sansovino (1486–1570)   Wax and wood   Italian (Rome) 1510   *H. (relief) 76.3 cm W. 72.4 cm*
Painters were recommended by Renaissance theorists to study from sculptural models; according to Vasari, a model of the Deposition was made in Rome for Perugino. This model, of gilded dark-red wax and wood is set in a contemporary wooden tabernacle. The painted scene behind is of a landscape, riding figures, and flying putti. Sansovino trained in Florence as an architect and sculptor and subsequently went to Rome. After the Sack in 1527, he fled to Venice where he became the leading High Renaissance architect and sculptor, a close friend of Titian and the writer Pietro Aretino. His figure style is richly classical, tending towards Mannerism in the elegant and elongated proportions.   7595–1861

Slave by Michelangelo Buonarroti (1475–1564)   Red wax   Italian (Florence)   c.1510   *H.16.7 cm*
This dark-red wax model is related to the figure of the Young Slave designed for the tomb of Pope Julius II, one of Michelangelo's innumerable unfinished projects, and one which dragged on for forty years. In the malleable medium of red wax, he was able rapidly to embody his ideas; even the small *modello* gives a sense of the power of the figure struggling within the stone block from which it was to be carved.   4117–1854

◁
Monument to Cardinal Niccolo Forteguerri by Andrea del Verrocchio (c.1435–88)   Terracotta   Italian (Florence)   c.1476 *H. 39.4 cm W. 26.7 cm*
Verrocchio, the master of Leonardo, trained as a goldsmith. The monument was commissioned in 1476 and Verrocchio and his assistants executed the upper part in Pistoia Cathedral before his departure to Venice in 1483. This sketch-model is important as it is the only one of its kind to survive from the 15th century. The figures of the angels and Faith and Hope show Verrocchio's mastery in rendering movement; the influence of the elaborate, fluttering draperies can later be seen in both painting and sculpture.
7599–1861

Miraculous Draught of Fishes by Raphael Sanzio (1483–1520)   Tempera on paper   Italian (Urbino) c.1515   *H. 3.19 m W. 3.99 m*   Lent by Her Majesty the Queen

These cartoons, among the greatest works of art to survive from the High Renaissance, were designed for a set of ten tapestries commissioned by Pope Leo X to hang in the Sistine Chapel below Michelangelo's ceiling. Three cartoons have been lost, but the Museum has on loan from the Royal Collection the remaining seven. The subjects are drawn from the lives of Sts Peter and Paul: the *Miraculous Draught, Christ's Charge to St Peter, Healing of the Lame Man, Death of Ananias, Blinding of Elymas, Sacrifice at Lystra,* and *St Paul Preaching at Athens.*

The cartoons, looked upon almost immediately as works of art in their own right, were sent to the Brussels weaver Pieter van Aelst to be executed. Sets of the tapestries were owned by some of the most famous Renaissance names, François I, Henry VIII, and Margaret of Austria. The cartoons were returned to Italy by 1623; in March of that year, they were bought by Prince Charles, later Charles I of England, and were ultimately sent to the Mortlake tapestry works, where copies were made and new borders designed to replace the hardly suitable symbolic and papal borders intended for the Sistine Chapel. The Mortlake version of the *Miraculous Draught* hangs opposite the cartoon in the Museum.

The cartoons have remained in the Royal Collection ever since; Prince Albert was himself a scholar of Raphael and his works. In 1865, Queen Victoria approved the loan of the cartoons to the South Kensington Museum, as it was then known.

Raphael was at the peak of his career at the point when the cartoons were designed: a painter with numerous commissions for easel paintings and frescoes, he was also an architect and Papal Inspector for Antiquities. His antiquarian interests are evident in the details from classical architecture in the cartoons, such as the altar in the *Sacrifice at Lystra*, the classical buildings in the *St Paul Preaching*, and the column in the *Healing of the Lame Man*. Also visible in these cartoons is the transformation of Raphael's style, from the manner of his early Umbrian days in the gentle, sad face of Christ in the *Charge to Peter* and in the lyrical landscape of the *Miraculous Draught*, to a grandeur of form recalling Masaccio, and individual psychological characterization, in the *Sacrifice at Lystra*.

Altar frontal Embroidered velvet   Spanish   Mid-16th century   *H. 104 cm W. 220 cm*
The top and side borders are of red silk velvet embroidered with gold and silver thread and
coloured silks, in a design of intricate scroll-work, with birds, gryphon heads, and leaves. The
middle portion of the frontal is made of a silk velvet. The repeating pattern of broad curving
stems forming large pointed oval compartments with lobed leaves and other plant forms is
typical of Renaissance woven textiles.   T.371–1976

Lucretia's Banquet Embroidery Franco-Flemish 16th century *H. 167.6 cm W. 297.2 cm*

As a contrast to the two altar frontals shown on these pages, this secular hanging (of which only the central panel is reproduced) shows the type of furnishing common in prosperous 15th- and 16th-century interiors. It is embroidered with tent stitch in coloured wools and silks on canvas. The embroidery design is typical of its period in taking its inspiration from literature. Lucretia, the wife of Tarquin, suffered outrage at the hands of Sextus; having revealed this to her husband, she took her own life. Here, at her banquet, the figures are shown in late 16th-century costume. T.125–1913

Altar frontal Embroidered velvet Spanish c.1530 *H. 132 cm W. 274 cm*

Formerly in the Church of San Juan de los Reyes in Toledo, this splendid altar frontal is made of gold, silver, and silk thread, and cloth of gold and silver embroidered on rich red velvet. In the two large roundels are scenes of the Baptism of Christ and the Virgin and Child with St John. The eagles which appear in the elaborately arabesqued border are the symbol of St John the Evangelist, after whom the church was named. Although this frontal and the one illustrated above were made in Spain, they are very similar to Italian work, which exercised a strong influence on early 16th-century Spanish embroidery. T.141–1969

Agony in the Garden by Antonio Allegri, called Correggio (c.1489–
1534)   Oil   Italian (Parma)   c.1528   *H. 37 cm W. 40 cm*
Apsley House
The lyrical sweetness of Christ's figure, the glowing colours,
dramatic light effects, and the *sfumato* (blurred effect of the outlines),
are all hallmarks of Correggio's style. So also are the expressive
hands and the foreshortened airborne angel, its foot almost piercing
the picture plane, and the agitated, windblown drapery, denoting the
inner drama. Influenced by Leonardo and Raphael, among others,
Correggio's style was to have a profound effect on Roman baroque
art nearly a century later.   WM.1585–1948

Smeralda Bandinelli by Sandro Botticelli (1445–
1510)   Tempera on panel   Italian (Florence)
c.1471   *H. 65.1 cm W. 40.9 cm* (Ionides Collection)
The motif of setting a figure within a casement window
comes from 15th-century Flemish painting. A strong light
falls from the left, creating the sense of light and airiness
typical of Florentine *quattrocento* painting. The picture was
once owned by Dante Gabriel Rossetti—Botticelli was an
important source of inspiration to the Pre-Raphaelites.
CAI.100

Lid of a virginal   Tempera on panel   Italian   16th century
The virginal is essentially a small harpsichord. It was fashionable in the 16th and early 17th
centuries. The inside lid of the instrument was often painted; this one shows a scene of an outing
to some idyllic spot, perhaps for a picnic.   363–1891

Chest (cassone) Walnut Italian (Rome) c.1560 *H. 64 cm L. 152 cm*
The carved scrollwork of this heavily ornate *cassone* is typical of late 16th-century
Roman furniture. In the centre, an unidentified shield is supported by two putti,
and the cartouches on either side contain the figures of cupids in chariots drawn by
dogs and bulls. The corners are decorated with the sinuous shapes of winged
female forms, ending in claw feet.   4414-1857

Octagonal table Walnut intarsia Italian (Tuscany) Late 16th century
H. 83.8 cm Diam. 141.6 cm
Intarsia, or marquetry, was used also in furniture, and this table illustrates the
extremely complicated effect which could be achieved; before the woods darkened
the effect of the contrasting colours must have been quite astonishing. The top is
covered in a myriad of allegorical figures, while the sides and legs are decorated
with characteristic Renaissance arabesques. Pseudo-volutes support the eight
corners, and end, as does the *cassone* above, in claw feet.   102-1869

Chair, *sgabello* Walnut, partly gilt Italian
(Venice) c.1560 *H. 101.6 cm*
This richly carved chair bears the device of a
star, and was made for the Steno family of
Venice. The back is heart-shaped, decorated
with strapwork and running scrolls, and with a
foliated grotesque mask, a motif which is
repeated below.   5690-1859

Virgin and Child by Veit Stoss (c.1447–
1533)   Boxwood   German (Nuremberg)
c.1520   *H. 20.3 cm*
Stoss, the leading wood-sculptor of
Nuremberg, worked in Cracow from 1477 to
1496; in both places he worked on large
memorials and altarpieces. Although it is
probable that in later life he produced many
small virtuoso statuettes, this Virgin and Child
is the only such statuette to be regarded as
indisputably by him. The pose, with the Virgin
leaning to the left, balanced by the Christ
Child held up and out to the right, is typical of
Upper Rhenish sculpture, but here, unusually,
the Virgin and Child do not incline towards
each other but both face the spectator. The
figures are caught up in the rich display of
swirling, deeply cut drapery, characteristic of
Stoss's work, which continues in a daring
sweep behind the Virgin's head. Her hair,
carved in fine, curvilinear grooves, cascades
down her back. The crescent moon is the
symbol of the Immaculate Conception.

646–1893

Late Gothic, Mannerism

Styles in art are often talked about as if they grew like plants or animals. First, a period of green unripeness or clumsy puppyhood, then full bloom, or strapping maturity, lastly a running-to-seed or slack decrepitude. The later, profusely decorative, phases of the Gothic style, especially in fifteenth- and sixteenth-century Germany, are often regarded in this light: Late Gothic foliage has something rank and autumnal about it. But the Late Gothic style has fresh as well as stale features.

The revival of antique styles in fifteenth-century Italy had no immediate parallel in Northern Europe, where Renaissance styles had to be imported by northern artists or patrons. Thought, however, crossed frontiers more easily. In the north as in the south, intellect and imagination began to explore regions outside the mental territory ruled by the Church. Signs of self-confidence in inquiry, self-advancement through commerce, and (especially in the North) self-reliance in religious matters, may be detected beside the more fantastic, lugubrious aspects of the Gothic mind. In art such attitudes are reflected in what is most conveniently labelled naturalism: an interest in the individuality of human beings and in the accurate representation of appearances. Naturalism appeared in advanced and prosperous regions of Northern Europe in the fifteenth century: in the work of painters like the Van Eycks and Memling in the Netherlands; and in South German sculpture, especially just after 1500 in the work of Stoss and Riemenschneider.

In Italy, the strong, straightforward qualities of early Renaissance art and the amplitude of the High Renaissance gave way to something more nervous and complicated. Art historians used to imagine that the dignified Renaissance eventually declined into the overblown Baroque, but they became aware that certain aspects of Italian art from c.1520–80 seemed not to fit into either category, and devised a new label, 'Mannerism'. This can be applied only to the visual arts: there is no interlude of Mannerist politics or philosophy; and, unlike 'Baroque', which has a fairly wide cultural reference, Mannerism can hardly be applied to literature or music. The word is, of course, primarily used to describe human behaviour: it suggests affectation and exaggeration, and it is to such tendencies that it refers in art. It is most clearly distinguished in nude figures, which are lanky, twisting, and languidly seductive. And it may be seen in artists' cunning attempts to confuse the spectator: by deceptively organized planes in pictures; in sculpture, by producing figures and groups that do not demand to be viewed from a particular point but draw the spectator all round them as they turn in upon themselves; in architecture, by distortion of proportion and perspective; in decoration, by inordinate richness and complexity.

When northerners imitated the art of Italy, it was up-to-date Mannerism that they took as their model. In France, François I commissioned Italian artists (including Benvenuto Cellini) to decorate his palace at Fontainebleau, and thus imported the Renaissance—or rather, Mannerism—to France at one stroke. Elsewhere, Italian forms spread more gradually, especially through engraved ornament. Grotesque ornament, revived in the Renaissance, provided Mannerist artists with material for more feverish invention. The poised, airy, if somewhat incongruous, gatherings of living creatures, swags of plant growth, and fragments of architecture were elaborated (especially when northern strapwork ornament was added to the mixture) into labyrinthine constructions entrapping uncanny monsters. The prints of Cornelis Floris, Cornelis Bos, Wendel Dietterlin, and Vredeman de Vries ensured that this ornament was widely circulated in the North, where more orthodox Renaissance ornamental motifs also became known in the prints of Dürer (which influenced, for example, the sculptor of the V&A's altarpiece from Troyes), Holbein, and the German 'Little Masters'. Borrowings from prints reshaped quite localized art-forms, such as the stoneware pottery of the Rhineland or the painted enamels of Limoges.

The Mannerist style was most astonishingly realized in goldsmiths' work, especially by Cellini in Italy and by the craftsmen of Augsburg and Nuremberg. In metalwork more than any other medium, ornament can be modulated without disjunction from flat to three-dimensional, from abstract to figurative; so, granted the virtuoso skill of the craftsmen, metalwork provided the occasion for the wildest flights of Mannerist fancy. Although not dependent on engraved ornament, the lurid, reptile-encrusted pottery of Bernard Palissy, and the glassware of Venice, blown with swift deftness into extraordinary shapes, and wrought about with beads and threads of glass, are fully in the spirit of Mannerism.

Mannerist art was not for the man in the street. It was highly sophisticated and expensive, delighting in precious materials and bizarre effects, and inviting a response not far from gloating. It almost asked to be collected, and in the sixteenth century any prince with cultural pretensions would assemble a little private museum of costly curios. It would include freaks of nature: fossils, meteorites, dragons, pickled mermaids. And it would also contain prodigies of workmanship, sometimes ancient but usually modern: engraved gems, carvings in precious substances like jade, amber, and rock-crystal, ivory-turning, goldsmiths' work (often incorporating oddities like coral, shells, and coconuts), clocks and mechanical toys. These collections were often stored in the cabinets that are Mannerism's chief contribution to furniture: intricate in construction, containing many little drawers, cupboards, and secret compartments, and decorated so exorbitantly that they hardly seem to need contents at all. Mannerist art is museum art *par excellence*; it is hard to imagine it looking appropriate anywhere but in showcases.

Pastoral Tapestry Flemish
c.1490 *H. 340 cm W. 343 cm*
This is a detail of a tapestry woven in wool and silk, depicting rustic sports such as hunting and hawking, shooting, and amorous dalliance. Set against the background of a Gothic castle, lively, jolly figures carry on their daily occupations. Here, a young woman who has obviously been dipping her feet in the stream, is helped by her swain to don her stockings and shoes, while a young boy cools his heels a little further up the stream. The elaborate, flowery background is typical of 16th-century Flemish hangings.
5668A–1859

Candle-bearing angels by Tilman Riemenschneider (c.1460–1531)   Limewood, formerly painted   German (Würzburg)
c.1500   *H. 63.5 cm each*
Limewood, a light and elastic wood, cuts easily and allows for fine sharp-edged forms and, because it has no strong grain marks, can be cut in all directions. These angels were designed as altar candlesticks, and the coarse cutting of the eyes and hair suggests they were probably originally intended to be painted. Riemenschneider's workshop was very large and productive over the space of forty years, and these angels are of an obviously lower grade of quality than the figure group below. Sculptors kept stocks of smaller sculpture of standard types such as crucifixes and Madonnas, and the angels may have belonged to this category of work.   A.16,17–1912

Mary Salome and Zebedee by Tilman Riemenschneider
Limewood, glazed   South German   c.1520   *H. 119.4 cm
W. 49.5 cm*
These figures formed the right side of a larger group of the *Holy Kindred*. The centrepiece would probably have been St Anne with three husbands, the Virgin, St Joseph, and the Christ Child. In this group, Riemenschneider uses forms natural to his material, exemplified in the soft, rounded, headdress of the woman and smooth, delicately modelled face with its beautiful high cheekbones and slanted, asymmetrical eyes, contrasting with the deep angular folds of drapery; it shows Riemenschneider's absolute mastery of the blade through the soft wood.   110–1878

185

Altarpiece of the Passion   Limestone,
painted   French (Aube)   c.1526
*H. 186.7 cm W. 86.4 cm; Wings: H. 77.5 cm
W. 91.4 cm*
The altarpiece is made up of three large blocks
of limestone, with two principal narrative
scenes in each. In the centre is the *Crucifixion*
with the *Annunciation* above, and below, the
Flagellation, *Road to Calvary*, *Entombment*, and
Resurrection. The donor, a lawyer, who became
a canon of the Church of St Peter and Paul in
Troyes after 1487, was Jean Huyard l'Aîné,
portrayed kneeling at the foot of the Cross.
Late Gothic elements such as the ogival frame
of the *Crucifixion* combine with Renaissance
ones (see the Virgin's *prie-dieu*). The influence
of Dürer and Martin Schongauer can be seen
in the roguish soldiers in their outlandish
costumes, and in various compositional
features.
Detail (*left*): **The Fainting Virgin supported
by St Mary Magdalene and St John the
Evangelist**. Now that later repaintings have
been removed from the altarpiece, it is
possible to see the sensitivity with which the
artist originally painted the faces in this detail,
where the eyes of the mourning women are
reddened with weeping. The soft limestone
allows fine detail in the carving of faces, hair,
and drapery.   4413–1857

Three Fates *Mille fleurs* tapestry   Flemish   Early 16th century   *H. 307 cm W. 264 cm*
The theme of the Triumph of Death over Chastity was extremely popular from the 14th to
the 16th century. It was suggested by Petrarch's poem *I Trionfi* (*The Triumphs*), finished by
1374 and inspired possibly by the death of Laura, the poet's mistress. The poem describes a
succession of triumphs in the manner of triumphal processions of ancient Rome. Here,
Chastity, a beautiful young woman with pearls decorating the hem of her gown, lies prostrate,
seemingly unconcerned, under the figures of Clotho, holding a distaff, Lachesis spinning the
thread of life, and Atropos cutting it. The flowering plants, birds, and animals in the
background are beautifully depicted, showing the Renaissance interest in nature and
realism.

Louis XII triptych Painted enamels on copper with gilding French (Limoges) c.1500 *H. 25 cm W. 41.5 cm*
Louis XII and Anne of Brittany kneel, their patron saints, Louis and Anne, behind them. Enamel painting superseded champlevé enamelling in the mid-15th century. The unknown enameller named after this triptych was active between 1490 to c.1515. Royal portraits rarely appeared in enamel triptychs at this date and are probably due to the influence of Italian art introduced by Jean Fouquet (c.1420–81), who travelled to Italy and brought back with him the architectural and pictorial styles of the Italian Renaissance.

552–1877

Esther before Ahasuerus (detail) Tapestry Flemish (Brussels) Early 16th century *H. 3.04 m W. 3.9 m*
In this detail of the central part of the tapestry, Esther kneels before Ahasuerus, surrounded by courtiers. Out of the picture, to the left, Esther is crowned by the king, waited on by beautiful handmaidens; on the right, they are seated in a garden, listening to music. The tapestry is woven in sumptuously coloured wools and silks. The artist has managed to individualize the figures to a certain extent by giving them different movements and expressions.   338–1866

Coat-of-arms of the Counts of Kyberg by Lukas Zeiner (active 1479–1512)   Stained glass   Swiss (Zurich)   *H. 31.1 cm W. 26 cm*
Coats-of-arms were popular motifs in domestic stained glass, used in decorating houses and castles. Here the Kyberg shield is held by a hirsute wild man and woman.   c.9–1923

St George and the Dragon   Stained glass   Swiss (Zurich) c.1500   *H. 31.8 cm W. 22.2 cm*
Glass-staining became widespread in 15th-century Switzerland. This lively panel once decorated a church.   c.208–1923

Tobias and Sarah   Stained glass   German   16th century *H. 65.7 cm W. 55.9 cm*
In this delightful panel, Tobias and Sarah lie in their 16th-century bedchamber, nightcaps on and slippers neatly placed.   c.219–1928

Crucifixion   Stained glass   Germany, from Altenberg Abbey c.1500   3 panels each *H. 254 cm W. 58.4 cm*
The richly coloured scene is set with fictive piers and tracery imitating the window in which the glass was set. Christ is flanked by the Virgin, St John the Evangelist, and Mary Magdalene.   c.68–1919

Month of April, from the Kalendar of a Book of Hours by Simon Benninck (1483?–1561)   Watercolour on parchment   Flemish   Early 16th century   *H. 9.5 cm W. 15 cm*
One of a family of 15th- and 16th-century Flemish book illustrators, Simon was the son of Sanders, the leading miniaturist of Bruges and Ghent. Kalendars were placed at the beginning of Books of Hours (see p. 194) to indicate Church feast days; their illustrations often provide a fascinating account of rustic and courtly life, precise enough to suggest the region where the book originated. In this scene courting couples stroll and play music set in a highly naturalistic landscape in which flora and fauna are painted in microscopic detail.
E.4575–1910

Ommeganck at Brussels by Denis van Alsloot (active 1599,   ▽
d. before 1628)   Oil on canvas   Flemish (Brussels)   1616
H. 117 cm W. 381 cm
This is the fifth of six paintings depicting the Ommeganck or procession held in honour of the Archduchess Isabella on 31 May 1615. In the 16th and 17th centuries such ceremonies were the occasion for the creation of magnificent artistic and architectural works which, however, perished almost at once, and are now recalled only through engravings and books and, occasionally, paintings such as this. The scene shows the Triumph of Isabella, a procession headed by four camels and followed by a strange assortment of cars representing, among others, Semiramis, Diana and Phoebus Apollo, Isabella and her court, the Nativity, and a ship made for the funeral procession of the Emperor Charles v in 1558.
5928–1859

Garden of Eden by Jan Brueghel the Elder (1568–1625)   Oil on
panel   Flemish   *H. 53 cm W. 84 cm*
The son of Pieter Brueghel the Elder, Jan was born in Brussels but lived in Antwerp, where
he became a close friend and collaborator of Rubens (the latter's influence can be seen in this
painting, in the white horse, which appeared in Rubens's *Riding School*, now in Berlin). Jan,
called 'Velvet Brueghel', specialized in very small wooded scenes like this one, brilliantly
coloured and finely executed, and his landscapes and animal scenes were extremely popular;
there are many versions and copies of this particular painting. The glade in the background is
the setting for the Temptation of Adam and Eve.   340–1878

Neptune taming a Sea-horse by
Alessandro Vittoria (1525–1608)
Bronze   Italian (Venice)
c.1580   *H. 49.5 cm*
This small, elegant bronze with its
elongated proportions is typical of
Vittoria's Mannerist style. The
tightly welded spiralling forms,
called in Italian *figura serpentinata*,
are derived from Michelangelo's
Victory. Vittoria's treatment of the
surface is brilliant and painterly. He
gives greater psychological
emphasis to his figures than does
Giambologna, his Florentine
contemporary. The musculature is
taut and the body tense, with head
to the right, arm swung across the
body, and the horse's head
diametrically opposite. A pupil of
Sansovino, Vittoria became after the
latter's death the leading
monumental sculptor in Venice.

A.99–1910

Head of Medusa by Benvenuto Cellini
(1500–71)   Bronze   Italian
(Florence)   c.1545–50   *H. 13.9 cm*
Cellini, a goldsmith and metalworker, became
one of the most important Mannerist
sculptors. This head is a model for the head of
Medusa in his great bronze statue of *Perseus*,
commissioned by Cosimo de' Medici in 1545.
Showing two stages, it is almost rough on the
right side, whereas the left is chased with the
delicacy and precision for which Cellini is
renowned.

Samson slaying a Philistine by Giambologna Marble Italian (Florence) c.1560–2 *H. 209.9 cm*
By the mid-1560s, Giambologna was established as court sculptor to the Grand Duke of Tuscany. This is the first of his series of group sculptures in marble, and it originally formed the apex of an ornamental fountain. The composition was influenced by Michelangelo's design for Samson and two Philistines in its twisting, spiralling form, but unlike Michelangelo and Vittoria, Giambologna is concerned less with psychological content than with form and composition. His source of inspiration was late Hellenistic works showing violent movement in carefully balanced compositions; his figure style is also that of late classical, and High Renaissance art. It is a less mannered style than that of the *River-god* sketch-model and his brilliant bronze statuettes, examples of which are in this Museum. The *Samson and Philistine*, in its mastery of form and material, shows Giambologna to be the link between Michelangelo and the genius of the Italian Baroque, Gianlorenzo Bernini. A.7–1954

◁

River-god by Giovanni da Bologna, called Giambologna (1529–1608) Terracotta Italian (Florence) c.1580 *H. 33 cm W. 39.7 cm*
Born at Douai, Giambologna trained in the workshop of Jacques Dubroeucq before travelling to Italy in c.1555. In his lifetime he was the leading sculptor of the Mannerist period, and his reputation was second only to that of Michelangelo. The Museum has a large collection of his *oeuvre* including a major work, the *Samson and Philistine* (see right) and models for many other important compositions.
Giambologna always made several sketch-models when working out his ideas, and this clay model shows the method of working with thumb and spatula. 250–1876

Intermezzo, 'L'Armonia delle Sfere' by Bernardo Buontalenti (1536–1608)   Pen and watercolour   Italian (Florence)   c.1589   *H. 38.1 cm W. 55.8 cm*

Buontalenti, a Mannerist follower of Michelangelo, was an architect, military engineer, painter, and sculptor. He worked mainly for the Medici grand dukes, who saw themselves as great patrons of the arts, and designed stage sets and firework displays for their extravaganzas. *Intermezzi* were entertainments with allegorical or symbolical characters; in this sketch (showing scenery and costume designs), Necessity appears in the opening of the clouds, holding a spindle which, according to Plato, united the two Poles of the Universe. Below her are the Three Fates, flanked by nymphs. The *intermezzo* was presented in Florence in 1589 on the occasion of the marriage of Ferdinand I of Tuscany and Christina of Lorraine, niece of Catherine de' Medici.   E.1186–1931

Book of Hours of Eleonora da Toledo: Flight into Egypt   Illumination on vellum, signed and dated 10 February 1540 by the scribe Aloysius   Italian (Florence)   *H. 13 cm W. 7.5 cm*

Books of Hours were personal prayerbooks for lay people, containing devotions to be recited at specific times, hence 'hours'; the *Flight into Egypt* was meditated upon at Vespers. This beautiful little book was made for Eleonora da Toledo (d.1562) after her marriage in 1539 to Cosimo de' Medici (d.1574). Like many such books it was designedly a precious object. The miniature is painted in expensive pigments and decorated round the border with cameos, emblems, and Renaissance ornament.   L.1972–1953

Apprentice grinding pigments by Francesco Mazzola, called Parmigianino (1503–40)   Red chalk   Italian (Parma)   c.1500   *H. 19.9 cm W. 15.5 cm*
Parmigianino, a painter and etcher, was one of the most elegant and sensitive of the early Mannerists, and was widely imitated in both his own country and north Europe. His figures have long hands and necks, and an air of being about to swoon in their religious ecstasy. This chalk drawing in his last style shows an apprentice grinding colour on the lid of a chest, and is an example of Parmigianino's exquisite draughtsmanship.   D.989–1900

Design for a chandelier by Jacopo Ligozzi (1547–1627)   Pen and wash   Italian (Florence)   1585   *H. 25.1 cm W. 30.5 cm*
This is a drawing of the type of elaborate chandelier which lit the great halls of Florence in the 1580s, and is similar to one used during the festivities celebrating the marriage between Cesare d'Este and Virginia de' Medici in 1585, for which Ligozzi designed the *intermezzi*. It shows alternative designs, with an eagle on the left and a winged harpy on the right. The shaft is in the form of a vase covered with ornament such as the scallop shells, which would have concealed lamps.   573–1874

Cabinet   Ebony with silver and gilt mounts   German (Augsburg)   c.1600   *H. 38.1 cm*
W. 37 cm
This miniature cabinet, made to house jewellery and other knick-knacks in its tiny drawers,
contains a silver ink pot and sander. It is elaborately decorated in silver and gilt, with strapwork,
mascerons, and flower vases, and medallions containing figures drawn along in triumphal cars
with signs of the zodiac. In the central niche is the figure of Charity, flanked by smaller allegorical
figures. It is surmounted by a reclining female figure with winged gryphons below.   M.511–1956

Games board   Wood and ivory
German   Second half of 16th century
43 cm square
This multi-purpose games board is for playing
chess, draughts, backgammon, and merelles.
Made of wood veneered with ebony and
engraved ivory, it is fitted with a lock and hasp.
On this, the backgammon, side, the outer
border is decorated with a lively procession of
knights in combat, while the inner borders
beside the hinges contain the figures of jolly
burgher couples dancing; fabulous monsters
decorate the centre panels. The other side, for
playing chequers, has a border design with a
hunting procession, sea monsters, and double-
tailed mermen.
567–1899

Writing desk   Walnut inlaid with whalebone   South German   c.1600   *H. 15.2 cm*
W. 48.3 cm
This exquisitely made desk bears on the inside the arms of Francesco Maria II, Duke of
Urbino (reigned 1574–1626) and is likely to have been a gift from a German prince. The
surface is decorated with inlay of engraved bone consisting of strapwork cartouches containing
trophies of arms, fruit, and flower vases, and medallions with biblical subjects such as Adam
and Eve, Cain and Abel, and the Tower of Babel, after engravings by Etienne Delaune (1519–
83). This technique of inlaid decoration was also used on gun stocks, and the maker of the desk
may well have been a gun stock maker.   W.1–1958

Flagellation of Christ by Guglielmo della Porta (d.1577)   Gilt bronze
Italian (Rome)   c.1575   *H. 20.1 cm W. 13.5 cm*
From 1555 to 1575, Guglielmo worked on a series depicting the Passion of
Christ, a project for bronze doors which was never realized. This bronze gilt
relief is taken directly from the original wax model and probably chased by
the sculptor himself; the highly sensitive treatment of hair and flesh is typical
of this fine sculptor's work. The Mannerists insisted upon the supremacy of
the human figure; here Guglielmo has placed such figures against typically
Mannerist architecture.   A.1–1977

Astronomical globe by Georg Roll and Johannes Reinhold   Bronze gilt   German (Augsburg)   Dated 1584   *H. 42 cm*
This example of the remarkable technical skills of the Augsburg instrument makers of the 16th century is both a mathematical instrument and a work of art in the South German Mannerist style. According to tradition, it was made for the Emperor Rudolph II (1576–1612).   246–1865

△ **Watch** by S. N. Lemaindre   Gilt and silver
French (Blois)   Early 17th century
L. 7.6 cm W. 2.8 cm
This solid, heavy little watch has a double dial of silver engraved with figural subjects. On either side small apertures show the day and date. The case, of gilt metal, has modern silver additions.   M.132–1923

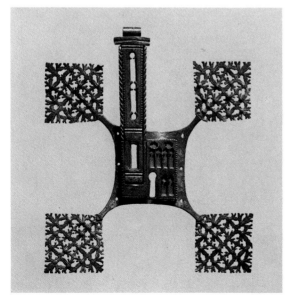

Mirror   Damascened steel   Italian (Milan)   c.1550   *H. 117 cm*   ▷
Damascened decoration is made by hammering wires of soft metal, such as gold, into engraved incisions in a hard metal, such as steel. This kind of decoration covers the surfaces of the rather heavy architectural forms which support this mirror, which was made for the House of Savoy.   7648–1861

Mirror and stand   Wood and mother of pearl   Italian (Milan) ▷ ▷
c.1575
The architectural frame and stand are decorated with moresque ornament in imitation of the damascened steel work for which Milan was famous in the 16th century.   506–1897

Lock   Wrought iron   Italian   End of 15th century   *H. 31 cm*
W. 28 cm
While blacksmiths worked hot metal, locksmiths mostly worked on cold metal at the bench, often producing extremely delicate and refined work. This lock, with decoration based on Flamboyant Late Gothic architecture, demonstrates both techniques.   4855–1858

Games board Chestnut and ivory
Italian c.1500 H. 53.3 cm W. 48.3 cm
The games board consists of a chess board
facing this side and a backgammon board
on the reverse, and is made of wood, partly
painted green, and ivory. 7849–1861

Philip II of Spain by Pompeo Leoni (?)
Shell cameo Italian or Spanish Late
16th century H. 51 cm W. 32 cm
Leoni (d.1610), a goldsmith and medallist,
worked for the Hapsburgs in Spain.
Philip II was married briefly to Mary
Tudor. 2628–1855

Stirrups probably by Bartolommeo Campi
Iron, gold, and silver   Italian (Pesaro)
c.1545   *H. 20.32 cm*   (Salting Bequest)
These iron stirrups, encrusted with gold and
silver, were probably intended to go with a suit
of armour made in 1546 by the armourer
Bartolommeo Campi for Duke Guidobaldo II
of Urbino. They are believed to have been
given by Guidobaldo to the Emperor Charles V.
Campi was a celebrated goldsmith from
northern Italy. The floral design and finely
chased masks in silver *appliqué* on the outer
face are inspired by classical antiquity in true
Renaissance style. The inner side is beautifully
damascened, imitating the craftsmen of the
Near East.   M.662, 662A–1910

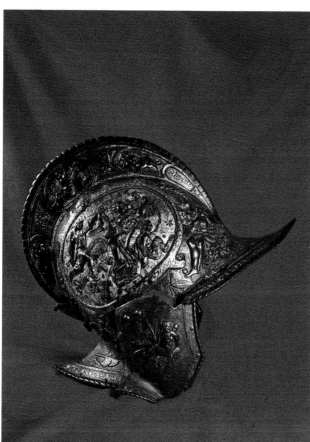

Helmet   Steel   Italian (Milan)   c.1560   *H. 30.5 cm*
This highly decorated helmet is embossed and damascened with
gold, and probably comes from the workshop of Lucio Picinino of
Milan. Panels of vine-leaf damascening in gold are typical of
Milanese work of the period. The surface is divided up by strapwork
into panels embossed with lively and somewhat lecherous scenes
from classical mythology. On this side, Mercury places a wreath on a
woman seated on a satyr's back, and the figures of Fame and Victory
decorate the helmet peak.   M.189–1921

Nautilus shell cup   Silver mounts   Dutch   1613   *H. 30 cm*
This cup bears the town mark of Utrecht for 1613, and the maker's
mark of Nikolaus van der Kemp. The shell and silver gilt mounts are
incised with a delicate foliate design, and the upper curve decorated
with the head of a sea god with a curly beard and scales running down
the spine of the shell. The figure of Neptune kneels on the back
holding his trident. The stem and chasing are characteristic of Dutch
Mannerist art.   4869–1858

Canning Jewel Pearl mounted in gold and enamels. Possibly Italian c.1560
L. 10 cm W. 7 cm
The Canning Jewel is a mis-shapen pearl ingeniously set so as to form the body of a triton, which is encrusted with rubies, diamonds, and brilliant green, blue, and gold enamel. The bizarre form and rich materials combine to make a characteristic example of Mannerist taste. Such jewellery was made in Italy, Flanders, and South Germany.

M.2697-1931

Tazza by Adam van Vianen Silver Dutch Early 17th century *H. 16.5 cm Diam. 20.3 cm*
A *tazza* is a shallow drinking vessel, of a form developed in the Renaissance. The bowl is embossed with the Judgement of Solomon in different degrees of relief, and the stem is decorated with fruit, masks, and escutcheons.

2125-1855

Inkstand by Theodor de Bry (1561–1623) Ebony and silver German (Frankfurt)
c.1580–1600 *H. 10.8 cm W.24.1 cm*
The inkstand is made of ebony overlaid with pierced silver, and contains an inkwell, pencase, and sander. It is chased with a shield of arms, symbols of the Evangelists, and putti, set among scroll foliage. The figures of the four Evangelists decorate the top of the lid, with Moses and Isaiah on the inside. Quotations in Latin from the gospels of St John are set in frames of foliage and grotesques.

840-1882

Vase Blue glass engraved with diamond point   Austrian (Tyrol)
Second half of 16th century   *H. 16.5 cm*
Italians set up glassworks in the Netherlands and Germany, and the art
of glass making was thus diffused throughout northern Europe. The
Italian style was assimilated into northern products, and was followed
with variations at an important glasshouse at Hall-in-Tyrol, which
flourished especially in the last quarter of the 16th century. As a means
of decorating glass, diamond engraving was capable only of quite
simple linear or shaded effects.   690–1884

Beaker and cover (Reichsadlerhumpen) Glass with enamel   △
colours   South German   Dated 1604   *H. 49.2 cm*
While Venetian glassmakers delighted in fancy, delicate forms,
Germans sought to achieve heavy, solid effects. The *humpen* was a
favoured form in the 16th and 17th centuries. In theory a drinking
glass, it was primarily a ceremonial rather than functional object,
sometimes enamelled with the *Reichsadler*, the eagle of the Holy Roman
Empire, with the coats of arms of the Imperial states on its wings.
   C.314+A–1936

Römer Glass   German or Netherlandish   c.1600   *H. 18 cm*
The *römer* was a sturdy wine-glass, a form developed in the 17th
century, with a plain bowl and a stem decorated with blobs or
'prunts'—a characteristically German form. Green glass was
traditionally produced by the forest glass-houses of northern
Europe.   C.284–1936

Lady Onyx cameo North Italian c.1550–1600 *L. 7.6 cm*
Cameos are gems which have two layers of different colours so that the upper part may be carved in relief while the lower half forms the base. This cameo, supported by an acanthus, imitates the classical manner in its hair-style and veil; it was in the collection of Thomas Howard, Earl of Arundel (1585–1646).   A.45–1978

Vase Clear glass with enamel colours Spanish (Barcelona) △
16th century *H. 27.3 cm*
Catalonia, and especially Barcelona, had trade connections with Venice and the Levant, and was much influenced by Venetian glass in the 16th century. In this delicate vase, the Venetian forms are exaggerated and distorted; an Islamic influence perhaps appears in the motifs of the somewhat primitive enamelling, painted in the characteristic light yellowish green, yellow, white, and lavender blue.   C.138–1914

Vase and cover, probably by Ferdinando Eusebio Miseroni ▽
(d.1684) Rock crystal, gilt bronze mounts Bohemian (Prague)
c.1650 *H. 43 cm*
A member of the famous Milanese family of carvers and engravers of precious and semi-precious hardstones of the late 16th and 17th centuries, Ferdinando Eusebio Miseroni worked in northern Europe, especially in Prague for the Imperial Court. The body of this vase is carved with lion masks, with leaves in high relief and festoons, flies and spiders in intaglio. The mounts and knop are of later date.   A.22+A–1977

△ **Bottle** Soft paste porcelain Italian (Florence, Medici factory) c.1580 *H. 17.5 cm*
Only some sixty pieces survive from the Medici factory, generally acknowledged as the first to produce soft paste porcelain in Europe. This bottle has the characteristic appearance of opaque glass and distinctive blue pattern outlined in manganese purple.   229–1890

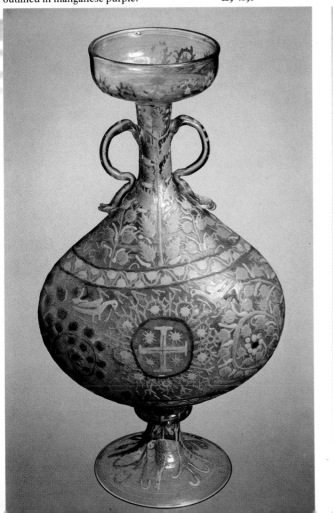

House-altar Amber, ivory German
c.1650 *H. 122 cm*
This ornate altarpiece is an example of
the Baroque insistence upon the
substance, colour, and texture of objects.
Following the design of a typical northern
Baroque altar, the ivory and coloured
amber replace the variegated marbles and
stone. A casket represents the altar,
above which is a scene of the *Adoration of
the Shepherds*, set in an elaborate
architectural frame, which in turn
supports a third storey containing
medallions of the *Baptism* and
Transfiguration. This is surmounted by a
relief of the *Agony in the Garden* and the
Crucifixion and *Resurrection*. On the back
there is a perpetual calendar with the
signs of the zodiac and Old Testament
scenes. A.1–1950

Baroque, Rococo

For much of Europe, the seventeenth century was a period of turbulence. The German States were harassed by the Thirty Years' War, which disrupted artistic patronage and caused the dispersal of many artistic collections; England's entry into the artistic life of Europe was set back by the Revolution and the sale of the Royal collection; Spain entered upon its long decline. However, France emerged from its religious strife into a splendid absolutist rule (in art as well as politics), and the United Netherlands, now independent of Spain, enjoyed a great surge of commercial and artistic creativity. Any generalizations about a Baroque style, assumed to persist through this troubled period, must be hazardous.

Nonetheless, a change of mood is quite evident in the arts of the time. In both Mannerist and Baroque art conventional forms, inherited from Renaissance art, are put under strain; but Mannerism irritates forms for forms' sake, while in Baroque art forms are forced by content. This notion may perhaps be more easily demonstrated in literature and music, where a distinction can fairly clearly be made between emotional content and forms of expression; but it holds good for Baroque architecture, in which spatial experiments frequently compel the rigid framework of the classical style to bow and buckle.

Baroque art, striving to express meaning even at the cost of form, addresses itself to an audience. Where Mannerism turns away into an intimate, clinging embrace, Baroque opens its arms to its audience. It is a theatrical art, and the artist is a kind of stage manager, co-ordinating various effects so as to catch up his audience into a single overwhelming illusion. That is why Baroque art is rather disappointing in museums. Architecture is the basis of the illusion; much of the best Baroque painting (the hectically receding ceiling and wall frescoes) is inextricably involved in the architectural effect, and so are furniture and the decorative arts. A visit to a great Baroque building, Versailles or St Peter's in Rome, will teach far more about Baroque art than a museum can.

Baroque artifacts are rich and showy, no less than Mannerist objects. But where the latter tend to be intricate and slender, the former are fat and burly, even coarse. What marks out a Baroque pot, bookbinding, embroidery, or silver dish is an enlargement in the scale of the ornament (which is less easily apprehended from a photograph than from the real thing). While in Mannerist furniture architectural forms exercise a discipline over decoration (however rich this may be), in Baroque furniture structural members (table-legs, for example) often become entirely sculptural. Terms and caryatids (i.e. supports in human form) are everywhere in baroque architecture and furniture.

Renaissance artifacts seem classless: a maiolica plate, sturdily graceful, would be as happy in a peasant house as in a palace. Mannerism, seeking the summits of refinement, can have no truck with the lower end of the market. But the Baroque style, going for big effects, can successfully be simplified and popularized: it is, in fact, the source of much folk art, and the only complete European baroque interior on show in the V&A is, as it happens, from a farm.

In the later seventeenth century, France again became the artistic leader of Europe. Until the end of the following century, the styles of French art are distinguished by the names of the French monarchs, not unreasonably since taste was dictated by the Court. In the Louis XIV style the pomp and richness of Baroque is constrained within a heavy formality. The Louis XVI style is also regular and restrained, but lighter and more deliberately neo-classical. Between them is the Louis XV style, irregular and playful. Since it was imitated all over Europe, and in Germanic countries unfolded from the Baroque with no interruption, it is perhaps better labelled as 'Rococo'. This word was specially coined to describe the style (unlike 'Baroque', which was originally used, albeit discrepantly, in other connections), and is a kind of visual onomatopoeia, since it vividly suggests the asymmetrical scrolling shapes which are the essence of the style. It had its origin in grotesque ornament and, like grotesque, was transmitted through prints; its energy lies in curling lines rebounding from each other, but this linear structure was in some art forms ingeniously extended into three dimensions, so as to produce restlessly counterpoised planes and solids.

Rococo is generally characterized as frivolous, but in painting the frivolity of Watteau and Fragonard is a profound, even rather costly, emotion, not a facile one. Rococo decorative art can hardly embody such feelings—although tapestry followed very closely upon painting in the seventeenth and eighteenth centuries, it inevitably spoke with a more muffled voice—but it often displays supreme craftsmanship, especially in the cabinets, commodes, bureaux, and occasional tables of the French furniture-makers. Such skill can hardly be called frivolous.

The phrase 'porcelain shepherdess' serves as a compact disparagement of Rococo art, but the development (from 1709 at Meissen) of hard-paste porcelain is an unexpected story of princely one-upmanship and industrial espionage; furthermore, porcelain figures are an important branch of small sculpture. Porcelain preens itself happily in a museum, and other small sculpture, especially in bronze and terracotta, fits in well. But Rococo garden sculpture, and the decorative sculpture and plasterwork of Rococo churches can, in the nature of things, hardly be represented. Such art must be visited, in the gardens of Nymphenburg or Veitshöchheim, and the churches of Einsiedeln or Vierzehnheiligen. And yet the Rococo spirit can be as perfectly realized in one small exquisite object as in a large festive set-piece.

Design for a mace by Pietro da Cortona (1596–1669)   Pen, wash, and chalk Italian (Rome)   *H. 41.2 cm W. 18.3 cm* Pietro, leading architect and painter of the Roman High Baroque, was patronized by the Barberini family whose emblem, the bee, is shown with the papal tiara and keys, and the Maltese cross.

D.1708–1885

Samson and Delilah by Luca Giordano (1632–1705)   Oil on canvas Italian (Naples)   c.1660   *H. 58 cm W. 142 cm* (Apsley House) The most important decorative painter of the second half of the 17th century, Giordano was nicknamed *Luca fa Presto* ('Luke paint quickly') because of the speed with which he worked. He was prolific and a good imitator, combining Neapolitan and Venetian art in a light and colouristic manner.   WM.1631–1948

Portrait of an Unknown Man ascribed to Bartolomé Estebán
Murillo (1617–82)   Oil on canvas   Spanish   *H. 119 cm W. 96.5 cm*
(Apsley House)
This fine portrait, showing the influence of Titian and Velasquez in
the sensitive handling of the face and different textures of the
materials, is traditionally ascribed to Murillo, who, born in Seville,
was brought up in the Naturalistic style of painting, working mainly
for the religious houses in Seville. He is best known for his somewhat
saccharine paintings of street urchins and numerous *Immaculate
Conceptions* with their Baroque fluttering draperies.   WM.1546–1948

The Waterseller by Diego Velasquez (1599–1660)   Oil on canvas
Spanish   c.1618   *H. 106 cm W. 81 cm*   (Apsley House)
Velasquez was born in Seville. His apprenticeship with Pacheco gave
him a firm technique and knowledge of Italian and northern
Renaissance masters. He painted several *bodegon* ('tavern') scenes, a
genre in which still life predominates. His fondness for cylindrical
shapes can be seen in the brilliant painting of the pottery and glass,
water and light glistening on them. He uses a sober palette with
ochres and dark browns on a warm ground; his monumental figures
stand out as silhouettes against a dark background.   WM.1600–1948

Judith and Holofernes by Adam Elsheimer (1578–1610)   Oil on
copper   German   c.1605   *H. 23 cm W. 17.8 cm*   (Apsley House)
Elsheimer's works are always on a small scale and sometimes on
copper, his subject matter drawn usually from the Bible or Ovid.
Born in Germany, he went to Italy in 1598 where he acquired a new
warm and jewel-like sense of colour in Venice and Rome. After 1600,
he lived in Rome, where he was probably in contact with Caravaggio
himself or his followers, as is shown in the painting of light on the urn
and water flasks, and the dramatic foreshortening of Holofernes.
                                                           WM.1604–1948

Thomas Baker by Gianlorenzo Bernini (1598–1680) Marble
Italian (Rome) 1636 *H. 81.6 cm*
In 1635, Bernini was commissioned to do a marble portrait of Charles I
(destroyed in 1678). Thomas Baker, who was also in Rome at the time,
persistently demanded a bust of himself from Bernini, who finally gave
in, persuaded by the financial reward. His genius at capturing and
caricaturing the sitter's expression is exemplified here, in the brilliantly
executed face of the dashing and faintly ridiculous cavalier. A.63–1921

Cardinal Paolo Emilio Zacchia by Alessandro Algardi (1595–1654)
Terracotta Italian (Rome) c.1650 *H. 82.2 cm*
Algardi, born in Bologna, settled in Rome in 1625, where he became
after Bernini the most important sculptor. A Baroque artist, his works
are less extreme than those of his rival and his portrait busts lack the
panache of Bernini's. They are, however, possibly more sensitive and
true to life. This terracotta model for the posthumous portrait of
Zacchia is a brilliant recreation of a living person in the modelling of
eyes and mouth and the expressive treatment of the hands. A.78–1970

Emperor Rudolph II by Adriaen de Vries (1560–1627) Bronze on
touchstone Signed and dated 1609 German *H. 71.1 cm*
W. 52.7 cm
Rudolph's court at Prague was steeped in Neo-Platonic astrology,
alchemy, and magic, acting as a magnet to Mannerist artists. De Vries,
Netherlandish by birth, trained in Florence with Giambologna,
assuming his master's style in elegant bronzes, but developing an
interest in more painterly surfaces. He became court sculptor at Prague
in 1601. This magnificent bust, a symbol of Hapsburg power, is
supported by the Imperial eagle; Rudolph wears the insignia of the
Golden Fleece and the armour is chased with reliefs showing Hercules
and Minerva. 6920–1860

Neptune and Triton by Gianlorenzo Bernini   Marble   1623   *H. 182.2 cm*
This powerful sculpture was commissioned by Cardinal Montalto, as part of a fountain at his villa. The story comes from Ovid's *Metamorphoses*: Neptune calms the waters summoned by Jupiter to flood the earth, and Triton blows his conch to make them recede. Neptune strides forward, while Triton twists through his legs, both figures embodying extreme physical and emotional intensity. Constantly aware of the play of light and water on surfaces, Bernini maximizes the effect by deeply undercutting details such as the hair and the cloak spiralling out behind Neptune.

A.18–1950

Mandore by Boissart   Pearwood
French (Paris)   Signed and dated 1610 or
1640.   *H. 42 cm.*
The mandore is the smallest example of
the lute family, especially popular in
France in the latter half of the 16th
century. The back of this instrument is
carved with an exquisite *Judgement of Paris*
set in an elaborate cartouche and
scrollwork. The figure style and ornate
hair-styles show the survival into the 17th
century of the Mannerist nudes of the
Fontainebleau school which flourished in
the early 16th century. The neck is carved
with a mask of Medusa.   219–1866

Theorbo by Cristoforo Choco (Koch?) ▷ ▷
Wood and ivory   Italian (Venice)   17th
century   *L. 106 cm W. 31 cm*
A theorbo is a double-necked lute which
appears to have come into use in the 16th
century. This pretty instrument has a back
of fifteen ribs of alternately rosewood and
ivory. The back of the neck is decorated
with marquetry in snakewood and ivory,
consisting of floral scrolls, a bird, and
double-headed eagle. The ivory
fingerboard panels are engraved with
figures and a landscape.   7756–1862

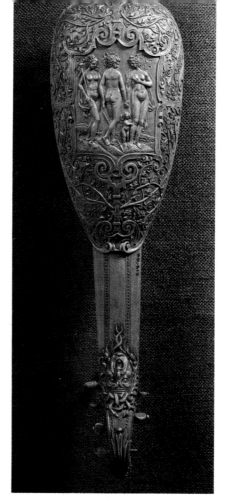

Bass viol by Martin Voigt   Ebony and pine   German (Hamburg)
1726   *L. 121 cm*
A bass viol or *viola da gamba* derives its name from being held between
the knees. The instrument is inscribed 'Martin Voigt in Hamburg me
fecit 1726'. The belly is of two pieces of pine, ornamentally bordered in
ebony, and the neck, fingerboard, and hook bar are richly and
delicately executed in mother-of-pearl, ivory, and ebony.   1298–1871

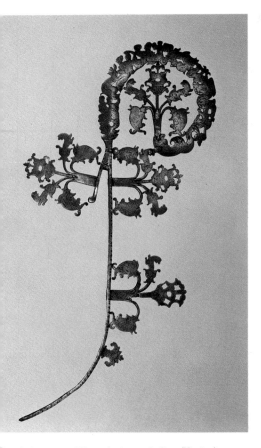

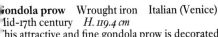

Gondola prow Wrought iron Italian (Venice)
Mid-17th century *H. 119.4 cm*
This attractive and fine gondola prow is decorated with a
flat foliage pattern, pierced and engraved, and the crook-
shaped top cut with animals and leaves. 9091–1863

Sword hilt by Gottfried Leigebe (1630–83) Steel
German (Nuremberg) c.1670 *Total length 106.7 cm*
Swords have always been regarded not only as weapons
but also as masculine jewellery because of the rich
decoration often applied to them. This hilt, decorated
with the figures of Hercules and Samson, is of a form
fashionable at the late 17th-century court of the Electors
of Brandenburg. M.59–1947

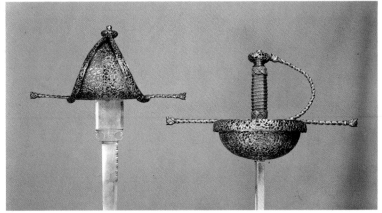

Rapier and dagger signed by Antonio Cilenta Steel Italian (Naples) c.1650
Rapier 114.3 cm Dagger 59.7 cm
The rapier was the civilian sword of the 16th and 17th centuries. The guards of
these weapons are delicately chiselled with beasts' heads, satyrs, fruits, and
flowers. M.56–1947; M.124–1921

Gates Wrought iron Italian *H. 152.4 cm W. 101 cm*
Iron, when heated, can be worked into elaborate shapes; in these gates (probably
for a chapel) it has been forged into finely balanced Baroque scrollwork.
619 + a–1875

Monstrance Silver and parcel gilt German (Augsburg) c.1700
H.99.1 cm W. 40.6 cm
A monstrance is used to display a consecrated wafer from the Mass in subsequent devotional services. Medieval monstrances often took the form of Gothic shrinework, but Baroque monstrances sought rather an unashamedly theatrical effect. In this one the wafer would be placed at the centre of the sunburst. In front of the lower rays is a lively scene of the Last Supper, and the theme of the Divine feast is taken up in two parcel-gilt cornucopiae at the sides, containing corn and grapes. At the top, characteristically Baroque angels with swirling, agitated drapery pull back the curtains of the baldachin to reveal the Dove, the Holy Spirit. M.3–1952

Chasuble Silk embroidery Italian c.1650–1700 *L. 115.6 cm*
Part of the Roman Catholic Church's response to the Protestant Reformation was the encouragement of splendid ceremonial in which fine vestments played their part. Baroque vestments were embroidered in bold and colourful patterns like the one illustrated, where the brightly coloured exotic birds perched among the flowers and foliage are embroidered with floss silks and silver gilt thread inlaid, and couched work with long and short stitches. T.295–1972

Pendant Gold, enamel, and diamonds
French or Dutch c.1620 *H. 12.4 cm*
W. 7.4 cm
Early 17th-century jewellery design became
abstract, with little verisimilitude in colour
and natural forms becoming stylized. In this
pendant, geometrically shaped stones are set
in foliage; the back-plate is enamelled and
the stones are screwed through both layers to
hold them together. M.143–1975

Pendant and earrings Gold and silver
French or Dutch c.1670 *Pendant
L. 11.5 cm Earrings L. 1.72 cm*
Ribbons and bows were popular motifs and
this *demi-parure* shows how the foliage
settings of the earlier period were adapted to
the bow shape. M.98–a,b,c–1975

Tankard (*humpen*) by Bernhard Straus (active 1640–81) Ivory,
silver, and gilt mounts German (Augsburg) Signed and dated
1651 *H. 48.5 cm*
This is one of the most magnificent examples of German Baroque art
with its heavily ornamented handle, figure group of Hercules and the
Centaur on the lid, and knobbly sculpture round the body. The painter
and art-historian, Sandrart, praised Straus for his sculpture in ivory,
precious stones, silver, and woods. Subjects round the side include
Venus and Cupid, Minerva, Silenus, Triton, Neptune, and Amphitrite.
4529–1858

Tower clock Gilt copper, silver, and enamel German (Augsburg)
Mid-17th century *H. 36 cm*
The top of this clock is in the form of a cupola supported on two
storeys of open arcades, each arcade being surrounded by a balustrade
with baluster finials. The upper half rests on detached doric columns
which act as a frame for the silver dials on each side of the case; the
smaller dials are enriched with translucent enamel. The large dial on
the front is a perpetual calendar; there are also astronomical and
astrological dials. M.52–1952

Wall-hanging 'Gilt leather' Dutch c.1700 *H. 86.4 cm W. 45.7 cm*
A pretty little Bacchus holding a cup out of which a bird is drinking is the central decoration of the panel. The leather skins, after being covered with tinfoil, were embossed, then painted and coated with a golden-coloured varnish. w.38–1974

Armchair Walnut, carved and gilt French (Paris) c.1675–80 *H. 109.2 cm W. 66 cm*
This armchair is paired with a chair without arms, and both may have been acquired in Paris by Ralph, Duke of Montague, while he was ambassador to Louis XIV from 1678–80 to furnish his London home, Montague House. The arms are carved with a heavy foliage design, and the chair has claw feet. The upholstery is a restoration done in 1974, based on a careful study of contemporary illustrations. w.32–1918

Table Tortoiseshell inlaid with pewter Flemish (Antwerp) c.1675 *W.104 cm* (From Mentmore Towers)
Boulle marquetry, the technique used here, was originally invented in Italy in the 16th century and brought to France in the 17th century. It was perfected by André-Charles Boulle (1642–1732), the great French *ébéniste* and most famous Louis XIV furniture designer and maker. He gave his name to the sumptuous furniture of the period covered in this striking form of marquetry with pewter and tortoiseshell. w.33–1977

Cabinet Wood, veneered in ebony, with silver mounts French 1675 *H. 183 cm W. 126 cm D. 53 cm*

This cabinet came from the collection of the Earls of Rosebery at Mentmore Towers. The wood, veneered in tortoiseshell and ebony, is decorated with embossed scenes from Ovid's *Metamorphoses*; the sculptor appears to have used pictorial sources for his own scenes—the panel depicting Venus and Adonis is a direct borrowing from Titian's painting for Philip II. The central part opens to show a miniature room with tortoiseshell columns. The base was altered in the 19th century to form a display cabinet.   M.320–1977

Cabinet Ebony and gilt metal mounts French c.1628 *H. 214 cm W. 155.5 cm D. 51 cm*

Formerly from Mentmore Towers, the cabinet was traditionally associated with Marie de Médicis (1573–1642), Queen of France, who was exiled in 1630. It is close to a design for a cabinet bearing the Queen's cypher in the Ashmolean Museum, Oxford. Architectonic in design, the upper half is supported by ionic columns and a cornice with swags. Scenes from Torquato Tasso's *Gerusalemme Liberata* are depicted in the gilt bronze reliefs, and may be to designs by Simon Vouet, who returned from Rome to Paris in 1627.   w.64–1977

Vincennes: July Tapestry From *The Months* or *Résidences Royales* (Gobelins: Jean de la Croix) French Late 17th century *H. 335 cm W. 345 cm*

The Gobelins factory was the most important tapestry factory of the late 17th and 18th centuries. Originally a dyeing workshop, it became a tapestry factory in the early 17th century and was taken over on behalf of the Crown by Colbert, Louis XIV's minister. Work was done mainly for the King, although there was also some private patronage. Designs were executed from cartoons made from the Italian Old Masters such as Raphael and Giulio Romano, and also from Poussin. Charles Lebrun (1619–90), who conceived and designed the series from which this tapestry comes, was the virtual dictator of the arts in France during the reign of Louis XIV; he became director of the factory, providing cartoons in the pompous, classicizing French Baroque style. In this detail, a woman in a striped gown and blue petticoat holds a basket of fruit, keeping an eye on the small dog which is investigating an urn on the right. In the background, the King and his courtiers hunt in the grounds of Vincennes.   T.371–1977

Wedding Party by Jan Steen (c.1626–79)   Oil on canvas
Signed and dated 1667   Dutch (Leyden)   *H. 97.8 cm
W. 15.3 cm*   (Apsley House)
Jan Steen is best known for his lively genre scenes of low-life
and peasant feasts, a world often inhabited by drunken and
somewhat grotesque characters, seen through satirical eyes.
He was extremely prolific (about 700 paintings still survive)
and versatile, painting portraits and historical and
mythological subjects. His palette is usually rose, salmon-red,
yellow, ochre, and a bluish green.   WM.1510–1948

Landscape with figures by Louis Le Nain (1593–
1648)   Oil on canvas   French   *H. 54.6 cm W. 67.3 cm*
With his brothers, Antoine and Mathieu, Le Nain was a
founder member of the Académie. He painted in the
naturalistic genre which had its roots in the work of
Caravaggio and Orazio Gentileschi. His large peasant scenes
are painted in silvery greyish-green colours, his figures having
the classical monumentality of the Dutch and Spanish schools.
They are treated simply and, unlike those of Steen, without
satire.   CAI.117

Departure of the Shunammite Woman by
Rembrandt van Rijn (1606–69)   Oil on
panel   Dutch   Signed and dated 1640
H. 39.4 cm W. 53.3 cm
Rembrandt painted Biblical and historical
subjects throughout his career and his interest
in old people and exotic costumes was present
from an early age. He was a master of
chiaroscuro and spatial effects, both of which
are evident in this painting. In the 1640s, after
a period of painting in the extravagant High
Baroque manner, his style changed, with an
emphasis on intimate, tender scenes expressed
through colour, atmospheric effects, and
chiaroscuro. It has been suggested that the
death of his wife Saskia in 1642 may have
helped to change his palette.   CAI.78

Putto Polychromed limewood German c.1725–50 *H. 69 cm*
This carving has recently been linked with the early work of the
Bavarian sculptor Ignaz Günther (1725–75), a prolific wood-carver
who used a Rococo style to create extremely emotional religious
works of art. This putto would probably have formed part of an
altarpiece, flanking the central part. A.7–1957

Sorrowing Virgin probably by Pedro de Mena (1628–88)
Polychromed wood Spanish c.1650 *H. 42.5 cm W. 49 cm*
Polychrome carving was popular in Spain from the end of the 14th
century; a concern for realism was a peculiarly Spanish development in
religious sculpture in wood, especially at Granada and Seville, e.g. the
violently decapitated head of St John by Montañes, the leading Seville
sculptor. De Mena carved many religious works and in his more
dramatic sculpture exemplified the theatrical side of the later Baroque
in Spain. The Virgin's realistically treated flesh and hair typifies the art
of the Counter-Reformation in Spain. 1284–1871

**St Diego of Alcala kneeling before the
Virgin and Child** by Luisa Roldan (1656–
1704) Polychromed terracotta Spanish
(Madrid) c.1675–1700 *H. 50.8 cm
W. 61 cm*
The rôle of saints was emphasized in
Counter-Reformation dogma, and many new
ones were canonized. In this devotional
figure group, the head of the saint is
extremely life-like, down to the greyish
stubble on his cheeks. With the help of the
beautiful angel, he presents the Cross to the
Murillo-like Madonna and Child. The
angel's wind-blown hair and agitated drapery
are typical of the Baroque means of arousing
the emotional participation of the
beholder. 250–1864

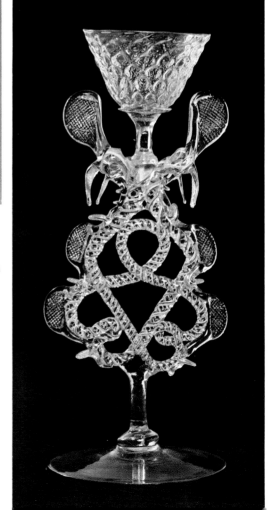

△

Goblet by Aert Schouman   Engraved glass   English, engraving Dutch   Signed and dated 1751   *H. 19.7 cm*
Stipple engraving originated in 17th-century Holland. A diamond point set in a handle is tapped to produce dots of varying sizes, creating effects of light and dark.

C.437–1936

Jug   Painted by Johann Schaper (1621–70)   German   c.1650   *H. 33.2 cm*
Schaper was one of the first to apply the art of stained glass to pottery, and this delicate black monochrome scene is typical of his work.

9–1867

Tazza   Glass with *lattimo* ornament   Italian (Venice)   Late 16th or early 17th century   *H. 12.7 cm*
The name of the white spiral filigree ornament comes from the Italian word *latte* (milk), and is applied to all glass in which white threads are used.

1860–1855

Wine-glass, façon de Venise   Netherlandish   17th century   *H. 23.5 cm*   ▷
The stem of this wine-glass (after the Venetian style) is in the form of a double-headed crested serpent elaborately coiled in red, yellow, and *lattimo* spiral threads.

594–1903

Sweetmeat stand by J. J. Kaendler (1706–75)   Hard paste
porcelain   German (Meissen)   1735   *H. 45.2 cm W. 32.5 cm*
White porcelain became extremely popular in the 17th century
owing to the large quantity being brought back from China by
the Dutch. The Rococo period coincided with the early years
of the European porcelain industry, producing elegant and
fragile *objets* painted in bright colours, like this sweetmeat
stand in the form of a Chinaman in an arbour, by the most
famous German porcelain modeller.   C.124 + a–1977

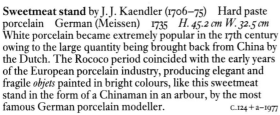

Part of a dinner service   Hard paste porcelain   German (Meissen)
c.1761   *H. 59.7 cm*
Kaendler modelled the group of Silenus and his Ass and the figures of satyrs
and fauns on this fruit basket; Frederick the Great of Prussia is believed to
have played some part in the design of the service.   C.238–56–1921

Columbine   Hard paste porcelain   German (Nymphenburg)   ▷
c.1760   *H. 19.7 cm*
This figure, from an Italian Commedia dell'Arte series modelled by Franz-
Anton Bustelli, is one of the most refined of all the small-scale statuettes
used as table-decorations in mid-18th century Europe. Nymphenburg was
one of the leading German porcelain factories.   C.82–1954

Armchair of the Duc de Choiseul Gilt, wood, and satin French (Paris) c.1770
The chair was made for the Duc's country house, Chanteloup, and bears the inventory brand of that estate. Its form is Rococo, but its classical decoration foreshadows Neo-classicism.   w10–1973

Writing table by J. F. Oeben (c.1721–63) Marquetry with ormolu mounts French c.1755 *H. 68.6 cm* (Jones Collection)
Sinuous and sensual forms were a hallmark of the high period of the French Rococo, or Louis XV, style. Furniture was often decorated with plant designs, as is seen in this elegant lady's desk.   1095–1882

Commode by Bernard van Riesenberg (d.1766) Black and gold lacquer, with gilt bronze mounts and Griotte marble slab French 1760 *H. 86.4 cm*
Fine Japanese lacquer was imported during the 18th century and was used by Parisian craftsmen for veneering especially luxurious pieces of furniture.   1094–1882

Reading-stand by Martin Carlin (d.1785) Wood inlaid with Sèvres plaque French c.1785 *H. with stand not raised 78.7 cm* (Jones Collection)
This is one of the most important pieces of furniture in the Museum, made by one of the most refined of Louis XVI period furniture makers. The stand, which can be raised, is decorated with a Sèvres porcelain plaque; the ormulu mount design of tasselled swags and drapery is distinctive of Carlin. The stand was given by Marie-Antoinette to Mrs Eden, later Lady Auckland, in 1786.   1057–1882

Bureau of Augustus III of Saxony
Inlaid woods, brass   German
c.1750   *H. 274 cm W. 127 cm*
Rococo persisted in Germany after it had
largely been abandoned in France. It
came into contact with the still-
flourishing Baroque interest in space and
plasticity, and emanated in an extremely
individual hybrid; fantasy was let loose,
producing extraordinarily beautiful
objects in architecture and sculpture. An
outstanding piece of German Rococo,
this cabinet was made probably by
Christian Friderich Lehmann for
Augustus III, King of Poland and Elector
of Saxony. It consists of an upper part
with arched doors with heavy ormolu
asymmetrical scrolling, ending in an
extravagant flourish. The surface is inlaid
with mother-of-pearl in the form of
flowers and leaves and decorated with
feathery scroll-work. Bought by Baron
Mayer de Rothschild in 1835, the bureau
was at Mentmore Towers from 1850.

63–1977

Fan Ivory and kid French c.1760 *W. open 53.7 cm L. 29 cm*
The painting on this side of the fan is of a very high standard. Painted in watercolour on kid, it shows a scene of fishermen bringing their catch into land to waiting village women. The landscape behind is Italianate and close to the work of Claude-Joseph Vernet (1714–89), a leading marine and landscape painter, whose sense of atmosphere made his work a foreshadowing of Romanticism. T.152–1978

Lady's dress Satin, raffia French c.1780
This sumptuous gown in cream satin has a sack back and matching petticoat. It is embroidered with sprays of flowers in coloured silks and chenille, and is trimmed with blue ruched and padded ribbon. Artificial flowers in shades of blue and pale green and curled feathers add to the richness of the full dress robe. T.180 + a–1965

Embroidered purse Silks, metal purl, silver and gold thread French Second quarter of 18th century *L. 11.5 cm*
The *grand sujet* was rejected by Rococo artists, and the pastoral became an extremely popular motif (see opposite). Here, Diana the Huntress is dressed as a shepherdess in a gaily coloured green dress and red apron. On the other side, a gentleman holds a gun and has a wild boar at his feet. The purse is edged with metal braid, and has a pinchbeck mount. T.44–1970

The Swing or **'L'Escarpolette'** by Nicolas
Lancret (1690–1743)   Oil on canvas
French   Early 18th century   *H. 70 cm
W. 89 cm*   (Jones Collection)
Fêtes galantes, pastoral scenes populated by
courtly ladies and gentlemen in shining silks and
satins, were a theme made popular by Watteau.
Lancret, the principal imitator of Watteau,
though less talented, painted many versions of
this composition. The rather coy lady is dressed
in a fashionable gown and the gentleman in
equally fashionable *déshabille*. The feathery
countryside adds to the airiness and grace of the
scene.   515–1882

Madame de Pompadour by François Boucher
(1703–70)   Oil on canvas   Signed and dated
1758   French   *H. 52.4 cm W. 57.7 cm*
(Jones Collection)
Jeanne Antoinette Poisson (1721–64) became
the mistress of Louis XV in 1745 and was
created marquise de Pompadour. Boucher was
the most important figure among the second
generation of French Rococo painters. His
paintings best demonstrate the frivolity and
elegant artificiality of 18th-century French life;
indeed, he complained that nature was 'too
green and badly lit'. The portrait is a charmingly
informal one, combining the Rococo pastoral
setting and interest in splendid materials with a
sensitive likeness of the sitter.   487–1882

Woven silk by Philippe de Lasalle (1723–1804) French (Lyons) c.1770 H. 55.9 cm W. 139.7 cm

Lasalle trained as a painter under Boucher, and became one of the leading Lyons silk designers and manufacturers of the latter half of the 18th century. He designed furnishing materials, incorporating naturalistic birds and sprays of flowers in an extremely elaborate style.   T.187–1931

Pastoral scenes   Plate printed cotton French (Jouy)   c.1775   H. 62.2 cm W. 94.6 cm

This piece of typical French Rococo printed cotton was designed by J-B Huet. Printed in red, it shows rustic scenes of Gothic ruins, cowherds and country lasses, stag-hunting, and a river scene.   T.449–1919

Pan grotesque in the style of Berain   Tapestry   French (Beauvais)   c.1700   H. 198 cm W. 284 cm

Fantastically clad, tambourine-bearing figures dance around a statue of Silenus in this tapestry, designed by J. B. Monnoyer. Grotesques became a popular decorative motif in the 16th century. Jean Berain (1637–1711) was a creator of the Louis XIV style, and his arabesques and grotesques started the movement which led to the Rococo style.   T.55–1955

Gobrias presents his Daughter to Cyrus
Tapestry Flemish (Brussels: Franz van der
Borght) 1771–75 *H. 401 cm W. 465 cm*
This brilliantly coloured tapestry is one of a set
of five surviving pieces ordered by Empress
Maria Theresa of Austria in 1771 (her arms
appear at the top), from cartoons by the court
painter Maxmilien de Haese. The son of
Gobrias the Assyrian had been slain by his
King, jealous of his skill in hunting. Gobrias
therefore offered support to Cyrus in his
campaign against Assyria, and as a pledge gave
to Cyrus the disposal of his daughter in
marriage. T.168–1969

The March: from **The Art of War**
Tapestry Flemish (Brussels: Judocus de
Vos) c.1715 *H. 417 cm W. 616 cm*
This detail comes from one of the seven
tapestries in the second series of the *Art of
War*, probably ordered around 1715 by
Augustus the Strong. Tapestries depicting
their victories were often commissioned by
military leaders, and Marlborough and other
commanders also ordered sets depicting
typical scenes of contemporary campaigning;
the *Art of War* belongs to this kind, and shows
scenes which are remarkably vivid images of
early 18th-century army life. The series
includes an army on the march and in camp, a
siege, an ambush, troops making fascines, a
halt on the march, and soldiers seizing
booty. T.283–1972

Coffee-pot   Porcelain   Painted by Jacob
Osterspey   German (Frankenthal)   (1730–83)
H. 28.3 cm
In the later 18th century the German porcelain factory
at Meissen lost ground to newer factories such as those
at Höchst, Ludwigsburg, and Frankenthal. This pear-
shaped coffee-pot from Frankenthal is decorated with a
scene of a naked girl surrounded by other naked
figures, a putto and satyr, the figures executed in stipple
by Osterspey, who specialized in mythological
subjects.   C.139 + a–1977

Vase   Porcelain   French (Sèvres)
c.1770   *H. 47 cm*   (Jones Collection)
The shape of this sumptuous object is a version of the
vase Bachelier à anses, and its colour, *bleu nouveau*, one of
the typical rich ground colours used at the Sèvres
factory. The scene of Jupiter disguised as Diana with
Callisto is adapted from an engraving after Boucher,
and is framed by rich gold leaves. It possibly formed
part of a collection sent in 1788 by Louis XVI to
Tippoo Sahib.   747–1882

Ewer and basin   Porcelain   Figures painted by
Catrice   French (Sèvres)   1763   *H. of ewer
16.5 cm*   (Jones Collection)
This ewer and basin are painted with the yellow
ground, *jaune-jonquille*, perfected by the Sèvres factory
in the 1760s. They are decorated with lively figures of
children playing, painted in blue, the flesh and hair only
in natural colours.   753–1882

Dish Tin-glazed earthenware Marked with LVE or LF in monogram Dutch (Delft: factory of Lambeth van Eenhorn, or Louwijs Fictoor) Late 17th or early 18th century *Diam. 49.5 cm*
The Dutch were the first to bring back pottery and porcelain from China, and by 1625 Dutch factories were already producing their own blue and white wares, imitating the Chinese. This dish has the typical Delft design of a floral medallion with sprays of flowers. C.647–1921

Tile panel Tin-glazed earthenware Portuguese (Lisbon) c.1720–30 *Entire panel H. 140 cm W. 38.8 cm*
Tin-glazed earthenware, especially tiles (*azulejos*), was made in Portugal from the 16th century. In the 17th century, beautiful items in blue and white were produced by a factory at Lisbon or Braga. This is one of a series of panels said to have decorated a music room in the Quinta Formosa, with scenes of ladies and gentlemen partaking of wine and listening to music, and of ladies being persuaded to dance. Each scene is bordered with masks, swags, and putti.
C.48–1973

St Augustine by Augustin Pajou
(1730–1809)   Terracotta
French   Signed and dated 1761
H. 56.16 cm
This over life-size bust was
probably a model for a marble statue
made for the Dôme des Invalides
and removed at the Revolution; the
lively and sensitive characterization
suggest that the bust was modelled
from the life. Pajou became Keeper
of the King's Antiquities at the
Louvre in 1777. His main work
consisted of portrait busts.   A.8–1974

Head of a Girl by Jacques Saly
(1717–76)   Marble   French
c.1750   *H. 48.9 cm*
Children were a popular subject for
18th-century French sculptors.
This charming bust, once thought
to be of the daughter of Madame de
Pompadour, is more probably of the
daughter of Jean-François de Troy.
8510–1863

Grotesque mask   Gilt bronze   French (Versailles)
c.1700   *H. 51.1 cm*
This is one of a pair of masks, typical of the decorative
sculpture produced for Versailles and other royal
châteaux under Louis XIV's patronage. They probably
formed part of a fountain.   AI.–1973

King Louis XIV of France   Bronze   French
c.1660   *H. 89.22 cm*
Louis, born in 1638, reigned from 1643 to 1715. The
bust was executed when he was about twenty-two years
old, around the time when he began to rebuild
Versailles.   A.54–1951

Cupid and Psyche by Claude Michel, called Clodion
(1738–1814) Terracotta c.1790 *H. 59 cm*
Related to, and taught by, L-S Adam, Clodion was the
son-in-law of Pajou. He produced many small statuettes,
terracottas, and bas-reliefs of nymphs and satyresses and
similar subjects treated in a sensual manner. Here a
nubile and swooning Psyche, supported partly by plump
little putti, is carried off to heaven by Cupid, with whom
she has been reunited after all her trials.   A.23–1958

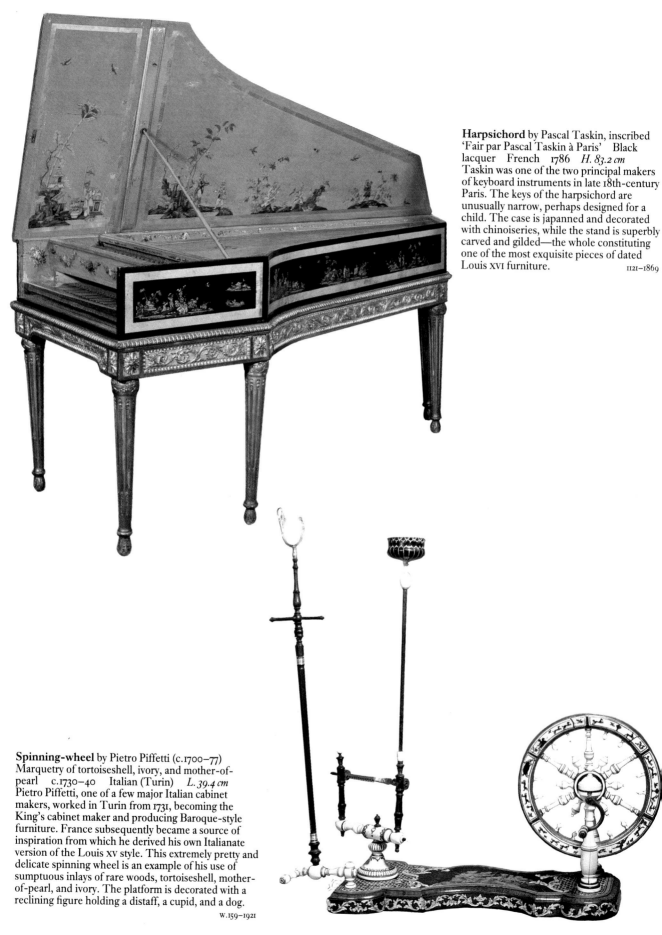

Harpsichord by Pascal Taskin, inscribed 'Fair par Pascal Taskin à Paris' Black lacquer French 1786 *H. 83.2 cm*
Taskin was one of the two principal makers of keyboard instruments in late 18th-century Paris. The keys of the harpsichord are unusually narrow, perhaps designed for a child. The case is japanned and decorated with chinoiseries, while the stand is superbly carved and gilded—the whole constituting one of the most exquisite pieces of dated Louis XVI furniture. 1121–1869

Spinning-wheel by Pietro Piffetti (c.1700–77) Marquetry of tortoiseshell, ivory, and mother-of-pearl c.1730–40 Italian (Turin) *L. 39.4 cm*
Pietro Piffetti, one of a few major Italian cabinet makers, worked in Turin from 1731, becoming the King's cabinet maker and producing Baroque-style furniture. France subsequently became a source of inspiration from which he derived his own Italianate version of the Louis XV style. This extremely pretty and delicate spinning wheel is an example of his use of sumptuous inlays of rare woods, tortoiseshell, mother-of-pearl, and ivory. The platform is decorated with a reclining figure holding a distaff, a cupid, and a dog.
W.159–1921

P 105

Box Red lacquer and gilt French Early
18th century *H. 10.2 cm W. 22.9 cm*
This japanned box was originally fitted with
several small boxes, one of which survives
and is exhibited in the case below. It is
decorated in the style of Berain, with an
arabesque design and a central medallion
containing the figure of a 16th century
woman having her hand read by an old
fortune-teller. This may be an example of
the Japan wares which were produced at Spa
in Belgium as souvenirs for those who came
to take the waters.   8506–1863

Snuff-box by Michel-Robert Hallé or
Hallet Enamelled gold French (Paris)
1750 *H. 3.6 cm L. 7 cm*
The tiny, heavy gold box is engraved and
enamelled *en plein* with birds amid trees in
brilliant and rich translucent colours. On the
lid are two peacocks, on the bottom two
ostriches, and the sides are decorated with
other birds.   M.115–1917

Snuff-box Soft paste porcelain with silver
mounts French (Mennecy) Mid-18th
century *H. 3.2 cm W. 7.6 cm*
The Mennecy porcelain factory was founded
in Paris in 1734 and transferred to Mennecy
in 1748. It produced objects in soft paste
porcelain only, in a restrained Rococo style,
decorated with flowers. This box is in the
form of an oblong wicker hamper with
rounded ends and a slightly convex top; it is
painted in muted enamel colours, including
the purple-rose distinctive of the Mennecy
factory.   C.315–1909

The Nineteenth Century

As historical surveys approach the present, generalizations crowd in more thickly, as more evidence survives and memory is fuller. For the historian of nineteenth-century art, styles move by at an increasing speed, and in confusing intermixture, because in this century almost all the discoverable styles of the past were revived.

Perhaps self-confident ages, which feel capable of mastering the world, are eager to annex the artistic past for their own purposes. The Renaissance gained new ground both intellectually and geographically, the nineteenth century through industrial technology: both also retrieved the past. Nineteenth-century revivalism, however, was stimulated equally by a desire to escape from the strenuously commercial present. The art of the late eighteenth and early nineteenth centuries is shaped by two almost counteractive revivals, Neo-classicism and the Gothic Revival, which must both be explained as part of a great impulse of recoil, the Romantic Movement.

Neo-classicism flagged first (although, of course, the language of classical architecture continued to be used in varied and original ways well into the twentieth century), because it was a search for pure archaeological perfection, bound to end in the chill of paralysis. Aesthetically authoritarian, it was apt for the service of autocratic powers: some of the grandest Neo-classical furniture was made for Napoleon, some of the severest Neo-classical paintings reflected the republican ideals of the French Revolution. Around a major Neo-classical work in a museum (the V&A possesses few, and even fewer are displayed, since the gallery displays end at about 1780) one can almost feel the temperature dropping.

But a kind of domesticated version of Neo-classicism pervaded the decorative arts and interior decoration in Germany and Austria in the early decades of the century; it was nicknamed the Biedermeier style, after a Pooter-ish literary character, but the name soon came to evoke the decent, cheerful qualities of the style, which needed no apology. It was in this pastel-coloured, highly polished, comfortably upholstered setting (the Regency interior is the English equivalent) that many Romantic poets and musicians cherished their most outlandish dreams.

It is a style poorly represented in the V&A, but it should not be overlooked, because it is a bourgeois style. Most artifacts that survive from earlier centuries are rich men's art, and objects selected for museums are usually exceptional pieces exemplifying superlative manual skill. In the nineteenth century middle-class taste came into its own. Mechanization made possible the mass-production of objects which were not expensive, but might nonetheless be well-designed, and exemplify high prowess of the imagination, if not of the hand. Mass-production overtook the different media at different rates. The creation of a mechanized textile industry was the first step in the Industrial Revolution; the technology of ceramics and glass was suited to larger-scale expansion; in furniture-making the change from workshop to factory was less easily made; working in precious metals remained a small-scale craft because of the sheer value of the materials. In general, however, there was an irresistible effort to make and sell more.

The collections of a museum like the V&A, in representing the decorative art of this period and later, try to register tastes at several levels. The Museum was, indeed, founded as part of a movement to improve taste in mass-produced objects. The art arbiters of the time believed that the way to do this was to train designers and artisans to reproduce styles of the past. All styles were taught, but the Gothic Revival movement, getting its second wind by the 1840s, was most

Cabinet by Henri-Auguste Fourdinois
(...1830)   Ebony, carved with inlay of
various woods   French   Signed and
dated 1867   *H. 251.5 cm W. 153.7 cm*
(Bethnal Green)

...ought from the Paris Exhibition of
...67 for the then vast sum of £2,750,
...e cabinet is by one of the most famous
...th-century cabinet-making firms,
...nd shows technical virtuosity of the
...ighest order. The taste for combining
...ecorative motifs derived from ancient
...gyptian architectural ornament and
...ymbols became popular in the 18th
...entury, and Napoleon's North African
...ampaign of 1798 gave this further
...npetus. Here, Egyptian caryatids and
...gures of Moors combine with
...lassically-inspired Renaissance motifs
...uch as the architectonic frame, the
...edallions containing Neptune and
...eres (?), Minerva in her temple, and
...utti carrying swags and scrollwork in
...his splendid, heavily-ornamented piece
...f Empire furniture.   721–1869

powerful in attracting followers, for it associated the Gothic style with doctrines of social reform.

In the second half of the century historicism luxuriated in the decorative arts. The exigencies of mass-production may perhaps have tended to smooth away some of the florid text-book detail in cheaper products, but at the great international trade exhibitions (London 1851, 1862; Paris 1844, 1855, 1867, 1878, 1889; Vienna 1873) every country strove to outdo the rest in *tours-de-force* of design and technique. Since the V&A's collection of European nineteenth-century decorative art (which is shown at the Bethnal Green Museum) was mostly acquired from such exhibitions, it shows European historicism in its richest colours.

A fresh and original style appeared in the 1890s and swept Europe almost at once. It must have been a relief to bestow upon it the simple label 'Art Nouveau' (which was borrowed from the deliberately boastful name of a Paris shop). A predominantly linear style, which, like Rococo, assumed three dimensions rather reluctantly, it was the first art style to be spread chiefly through art magazines. It was also one of the last styles of ornament to be based on forms in nature; for its sinuous curves, although thought by many to confess drooping degeneracy, are found everywhere in the movement of air, water, and sound waves, and in the growth of plants. It was a style fully capable of popularization (as the work of art-students at the time showed), but not sufficiently well suited to mass-production to hold public taste for more than a few years. At its best in metalwork (notably architectural ironwork) and textiles, but by a few designers extended brilliantly throughout the furnishing and decoration of complete rooms, it also influenced painting, and was the last style to dominate all the visual arts at once.

Baton   Gold mounts with translucen enamel   German (Hanover) c.1815   *L. 56 cm*   (Apsley House) According to the inscription, the baton was presented to Wellington by Ernst August, King of Hanover, when the former was appointed Field-Marshal o Hanover. It is decorated with a crown surmounted by a horse, the horse moti being repeated on the dark red velvet.   WM.1365–1948

Arthur, Duke of Wellington by Benedetto Pistrucci (1784–1855) Shell cameo   Early 19th century   Anglo-Italian   *H. 5.08 cm W. 4.3 cm*   (Apsley House) A Roman *emigré*, Pistrucci was employed at the Royal Mint from 18 designing and cutting dies for coins and medals. He is principally known as a carver of gems and cameos in the Neo-classical style. H also executed a large bust of Wellington, which is at Apsley House.   A.25–19

Necklace Cast iron and steel Prussian (Berlin) Early 19th century *L. 43.8 cm*
Cast iron jewellery was the speciality of the Prussian Royal Iron Foundry in Berlin. It became fashionable during the Prussian War of Liberation (1813–15), when more precious jewellery was surrendered to finance the war effort. The fine casting of such small objects was a considerable technical achievement, made possible by the 'cupole' furnace.   M. 136–1922

Lamp Silver Italian (Rome) c.1805
The Belli family of goldsmiths and silversmiths were makers of much of the best Roman plate from the mid-18th to the 19th century. This very ornamental lamp carries the figure of Cupid bearing a torch and strange, butterfly-like object.   436–1863

Tea service Silver and parcel gilt Prussian (Berlin) 1804–15 *Tea-pot 14 cm Coffee-pot 21 cm Cream jug 17 cm Hot water pot 17 cm Sugar bowl 6 cm*
The tea-pot has a classical lotus motif on the lid with reliefs of Neptune attended by Triton and a sea nymph, and probably Venus and Amor. The coffee pot bears a relief of a priestess pouring incense on a burner, with two cupids lighting torches, and Jupiter's eagle attended by Amor.   M.1a/b–1971

Panel from a skirt   Voided velvet with satin
ground   French (Lyons)   c.1850–60
The black silk velvet pile has been woven on to a
crimson satin ground in a cascade of scrolls and
flowers.   T.145a–1959

Evening dress by 'Pontecorvo, Rome' Italian   c.1893   △
This stately evening dress in pale-green striped grosgrain is trimmed
with orchid pink chiffon and velvet. The bodice is ruched and the wide
lapels embroidered with silver cord, sequins, and beads, as are the edge
of the overskirt and the hem of the underskirt.   T.47a–1973

Day-dress   Brown silk   French or English   1856–8
This smart outfit is in brown silk trimmed with black velvet and braid
edged with brown bobble and silk fringe. The jacket has open flaring
sleeves and the skirt, of matching silk, has rows of horizontal
flounces.   T.325a–b–1977

Jug   Lithyalin glass   Bohemian   c.1830   *H. 22.2 cm*
Lithyalin, a coloured glass simulating various stones, was developed by
Friedrich Egermann (1777–1864) in 1828–9.   C.139–1916

Tea-service by A. Greyton Silver-gilt and champlevé enamel French (Paris)
1862 *Coffee pot H. 21.5 cm* (Bethnal Green)
This silver-gilt tea-service is in pseudo-Arabic design. Comparison with the
service on p.109 shows that historicism is now in full flood. 8001/4–1862

Vase and stand by Barbedienne & Co Gilt metal and cloisonné enamel ▷
French (Paris) 1862 *H. 78.7 cm* (Bethnal Green)
Ferdinand Barbedienne (1810–92) was the best-known 19th-century Parisian
bronze founder. He produced imitation Chinese and Japanese bronze and
enamelled work, and in 1862 exhibited this amphora-shaped vase at the
International Exhibition. 8026–1862

Candelabrum by Salviati & Co Glass Italian (Venice) 1862 *H. 61 cm* ▽
(Bethnal Green)
The Salviati glasshouse was in the forefront of the revival of the Venetian glass
industry in the 19th century. Founded in order to manufacture mosaics for the
restoration of St Mark's, it also produced ornamental glassware such as this
candelabrum, which emulates 18th-century models. 9042–1863

Tazza Layered glass, cut, and gilt Bohemian c.1850 *H. 22.9 cm*
The *tazza* is made of clear glass coated with white and turquoise glass, which is cut
away to form the decoration. 4465–1901

Hush-a-bye-baby by Aimé-Jules Dalou (1838–1902)
Terracotta   French   c.1875   *H.55.9 cm*   (Bethnal Green)
The naturalistic movement arose in French 19th-century art as a
reaction to Idealism and Romanticism. The artist's duty was to
represent natural objects as they appeared; this, however, did not
prevent idealizing elements from being present! Dalou's work is often
sentimental in choice of subject, but in this statuette he manages to
capture a tender relationship without making it cloy.   A.39–1934

St John the Baptist by Auguste Rodin (1840–1917)   ▷
Bronze   French   1879–80   *H. 200 cm*   (Bethnal Green)
Rodin was the most celebrated sculptor of the late 19th
century. He created a new form in sculpture—the fragment as
a finished work—and was influential through his use of
symbols and expression of emotion and movement. The
spontaneity of the *St John* is achieved through having the
model begin to walk, and by a vivid characterization combined
with free handling.   601–1902

Elephant running by Antoine-Louis Barye (1796–1875)
Bronze   French   c.1855   *H. 13.7 cm*   (Bethnal Green)
Barye is known principally as an animal sculptor. A major
exponent of the Romantic movement, his subjects are usually
depicted in violent movement, and with an accurate portrayal
of animal forms, as in this running elephant.   62–1882

Bacchanales by Aimé-Jules Dalou   Terracotta   c.1879
Diam. 175 cm   (Bethnal Green)
This very large *tondo* of a woman, two men, and a satyr was exhibited
at the Royal Academy in 1879. Dalou later used the same
composition for a more successful marble version at Auteuil.
    434–1896

Theseus and the Minotaur by Antoine-Louis
Barye   Bronze   c.1855   *H. 46 cm*   (Bethnal Green)
An important early purchase from the Paris Exhibition of 1855, this
small figure group shows the strong influence of Greek archaic
sculpture, for which Barye was much criticized at the time. Theseus
struggles with the Minotaur, bronze being the perfect medium for the
expression of tension and power.   2708–1856

Partie de Campagne by Henri de Toulouse-Lautrec (1864–1901)   Colour lithograph
French   c.1897   *H. 51.4 cm W. 39.8 cm*
Lautrec's subject-matter was derived from the
life he led, in cafés and dance-halls in
Montmartre, circuses, and brothels. A superb
draughtsman, he conveyed intense
atmospheres with just a few lines and broad
areas of flat colour. His mastery of movement
and form can be seen in the galloping horse
and the minimal strokes which go to make up
the wheels of the buggy.   E.841–1949

Mountebanks or **Les Saltimbanques** by
Honoré Daumier (1808–79)   Pen and
chalk   French   c.1865   *H. 33.7 cm
W. 39.8 cm*   (Ionides Bequest)
Daumier worked as a cartoonist, and in 1835
joined *Charivari*, making lithographs for this
and other journals of political and social satire.
He combines a free and rhythmic drawing
style with strong chiaroscuro. Here, the clown
is drawn with a nervous line which emphasizes
the pathetic desperation of his appeal to the
crowd, for whom, evidently, the circus folk are
outcasts of society.   CAI–120

Ballet scene from Meyerbeer's 'Roberto il Diavolo' by Edgar Degas (1834–1917)   Oil on canvas   French c.1872   H. 75.6 cm W. 81.3 cm   (Ionides Bequest)

From 1862, Degas painted contemporary subjects, mainly scenes of racing, ballet, cafés, circuses, theatres, and laundresses. Influenced by Japanese colour prints and the new art form, photography, he was interested in conveying the sense of movement and spontaneity, although in fact his paintings were always carefully composed. In this one, loosely-handled paint suggests the ghostly figures of nuns on the stage while in strong contrast the audience, composed of Degas' friends, is tightly and firmly painted.   CAI–19

Wood-sawyers by J. F. Millet (1814–75) Oil on canvas   French   c.1850–2 H. 57 cm W. 81 cm   (Ionides Bequest) Millet, the son of a peasant, trained at Cherbourg and went to Paris in 1837. He was strongly influenced by Daumier. In 1849, he moved to Barbizon and devoted himself to painting scenes of peasant life— for which he was accused of socialism. His painting is extremely emotive in character, but his tendency to idealize the peasant, for example in *The Angelus* (1859), has led him to become less popular in the 20th century. His importance lies in his draughts- manship, where simplified forms are given a monumental weight and dignity.   CAI–47

Throne chair by Thomas Hoffmeister and Behrens   Carved oak, velvet   German (Coburg)   1851   *H. 205.7 cm*   (Bethnal Green)
Originating in England, the Gothic revival began in the 18th century as a romantic interest in medieval forms, but soon spread throughout Europe and America. This chair, one of a set of four, is carved with heavy Gothic architectural ornamentation, such as in the pinnacles, angels, gryphon arm-rests, and somewhat strangely-shaped legs. The back is carved with a suit of armour and fantastic beasts. As can be seen, the various Gothic styles allowed 19th-century artists a free reign to their imaginations.   w.10–1967

Bookcase designed by Bernardo de Bernardis (1807–1868), made by Leistler   Oak   Austrian (Vienna)   1851   *H. 579 cm   W. 457.2 cm*   (Bethnal Green)
This vast piece of furniture was presented to Queen Victoria by Emperor Franz Josef of Austria in 1851. Resembling elements of a Gothic church with its tracery and architectural ornament, it consists of four cupboards placed on nests of drawers. The outer cupboards are surmounted by miniature flying buttresses and pinnacles, the inner ones topped by domes and figures carrying an ecclesiastical building, and palette and chisel. Angelic and human figures represent various aspects of the visual arts, and others in medieval costume represent the performing arts.   w.12–1867

Cabinet by Louis Majorelle (1859–1926)
Mahogany and marquetry in various
woods   French (Nancy)   c.1900
H. 170.8 cm   (Bethnal Green)
Art Nouveau, the decorative style of the
1880s and 90s, is characterized by swaying,
curving lines, and the use of naturalistic
tendrils and flower and leaf motifs, fluid
female figures, and the ubiquitous waterlily.
The first Art Nouveau furniture by Gallé was
made in Nancy in the 80s; Majorelle adopted
the style and became the leading French
producer of it. Carved with waterlilies, the
graceful cabinet is marquetried in the upper
part with a scene of Gauguinesque females
bathing, and yet more waterlilies below.
1998–1900

Chair by Carlo Bugatti (1855–1940)
Walnut with metal inlay, vellum   Italian
(Milan)   H. 74.9 cm   (Bethnal Green)
Bugatti, the son of a carver of architectural
ornament, trained as an architect before
turning to furniture-making. His is a highly
inventive version of Art Nouveau, employing
as it does motifs from styles as diverse as
Middle-Eastern, Japanese, Turkish, and
Romanesque, and using metal and ivory inlays,
vellum, and cords. This chair, richly exotic in
design and materials, has vellum back-panels
decorated with heads of Egyptian inspiration,
and the pseudo-Arabic motif round the base is
made of pewter and brass inlay with copper
binding.   W.34-1969

Coffee-service by Tiffany & Co.   Silver inlaid with various metals   American (New York)   c.1878–80   *Coffee-pot H. 21.6 cm Creamer H. 7 cm Sugar bowl H. 5 cm*   (Bethnal Green)
Tiffany's, the famous New York jewellers, was established by Charles Louis Tiffany (1812–1902). It later manufactured silverware in the European Art Nouveau style, like this elegant and sinuous coffee service in imitation of Japanese Shakudo. The bulbous body, long neck, and long thin spout show the Oriental influence. It is decorated with inlay of silver and base metals in motifs of dragonflies, flowers, and fruits.   M.26–1970

Belt-buckle by René Lalique (1860–1945)
Silver and gold   French   c.1897
(Bethnal Green)
Lalique was the greatest Art Nouveau jeweller and glassmaker. Using all the favourite motifs such as flowers, serpentine female nudes, and dragonflies, he designed jewellery, combs, and buckles which are characterized by their asymmetrical forms and by the fact that the designer gave no predominance to one material over another. The auricular-shaped silver buckle is decorated with gold fronded leaves.   M.III–1966

Brooch designed by C. Desrosiers, made by Georges Fouquet   Gold with translucent enamels   French   Dated 1901
L. 12.8 cm   (Bethnal Green)
Another typically asymmetrical Art Nouveau design, the brooch is in the form of a long-stemmed flower in blue, grey, white, pink, and green enamels, being visited by a black and gold bee.   957–1901

Bowl and vase by Tiffany & Co.   Iridescent favrile glass   1902
Vase H. 7 cm   (Bethnal Green)
The bowl and vase are by Louis Comfort Tiffany, the maker of Art Nouveau glass lamps and vases. Louis (1848–1933) patented the iridescent glass called 'favrile' and founded the Tiffany furnaces in 1892. His glass designs are distinguished by their wavy outlines and abstract rainbow patterns, and satiny finish like mother-of-pearl.   1450/51–1902

Vase by Emile Gallé (1846–1904)   Amber glass with etched and painted decoration   Signed and dated 1900   French (Nancy)   *H. 47 cm*   (Bethnal Green)
A leading French glassmaker and exponent of Art Nouveau, Gallé established the school of Nancy. His vases, often elongated in shape, are decorated with tendrils, flowers and foliage, dragonflies, and sea creatures. The base of this vase has chrysanthemums and foliage richly painted in enamel colours.
1622–1900

Inkwell by René Lalique
Moulded glass   Early 20th century
H. 17.1 cm W. 11.4 cm
(Bethnal Green)
After 1902, Lalique designed a good deal of glass in the form of scent bottles, clocks, light fixtures, vases, etc. An amusing item, the square inkwell has corners moulded with figures of owls and a lid knob in the shape of an owl.   C.1491–1924

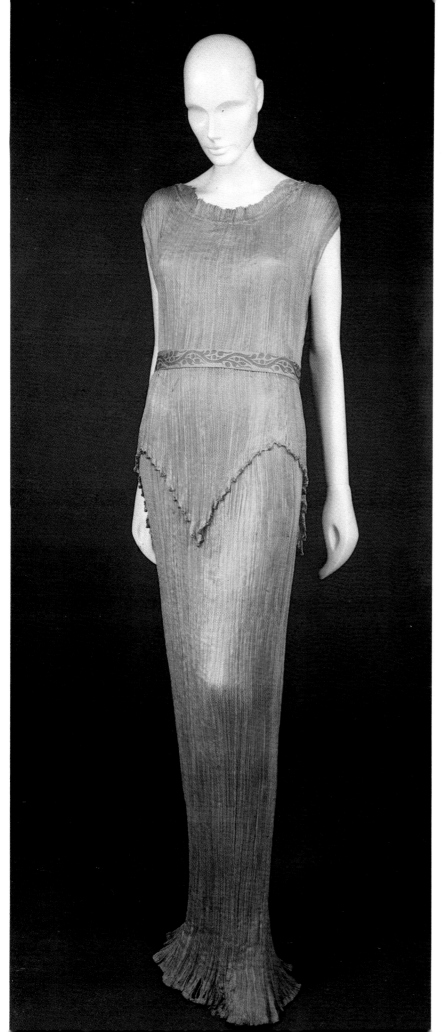

Evening Dress by Mariano Fortuny y
Madrazo (1871–1949)   Italian   c.1912
Born in Spain, the son and grandson of artists,
Fortuny spent much of his early life in Paris,
working for the theatre, before moving to
Venice with his family in 1889. It was there
that he developed a secret process for printing
colours and metals onto fabrics to achieve the
effect of brocades and velvets, the designs of
which he based on Renaissance examples. In
all his work Fortuny saw himself primarily as
an artist and took inspiration not only from
historic textiles of the West, but also from
Arabic and Far Eastern cultures. Thus it was
as an artist that, from 1906, Fortuny began to
design clothes which were quite outside
accepted convention. The following year he
produced what must be his best-known
costume design the 'delphos', named after the
tunic of the Delphic Augury, although actually
closer to the pre-classical 'chiton'. In 1909
Fortuny took out a patent for this simple
sheath of undulating pleats which cling to the
length of the body, and developed from it a
whole series of variations such as this beautiful
example in peach-coloured silk.   T.193 & A–197

The Twentieth Century

In the present century the decorative arts and architecture have lost touch with the fine arts of painting and sculpture. From time to time, there have been convergences: for instance, Cubist painters and those of the de Stijl movement seem to have shared the vision of contemporary architects and craftsmen; and, as in past ages, textiles, both woven and printed, have borrowed motifs from painting. But styles in painting and sculpture have changed so rapidly (at least eight distinct movements can be detected in the decade 1960–70) that they can hardly be plotted on the same graph as developments in the decorative arts. Perhaps it can be said that the foremost characteristic of all twentieth-century art has been Abstraction: a distaste for representation in painting has been matched by an abstention from ornament in architecture and the decorative arts (which can hardly therefore be called 'decorative' any longer).

Painters and sculptors have ceased to defer to the standards of their audience, and, taking whatever path attracts them, have left the audience to follow if it can. Architects, on the contrary, have more than ever before (or so they would claim) put their artistic skills at the service of technical and social imperatives. Architectural forms have been determined by new materials (reinforced concrete, steel-framed towers, plate glass cladding), and new building types have been devised for the modern industrial city. Architects have not simply become engineers, however. In the 1920s the work of Gropius, Mies van der Rohe, and Le Corbusier provided the inspiration for a powerfully influential aesthetic. The buildings of the Modern Movement (as these architects and their followers have come to be called) may or may not actually be functional and machine-made, but they are designed to look as if they are. They are overwhelmingly rectilinear, with a strictly geometrical articulation, a smooth finish, and no applied decoration. Although in the 1960s some more expressionist buildings have signalled a reaction against the Modern Movement, it remains the prevailing orthodoxy.

The decorative arts have found themselves rather nonplussed between the subjectivism of the fine arts and the functionalism of architecture. Now that decoration has been disallowed, they have tended to polarize between 'craft' and 'design'. The first term lays emphasis upon individual manual skill, and it has been a constant problem to reconcile this with the demands of the machine, satisfied by 'design'. The first attempts somehow to save the craftsman's position in industrial society were made in Britain at the close of the nineteenth century by the Arts and Crafts Movement (legatee of the social conscience of the Gothic Revival), which was soon emulated abroad by various groups. There was the Wiener Werkstätte, in Vienna in 1903–32, which made spherical teapots and square chairs with a teasing charm that owed much to Art Nouveau; and the more famous Bauhaus, at Weimar (1919–25), and then Dessau, a design academy which made spherical teapots and square chairs in a more deadly serious spirit. And there have been many reforming professional associations whose theory and ideology have been as important as their products.

The architects of the Modern Movement did not wish their buildings to be encumbered with too much furniture. Le Corbusier called it merely equipment, and reduced it to three components: chairs, tables and storage units. Since storage units are almost bound to be some kind of box, however beautifully finished, designers have lavished most creative effort on tables and chairs, especially the latter. There is a kind of apostolic succession of chairs by Rietveld, Breuer, Mies, Le Corbusier, Aalto, Eames, etc. (which are duly represented in the V&A). Some are ingenious cat's cradles of fireside engineering; some maintain traditional forms and materials, pared down with more or less subtlety (the speciality of Scandinavian designers); others use the tensile strength of materials in cantilevered forms to produce elegance out of stress; and recently, in reaction, some have been all upholstery and no structure.

Pots and pans have been successfully mass-produced in elegant, plain shapes; and household design has been extended by many new inventions, such as electric fans, radio receivers, and typewriters. Great skill has also gone into graphic design, which must take an important place in an applied arts museum. Perhaps the most significant development in twentieth century design has been the invention of synthetic plastics, which have made possible a new repertory of moulded forms.

The Modern Movement in the arts has been nothing if not earnest, but there has been room for some more frivolous interludes when ornament and representation have been in order. The world of 'Art Deco' (celebrated at the Paris Exhibition, 1925), a spectacle of shiny nude nymphs tiptoeing through gaudy zig-zag decoration, is preserved on many little decorative luxury objects. The art of the theatre was never more vibrant than in the scenery and costumes of the Ballets Russes. And fashion in dress has remained, in the western world, resolutely unfunctional and brilliantly inventive.

Fashion is not a bad note to end on, for, in its wayward absurdity, it discloses an element of caprice, of fun, that is always present, but not always obvious, in the arts. A book like this presents works of art neatly filed and docketed under styles and movements. While it is true that artists follow conventions, these are, after all, only fashions. Even the most academic student of art finds his greatest pleasure when he perceives how convention has been breached by some especially keen observation or surprising expressiveness on the part of the artist. The ordinary man may not spot this as quickly as the specialist, but if he looks out for the flash of caprice or fun in a work of art, this may be the clue which may give him entry to the creative imagination of the artist.

'Planta' hat stand by Castelli Plastic Italian 1978 *H. 170 cm Base diam. 38 cm* 20th-century office furniture has become more and more colourful, and influences home furnishing, so that chairs, lamps, desks, and tables now come in all the colours of the rainbow. This hat stand, designed in 1976, has six folding coat-hoo and two umbrella holders. w.57–1978

Commode by Dominique Ebony and silver French 1928 *L. 199.4 cm H. 90.8 cm* This very severe sideboard has doors, top, and sides veneered in macassar ebony and is complemented by silver lock plates. The silver mount is fluted and has a stepped outline, while the wooden plinth on which the carcase rests is likewise fluted. w.108–1978

'**Hammock chair 24**' designed by Poul Kjaerholm (b.1929) made by E. Kold Christensen   Stainless steel, cane   Danish (Copenhagen)   1965   *H. 87 cm D. 155 cm*
Kjaerholm was the leading Danish furniture designer of the Fifties and Sixties. The chair has simple and elegant lines and is made of stainless steel combined with natural materials—a handwoven cane seat and back, and a headrest cushion covered in African goatskin. The versatile chair is adjustable to any angle within a wide arc.   CIRC. 726–1968

Settee 'FS 48' by Finn Juhl (b.1912)   Teak with oxhide   Danish   *W. 141 cm H. 78.7 cm*
Danish furniture came to the fore in the 1950s with its emphasis on utility and comfort, and on the texture of the simple natural materials used. Here the moulded seat and back are supported by smooth dark teak but actually give the impression of being suspended over the frame, detached and hovering.   CIRC. 451–1969

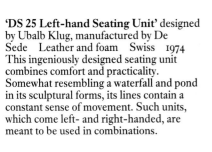

'**DS 25 Left-hand Seating Unit**' designed by Ubalb Klug, manufactured by De Sede   Leather and foam   Swiss   1974
This ingeniously designed seating unit combines comfort and practicality. Somewhat resembling a waterfall and pond in its sculptural forms, its lines contain a constant sense of movement. Such units, which come left- and right-handed, are meant to be used in combinations.

Stage design for Borodin's 'Prince Igor' by Nicholas Konstantinovich Roerich (1874–1947)   Tempera and body colour   Russian   *H. 50.8 cm W. 76.2 cm*
Roerich, a painter-archaeologist, was a prolific designer for the Russian ballet, theatre, and opera. In this stage set for Borodin's opera-ballet, he follows the naïve art of the icon painter, combining an almost oriental sense of rich colour with the decorative effects of Byzantine art, evoking the poetic scenery of a hot evening on the Steppes. He designed both *décors* and costumes for 'Prince Igor' which was first performed in 1909 under the aegis of Diaghilev in Paris.   E.2487–1920

Costume design for Pavlova by Natalia Gontcharova (1882–1962)   Water and body colour with gold and silver   Russian   *H. 61 cm W. 57 cm*
Gontcharova was instrumental in establishing the modern art movement in Russia, which led to the setting up of the Ballets Russes. Her familiarity with Russian folk art is evident in this attractive design for a peasant girl, created for Pavlova, prima ballerina of the troupe.   E.941–1927

Set for 'The Firebird' by Stravinsky by Natalia Gontcharova   Pen and ink, water and body colour, and gold   Russian   *H. 61 cm W. 62.2 cm*
Using Russian folk art motifs found in icons, brightly painted trays, and peasant prints, Gontcharova combined the simplicity of Cubist forms with the decorative effects of traditional craftsmanship. This design for the backcloth for Scene II is one of the very striking sets with bold colour contrasts of gay reds and yellows which painters like Gontcharova and Bakst designed for the Ballets Russes in the Twenties. 'The Firebird' was first performed at the Lyceum Theatre, London, in 1926.   E.2137–1932

Autumn leaves designed by Alexander ▷
Calder (1898–1976), woven by Pintou
Frères, Aubusson Cotton warp
tapestry French 1971 *H. 16.51 cm
W. 23.7 cm*
Calder, a sculptor, abstract painter, and
inventor of the mobile, originally trained as
an engineer and later became the leading
exponent of sculpture in welded metal. His
paintings were much influenced by the
Spanish surrealist painter, Joan Mirò
(b.1893); this clear abstract design is based
on his own mobiles, but at the same time has
elements of the decorative arabesques and
enlarged amoebic forms so often used by
Mirò. T.503–1974

Printed cotton by Madame de Andrada French (Paris) c.1925
H. 448.7 cm W. 72.5 cm
The cotton was probably originally designed as wallpaper, which was
produced by Paul Dumas and exhibited at the Exposition
Internationale des Arts Decoratifs et Industriels Modernes in Paris in
1925. The interlocking abstract forms include elongated triangles, fan
shapes, and chequer-board devices in purple, grey, yellow, green,
mauve, amber, and black. T.88–1973

Carpet by Voldemar Bobermann Hand-knotted wool French 1928–9 *H. 299.7 cm
W. 194.3 cm*
Bobermann was a painter and designer of furniture. This carpet was produced for the Maison
de Décoration Intérieure Moderne in Paris. It has a dark-brown ground with a sweeping linear
figurative design of three acrobats in action. The outline of the bodies and their ropes is in
cream and dark pink. It is signed in the pile in cream DIM. T.366–1977

Evening jacket by Charles James (d.1978)
Quilted satin   French (Paris)   1937
Worn over **sleeveless evening dress** by
Jeanne Lanvin (1867–1946)   Wool crêpe
French (Paris)   c.1938
By the Thirties, it had become fashionable to
show off a girlish figure. This was considerably
assisted by the new technique of cutting
clinging material on the cross. The square-
shoulder look was a distinguishing feature of
the immediate pre-War period. Charles
James' white quilted satin jacket is an evening
version. James, an Anglo-American, worked in
London, New York, Chicago, and Paris; the
Museum has a collection of his work. The
jacket is worn over Lanvin's black crêpe dress,
which is extremely simple in line, clinging to
the knee and then flaring out. Lanvin was one
of the most celebrated of French designers,
and her house became known for its graceful
feminine clothes.   T.385–1977 and T.4–1973

The South Court, from a drawing by John Watkins c.1876–81

Oriental Art
in the Victoria and Albert
Museum

The former India Museum in Whitehall Yard: an engraving published in the *Illustrated London News*, 1861, showing the Golden Throne of Ranjit Singh (see p. 340) in the right middle ground.

Introduction

This volume attempts to survey all that part of the Museum's collections which come from the continent of Asia: an area which apart from its size remains even today by far the most populous as well as, probably, the most racially varied on the face of the globe. The term 'oriental art', however widely used, is of course no more than a convenient fiction for the 'Orient' in fact has no real cultural identity, and exists only as a mirror-image of the Occident. This fragmented state of Asia has been ensured throughout history by a geography which divides the continent severely into east, south, west, and north: the mountain ranges and desolate plateaus of Central Asia, awesome in their extent and solitude, have proved a formidable obstacle which if not always sufficient to restrain conquest and trade, has until now thwarted any major assimilation of race by race, or culture by culture.

To the south of this barrier lies the sub-continent of India, largely tropical in climate, and the source of highly influential religions; to the west, the so-called Near Eastern lands which nourished the world's most ancient cultures, falling later under the spell of Islam; and far to the east, a more remote civilization which came to birth in China, later embracing the Korean peninsula and islands of Japan; also South-East Asia, a region powerfully influenced by India and China alike. The less hospitable north, the home of nomadic peoples, has aroused interest mainly as the source from which they have from time to time ventured to threaten or achieve widespread conquest, notable instances being the migrations which beat with ultimate success against the Roman Empire, and the Mongol domination of the thirteenth century. For all its cleansing vigour, however, their contribution has only marginally affected artistic and intellectual life.

Throughout history two further agencies besides large-scale migration and war have worked in favour of closer communication in Asia: religion and trade. From Asia have come all the world's major surviving religions. In India, Hinduism arose from a synthesis of Brahmanism and other existing beliefs allied to a caste system. Exerting a dominant influence in the early history of Indian art, and enjoying a late resurgence which has left it still very powerful today, it has also been a strong influence in South-East Asia. It is, however, the meditative traditions and practices of Buddhism, with its promise of salvation from the cycle of earthly reincarnation, which have most effectively crossed national boundaries. Transmitted by way of Central Asia in the early centuries A.D., Buddhist forms of thought came to permeate the fabric of Far Eastern societies and art, and in some parts of that area are still highly influential. Images of the Buddha first appeared in North-West India at Gandhara in the early centuries A.D., interestingly enough under the influence of Hellenistic models, although the ripest sculptural development came later in Gupta times. Various forms of Buddhism were later evolved showing a differing emphasis. The Tantric form, for example, with its many esoteric observances incorporating Hindu elements, took especial hold in Nepal and Tibet; while in medieval China and Japan the essentially meditative cult of Chan (or Zen) developed alongside the more institutional form. The practices of this sect were in some measure influenced by Taoism, a Chinese philosophical creed having as a central doctrine the attainment of harmony with nature. And we may note in passing that Taoism became a major creative force in the evolution of Chinese landscape painting. The third 'religion' of China, Confucianism, enshrines a social code of attitudes towards state and family which contributed greatly to the long stability of its culture. These various forms of belief have not only inspired great schools of painting and sculpture: they have

also fostered a rich world of symbolism and legend from which the decorative arts
have drawn continuously over the centuries. In the Near Eastern lands and North
Africa the religion of Islam, militant in its early aspects, iconoclastic, and with a
strict rule of observance and prayer, established its own traditions. Its power to
unify different races and cultures in worship has proved a lasting one. In the
sixteenth century, by means of the Moghul conquest, Muslim culture was carried
into India and beyond; so that a whole school of Mughal, Indian art is closely
allied to that of Persia.

Religions were not alone in traversing frontiers. From early times, caravans
travelled the long desert routes between East and West Asia carrying a variety of
rare, and often exotic products, and it was in this way that within the Roman
Empire Chinese silks came to be widely worn by the populace; the Han,
meanwhile, supplemented their military power by the use of horses imported
from Ferghana, or transported from Khotan precious boulders of raw jade. In
later times, trade by sea round the southern shores of Asia became increasingly
important, and Arab, Indian, and Malay ships brought a wide range of
commodities to and from the Malaccan straits, while both India and the Islamic
world enjoyed the luxury of Chinese porcelain from an early date.

Europe has taken its own place in this traffic. Throughout the Middle Ages,
merchants succeeded in carrying on a highly profitable trade with the Islamic
lands, and by the sixteenth century diplomatic contacts were becoming more and
more significant. At this time, too, their bent towards maritime expansion took
them round the Cape into the Indian Ocean, and beyond into the China Sea,
where they soon outclassed the indigenous traders. The riches of this trade led to
a growing involvement by rival nations in India, where mercantile colonization led
eventually to empire, as it did also, later, in South-East Asia and China. In all
these areas, from the seventeenth century onwards, contact with the developing
technology and consumer market of the West began to exercise a significant, and
not always beneficial, influence on developments in the arts and daily life of the
people.

Only in relatively recent times have the arts of the East been at all extensively
studied or collected by Westerners, and scholars today exert their energies to
interpret them more and more effectively in terms of the unfamiliar traditions we

have described. Fortunately, the works themselves seldom fail to speak directly in that international language of art to which all can respond.

History of the Collections

The Oriental collections of today date back to the foundation of the Museum and well beyond. They are conveniently treated in three main parts, two of which are today cared for by well-established specialist departments, the Indian Department and Far Eastern Department, while the third comprising the Near Eastern collections remains divided. The first is concerned with the Indian sub-continent and its extensions into South-East Asia and the Himalayas; the second, with China and its extensions similarly into Central Asia and the South-East Asian seas, together with Korea and Japan. Logically, the Museum has need of a further, Islamic, department to take sole charge of its Western Asiatic collections, which are at present variously allocated according to material.

The Indian collections have a particularly long and interesting history of their own for their origins may be traced back to the private museum of that great trading institution, the Honourable East India Company, which came into being at the end of the eighteenth century. This was situated within East India House in Leadenhall Street, in the City; and among its contents was the celebrated 'Tipu's Tiger', a model of an unfortunate Englishman being devoured with sound effects, which remains a most popular exhibit today (see page 340). When the company collapsed in 1858, the collections became part of the new governmental Indian

Hindu sculpture in part of the present
Indian Primary Gallery

The Primary Gallery of Islamic Art

Office, and were placed on display to the public at Fife House in Whitehall. An engraving shows this to have been a very rich and stimulating display: at that date it included all kinds of items such as marble busts of distinguished soldiers and statesmen, mineral products, agricultural models, and stuffed birds and animals, as well as works of art.

In 1879, well after the foundation of the (later so-called) Victoria and Albert Museum, the major part of the art objects was transferred to the control of the Department of Science and Art. Now set up in existing premises in South Kensington, they already numbered some nineteen thousand items and in the following decades the collections grew steadily, largely through purchasing expeditions sent to India for this purpose. Meanwhile, questions of their proper role and location were much debated in what was then a highly-charged Imperial context. The galleries themselves became directly linked with those of the newly constructed and grandiose Imperial Institute nearer to Hyde Park, while for a time the Museum's collections of Chinese, Japanese, and Near Eastern art were installed in the same complex. When the large-scale extension of the main Victoria and Albert Museum building was opened in 1909, these other Asiatic collections were re-installed there and following the Second World War, the Indian collections also joined them: provision for storage and display are, however, cramped and the promise of a more suitable setting has yet to be fulfilled. The most vital step since then, instituted in 1970, has been the long-needed integration of the Museum's scattered Chinese and Japanese collections to form a fully specialized and properly staffed Far Eastern Department. The further aim of achieving a logically organized and well laid-out oriental wing for the Museum remains, and plans for this have been prepared.

Outline of Dates

CHINA

Neolithic	to c.1700 B.C.
Shang	c.1700–1027 B.C.
Zhou	1027– 256 B.C.
Warring States	481– 221 B.C.
Han	206 B.C.– A.D. 220
Six Dynasties	220– 589
Tang	618– 906
Five Dynasties	907– 960
Song	960– 1279
Yuan	1279–1368
Ming	1368–1644
Qing	1644–1912

JAPAN

Jōmon	to c.200 B.C.
Yayoi	c.200 B.C.– A.D. 250
Kofun	c.250– 552
Asuka	552– 645
Nara	645– 794
Heian	794– 1185
Kamakura	1185–1333
Muromachi	1392–1568
Momoyama	1568–1615
Edo	1615–1868
Meiji	1868–1912

KOREA

Three Kingdoms	57 B.C.– A.D. 668
United Silla	668– 935
Koryō	918–1392
Yi	1392–1910

INDIA

Indus valley culture	c.2150–1750 B.C.
Vedic period	c.1500– 800 B.C.
Life of the Buddha	c.563– 483 B.C.
Maurya	c.322– 183 B.C.
Shunga	c.183– 71 B.C.
Kushan	c.50– A.D. 320
Gupta	c.320– 540
Pallava (South)	c.300– 893
Chalukya (Deccan)	c.550– 973
Pala & Sena (Bihar, Bengal)	c.750–1200
Chola (South)	c.830–1279
Hoyshala (Mysore)	1110–1327
Sultanate of Delhi	1206–1526
Vijayanagar (South)	1336–1564
Mughal	1526–1858
British rule	c.1757–1947

SOUTH-EAST ASIA

Thailand:

Dvaravati	6th–11th century
Srivijaya	8th–13th century
Lopburi	11th–14th century
Sukhotai	13th–15th century
Ayudhya	15th–18th century

Cambodia:

Funan	c.5th– 8th century
Khmer	8th–15th century

ISLAM

Ummayad (Damascus)	661– 750
Abbasid (Baghdad)	749–1258
Samanid (E. Persia)	819–1005
Fatimid (Egypt)	909–1171
Ghaznid (E. Persia)	971–1186
Seljuk (Persia, Iraq)	1038–1194
Ayyubid (Egypt/Syria)	1169–1252
Mamluk (Egypt/Syria)	1250–1517
Mongol (Persia, Iraq)	1256–1353
Timurid (Persia)	1370–1506
Ottoman (Turkey, etc)	1281–1924
Safavid (Persia)	1501–1732
Qajar (Persia)	1779–1924

Painted earthenware jar Banshan type Neolithic
period *c.*2500 B.C. *H. 38.8 cm*
This funerary urn comes from the Yangshao culture which developed
in the upper Yellow River valley and later spread west to Gansu. The
importance of the craft in Neolithic times is evident in these finely-
made pots, which were burnished smooth and then painted in purple,
red, and black: the swirling linear designs have a rhythmic life that is
already unmistakably Chinese. In eastern China, at the same time,
the Longshan culture was making a plain black pottery in thin,
metallic shapes of a quite different character. The historic Shang
culture which followed owed much to both. C.286-1938

The Far East

The Far Eastern Department takes care of about sixty thousand works of art which have come from China, Korea, and Japan. China has been the fountainhead of cultural development in this region, and it is above all the civilization developed there in early times which has nurtured the growth of its immediate neighbours. This is apparent in the wide spread of the Chinese language and philosophy and the transmitted religions such as Buddhism, as well as its highly distinctive traditions in the arts.

It was in Bronze Age China, under the first historic dynasties of Shang and Zhou (c.1700–200 B.C.), that the mould of this civilization was cast. Its origins remain somewhat obscure, although in recent years archaeological studies have yielded increasingly significant discoveries. In Han China (206 B.C.–A.D. 220), we find a united empire already capable of extending its power into Central and South-East Asia and Korea, and China soon became a centre of attraction for foreign emissaries who bore her cultural influence steadily outwards. The following disturbed period brought the gradual establishment of Buddhism and its spread to Korea and Japan. Reinforcing this influential tendency, the great power and wealth of Tang China brought new standards of social organization and sophistication to the arts and everyday life; the periods of the Song, Koryō, and Heian which followed in these countries consequently achieved a cultural level that is rare in world history.

The Mongol conquests of the thirteenth century constitute something of a cultural watershed. Under the Ming, state and society in China resumed their measured path, but in the arts the direct inspiration and poised assurance of the preceding age proved harder to recapture; in Korea, the calm brilliance of Koryō court art gave way in the Yi period to wilder and more folk-based forms. The workmanship of Chinese crafts, however, remained at a remarkably high level, even under the Qing dynasty of the Manchus (1644–1912), an age of great activity especially in ceramics, textiles, and the whole range of arts which we call 'decorative'. In Japan also, a flowering of native culture during the Momoyama (1568–1615) and early Edo periods underlines the unusual artistic talent and skills of its people, especially in decorative design.

While the archaic period of China is represented by good examples, the collections are most outstanding in the arts from the Han dynasty onwards, including that of Buddhist sculpture from the Six Dynasties to the Sung; they are especially rich in ceramics of all periods, and in Ming and later textiles, metalwork, lacquer work, jade carving, and furniture. Korean art is represented predominantly by ceramics. Apart from some fine early Buddhist sculpture and paintings, the Japanese collection is particularly strong in pottery and porcelain, and in lacquer work, carved netsuke, armour, and the arts of the sword; it also includes a large and important assemblage of prints and illustrated books.

China

The first historic culture of China, that of the Shang state, emerges from the Neolithic about 1700 B.C. in the northerly valley of the Yellow River. Its surviving monuments are the contents of its tombs: chiefly bronzes, jades, and ceramics. The bronze vessels represent a ceremonial art on which much labour was spent, with powerful forms and a mysterious, hieratic repertoire of designs which are cast with exceptional artistry. Its complex styles continued to evolve under the Zhou dynasty (1027–256 B.C.), and are reflected equally in jade carving, an art which was to maintain a special significance in later centuries. Many important characteristics of Chinese art, such as its subtle use of line, and its close adherence to the rhythmic patterns of nature, are already evident in this period.

By the time of the unified Han dynasty (206 B.C.–A.D. 220), bronze art had moved towards greater simplicity in design. Tomb art now included wall paintings and extensive sculpted reliefs in which legend and daily life are depicted in an extremely realistic manner, as they are also in the sets of pottery models placed there to accompany the dead. In its production of glazed stoneware, the ceramic industry stood poised for a major advance, while such arts as lacquer work and textile weaving also became important.

There followed a period of disunity and war which is chiefly noteworthy for the establishment of Buddhism, introduced through Central Asia. Under the patronage of the Northern Wei kingdom, there emerged a prolific art of stone sculpted images which filled cave temples and shrines right across North China. It was an art which was to flourish further under the Tang (618–906), and to a lesser extent under the Song (960–1279). Unfortunately, the great wall-paintings and scrolls which accompanied them are substantially lost to us.

Enough survives of the arts of Tang China to demonstrate its abundant prosperity, self-confidence and power as the leading world force of its day. Some splendid silver and gold vessels and lacquers still exist, as well as lavish tomb furnishings which show a further advance in ceramic technology. The colourful models of horses, camels, and other animals are much admired for their brilliantly executed vigorous forms, while glazed stonewares also are filled with a simple strength: more important still, however, was the invention of translucent white porcelain.

The classic development of Chinese ceramics in the following Song period included production of the creamy-white Ding porcelain and bluish-green Ru and Guan celadons, with their characteristic crackled glazes; while the brown-painted Cizhou, luminous blue Jun and green Longquan wares are no less celebrated. In addition to developments in painting—especially in landscape, which at this time became perhaps the leading branch of the art—the Song also brought a strong antiquarian movement within the scholar class. A renaissance of archaic styles followed, which is reflected from this time onwards in such arts as those of bronze and jade.

Jade ceremonial blade Shang 13th–11th century B.C. *L. 34.9 cm*
The curved and tapering form, honed edge and grooved tang display
the great vigour and refinement of Shang art. Jade was worked mainly
for ceremonial purposes from Neolithic times onwards, and objects
such as this were clearly not for ordinary use; the labour involved in
working the hard stone shows how highly they were regarded.

A.71–1936

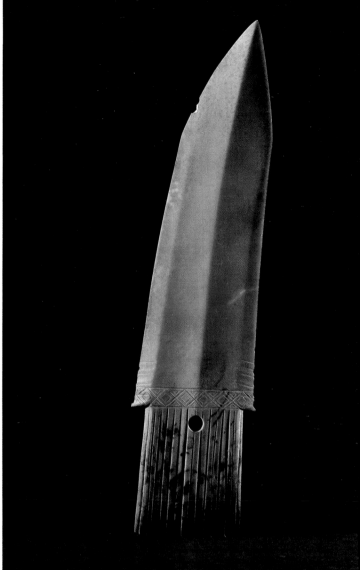

Bronze ceremonial axe Shang 13th–11th century B.C. *L. 16.2 cm*
The axe possibly formed a finial for a ceremonial pole: the
human head, perhaps that of a warrior, is a relatively
unusual and striking feature. It is beautifully decorated
with highly stylized animal forms combined to great effect
with incised detail. Present-day collectors admire the rich
green patina of these bronzes, but originally the metal was
clean and silvery-gold in appearance. M.15–1948

Bronze ritual food vessel (*ding*) Shang 13th–11th century B.C.
H. 19.1 cm
The form of the three-legged *ding* comes from that of a Neolithic
cooking-pot. Shang bronze vessels were used during solemn and
important occasions; they are elaborately decorated with the stylized
symbols of a hieratic religion, the creeds and practices of which have
faded into obscurity. The impact of their powerful designs and
superb technique remains a source of fascination today. M.60–1953

Bronze owl vessel (zun) Zhou 11th–10th century B.C.
H. 20.9 cm
In ancient China, the owl was probably endued with a
symbolic significance now lost to us. This rather quizzical
strutting bird actually forms a wine vessel, with its head as the
removable lid. Nature has, however, been deliberately transformed—the feathers have been rendered as scales and the
wings as spiralling snakes, no doubt adding further symbolic
meaning. M.5 & A–1935

Bronze mirrors *above:* Shaoxing, Jiangsu
2nd century A.D. *Diam. 18.4 cm*
below: Shouxian, Anhui 4th–3rd century
B.C. *Diam. 7.6 cm*
Early Chinese mirrors are highly polished on
one side, the reverse being generally decorated with cast ornament. The smaller
example is the earlier, its delicate formal
patterns recalling textile designs. The larger,
late Han dynasty mirror comes from South-
East China and is cast in strong relief with
figures of Taoist deities, including Xiwang-
mu, Queen Mother of the West and her
consort Dongwanggong. 200–1899
M.46–1939

Glazed earthenware dog Han 1st century
A.D. *L. 34.9 cm*
This fiercely-barking dog provides an illustration of daily life in a predominantly rural
community. Pottery models of farm animals
and equipment, as well as of solemn officials
and servants, were buried in tombs from
Han times onwards to cater for the future
needs of the dead. They were made of both
lead-glazed pottery and unglazed ware
painted in bright colours. C.167–1914

Earthenware tomb guardian Han 1st
century A.D. *H. 47 cm*
The more important tombs were built of
brick and for the official classes. Although
the ceremonial function of this expectant-
looking dignitary is uncertain, it was clearly
one of importance. He wears a Han-style
robe, and his hands are clasped as if he had
originally held some ceremonial object which
has since perished. Some traces of the
original bright pigment can be seen.
C.924–1935

Apsaras Limestone Northern Wei Early 6th century *H. 64.5 cm*
W. 64 cm
Part of a much larger composition, this relief may have come from the
cave temples of Longmen in north China, where innumerable
Buddhist carvings were executed over a period of centuries. This
apsaras, or music-making angel, is similar to the figures carved at
Longmen, shown descending to escort important deities to heaven.
In the flat relief treatment of the Northern Wei style, the pleated
folds of the draperies seem to take on a life of their own.   A.55–1938

Buddhist stone stele Northern Wei 520 A.D. *H. 173.4 cm*
Carved in reddish sandstone, this tablet would have originally stood
in a northern Chinese temple precinct. Successive dynasties greatly
supported the Buddhist faith which was introduced via Central Asia
from India. Such stele can either be flat slabs bearing a single large
figure group or, as here, carved on all sides with various themes, such
as the famous discourse of Vimalakirti and Manjusri. Depicting the
human body less sensuously than did their Indian counterparts, the
Chinese sculptors emphasized their message through a skilful
handling of linear rhythms. The inscriptions record the piety of the
numerous donors.   A.9–1935

Bodhisattva Sui *c.*600 A.D. *H. 95 cm*
The combination of sculptural forms and
rhythmic, flowing lines with a highly sensitive
treatment of the face makes this an outstanding piece of sculpture; it has a characteristic
air of great calm and reassurance. This is
possibly one of two Bodhisattva figures
which would originally have accompanied a
central Buddha to form a trinity or larger
composition.   A.8–1935

Glazed stoneware ewer Yue ware Deqing, Zhejiang province Jin Late 4th–early 5th century A.D. *H. 16.8 cm*
This rare stoneware ewer shows the smooth black glaze which had recently been discovered in the late fourth century. Of a pleasing globular shape, the vessel has a 'chicken-head' spout; it was probably recovered from a tomb, and used more as a ceremonial piece than for daily purposes.

FE.9–1972

Stoneware jar Probably from Zhejiang province S.E. China Han *c.*1st century A.D. *H. 32.5 cm*
This finely shaped jar is made of a high-fired type of pottery with a well-integrated olive-green glaze used as a decorative feature. It has neat loop handles and ribs and is decorated with lively incised patterns round the shoulder and neck. The earliest stonewares had already appeared under the Shang about 1500 B.C., and this advanced level of skill helps to explain the unique achievements of later Chinese pottery

C.138–1913

Glazed stoneware pilgrim's flask Early Tang 7th century *H. 21.9 cm*
The relief-moulded design of dancing and piping figures among branches of vine under the brown glaze vividly illustrates the growing intrusion of western Asiatic features into Chinese life and art during the late sixth and seventh centuries, when Chinese power extended far across the central deserts. Similar flasks were strapped to the saddles of camels traversing the long trade routes.

C.432–1920

Silver stem cup Tang 7th–8th century *H. 8.3 cm*
The popularity of gold and silver plate under the Tang dynasty reflects the new-found wealth and taste for luxury that characterized much of that era. Small dishes, bowls, and boxes predominate in the tombs, but as the Shōsōin storehouse in Japan proves, magnificent ewers and ritual objects existed also at Court. The chased and punched work is reminiscent of Persian Sasanian silver, and craftsmen from that area were no doubt instrumental in introducing and developing the techniques, as well as bringing in new designs.   M.31–1935

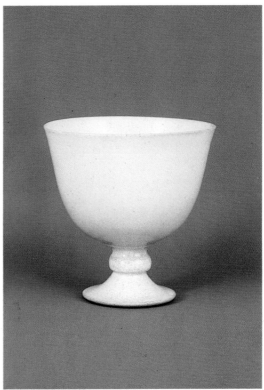

Glazed white stoneware stem cup Tang 7th–8th century *H. 7.6 cm*
A most important innovation of the north Chinese potters at this time was a dense white stoneware with a clear, glassy glaze, the immediate forerunner of the more homogeneous white 'porcelain'. It had appeared by the ninth century and soon achieved worldwide fame. The knopped stem here follows a shape found in silver ware; the stoneware is so fine that it is translucent.   C.138–1965

Stoneware bowl Yue ware Tang or Five Dynasties period 9th–10th century *Diam. 11.1 cm*
The Yue wares derived from a long-established tradition of green-glazed stoneware manufactured in south-east China. 'Celadon'-glazed wares, so-called after the colour of the garment worn by a rustic character of that name in a seventeenth-century French romance, were exported in quantities from China throughout Asia in later centuries. The Tang bowls and vases have lobed, flower-like forms which show great potting skill; according to early documents, the restrained glaze colour was much liked by tea drinkers. Similar wares were exported along the sea routes to western Asia, where fragments have been dug up at the sites of former trading-posts.   C.138–1973

Glazed earthenware horse Tang Early
8th century *L. 80.5 cm*
Strikingly bold in execution, with their
powerful bodies and fine, intelligent heads,
these pottery horses are among the Tang
potters' more ambitious and colourful crea-
tions. That such fine works of art should
have been made for placing in tombs is
remarkable evidence of the lavish burial
customs of that time. Together with the
related models of camels, they symbolize the
important role played by these animals in
pacifying the Empire.   C.50–1964

Earthenware figure of a foreign youth
Tang 7th–8th century *H. 25.8 cm*
This well-observed portrait in clay is a
reminder that the Tang capital served as a
focus for foreigners from every part of Asia.
The black-painted flesh areas suggest a
visitor from one of the tropical south-east
Asian lands, and perhaps ultimately of
Hindu or even African origin. With his
colourful clothing and gilt necklace, bracelet,
and anklet, the figure may have been a groom
or drummer heading a procession. C.827–1936

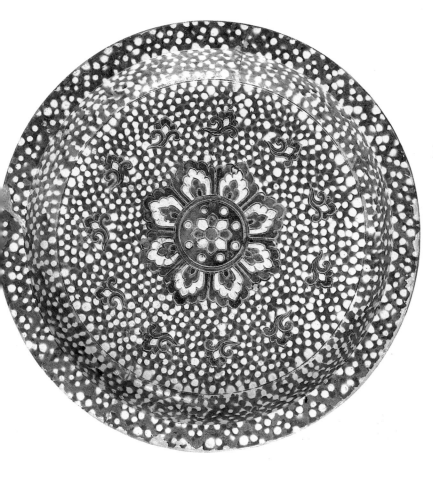

Glazed earthenware dish Tang Early 8th century *Diam. 38.1 cm*
The main floral design of this attractive dish was stamped in the clay and filled in with green, amber, and white, the ground then being decorated with a spotted pattern; the result is one of glowing colour and splendour. The dish shows the influence of metalwork techniques which underlies much of this funerary pottery. These wares are found mostly in the metropolitan areas of the Yellow River valley, but regional variations are now coming to light. C.II–1935

Jade camel Tang or early Song 9th–10th century *L. 9.8 cm*
Small jade animal sculptures have held a permanent place in Chinese art since they became popular under the Han. The purpose of this delightful carving of a camel biting its hump is unknown. The contrasting colours of the stone are cleverly exploited and, given the hardness of the material, the firm, sharply-drawn lines of the mane and stylized sinuous shapes are something of a *tour-de-force*.
A.28–1935

Glazed earthenware jar Tang Early 8th century *H. 27 cm*
Whether by accident or design, the splashed green and amber-yellow glazes running down the sides of this jar produce an unusually beautiful effect. Shaped like a gourd with its tiny lid, the design is simple, but at the same time has the vitality and sense of form characteristic of the Tang potters. C.867 & A–1936

Lacquer toilet box Song 10th–13th century *Diam. 16.4 cm*

Lacquer, a resin with strong preservative properties, is tapped from a tree of the same name which grows in many Far Eastern countries. In the Song period, simple but elegantly-shaped objects like this multi-tiered box, containing a tray and smaller box, were made for daily use, a few layers of lacquer in one or two plain colours being applied to a thin wood or fabric construction. More elaborate styles existed, such as in the intricately painted boxes found in Han tombs and the rich shell inlays of Tang lacquer wares. GARNER LOAN

Jade cup Song 12th–13th century *L. 8.9 cm*

Jade vessels from the Song period and earlier are rare, an indication of the precious nature of a material brought all the way from Central Asia. The carefully worked quasi-geometric designs are derived from the study of ancient jades and bronzes. A 'renaissance' of archaic style took place at this period which appealed especially to those of a scholarly bent. A.5–1968

Jade tiger Song 12th–13th century *L. 11.9 cm*

A conscious archaism is also evident in this boldly-conceived figure of a roaring tiger. The influence of the Han or Six Dynasties can clearly be seen in such details as the stylized jaw and arrangement of the paws with tail curling between them; the original effect of ferocity has been changed into one of repose. The beauty of the stone itself is an important element in this small-scale sculpture. A.72–1936

Bodhisattva Guanyin   Carved and painted wood   Song   13th century   *H. 96.5 cm*
Despite a general decline in Buddhism, many new temples were built in Song China, and these
were often furnished with painted wood images in a style both softer in outline and more realistic
than that of earlier stone carvings. The Bodhisattvas are beings who have attained full
enlightenment, but remain below for the salvation of man. In this sculpture, Guanyin is portrayed
in the serene *maharajalila* pose of an Indian prince, the smoothly rounded and painted flesh and
flowing gilt draperies conveying an ideal of perfected humanity.   A.7–1935

Celadon-glazed stoneware vase Probably from Yao-zhou, Shaansi Song 11th–12th century *H. 23.9 cm*
The Song potters were famous for developing a range of stoneware glazes of a variety and quality hitherto unknown. The vase form is of classic simplicity, the olive-green glaze flowing deeply over a carved peony scroll design.

c.810–1936

Painted stoneware jar Cizhou type perhaps from Guantai Song 11th–12th century *H. 24.1 cm*
The large flower sprays, butterflies, and insects painted over a white 'slip' layer recall the supremely assured brushwork of the great Song masters.

c.32–1935

Jun ware jar Song 12th–13th century *H. 12.5 cm*
This finely executed jar with its two neat handles has been fired with a characteristically luminous blue glaze, enlivened with random splashes of crimson-purple.

c.20–1935

Black-glazed stoneware bowl Song 12th century
Diam. 10.2 cm
Among many ingenious variations of brown or black based on kiln control is the so-called 'oilspot' glaze, with its spangled pattern of silver. The bowl was used for drinking tea.

c.18–1935

△
Longquan porcelain vase Song 12th–13th century *H. 25.4 cm*
Thick and lustrous, the celadon glazes of Longquan in south-east
China are applied to a near-white porcelain. The decoration is either
carved, or moulded and applied, as is the dragon on this funerary
vase. Stoutly-made dishes and bowls of this ware were exported
throughout Asia. C.28 & A–1935

Guan ware vase Hangzhou
Song 12th–13th century
Diam. 12.4 cm
Examples of Guan ware, the 'official'
pottery of the Court, are extremely rare.
The fine grey stoneware of this vase is
covered in several layers of a celadon-
type glaze, which also has an induced
pattern of 'crackle'. The forms of Guan
ware are sometimes flower-like, or based
on ancient bronzes. C.25–1935

Qingbai porcelain bowl Song 12th–
13th century *Diam. 14.6 cm*
These finely-potted, translucent porcelains come mainly from around the later
porcelain centre of Jingdezhen in south
China. On this bowl, delicate floral designs have been lightly incised under the
bluish-green tinted glaze. C.800–1909

Later Chinese Art

The Yuan dynasty of the Mongols (1279–1368) was hated in China, and many
refused to serve it. It was a time of new departures in painting, where the scholar-
artists cultivated a fine, studied style of landscape, and also in ceramics; when the
Ming restoration came, the arts already reflected a changed world. The invention
of underglaze blue-painted porcelain, reinforced later by brightly-coloured
enamels or glazes, exactly suited the taste for pictorial design and extrovert
colour. Yuan porcelains have more vigour, but the controlled style and perfected
technique of the fifteenth century make this a classic age of porcelain. The
building of the Forbidden City in Peking in early Ming days set a new
architectural standard, complemented in the crafts by plain, elegant furniture for
the scholar, and resplendent lacquered work for the Court. Similarly, silk textiles
such as the fine *kesi* tapestry were used in both furnishings and dress; vessels of

shining cloisonné enamel added further to the colourful effect of palace or temple buildings.

Under the Qing dynasty (1644–1912), this activity flourished with a new emphasis. The porcelain of the Kangxi and Yongzheng reigns is more finished but less vigorous than that of the Ming, while the novelties favoured by the Qianlong Emperor (1736–95) are at times over-ingenious; there is, however, much to admire in the *famille verte* and *famille rose* styles, among others. Magnificent screens and thrones of colourful lacquer work were made, and the variety of textiles and sumptuousness of Court robes became ever greater, with lacquers, jades, ivories, and metalwork all contributing to the splendour.

Buddhist Lohan Carved and painted wood Yuan or early Ming 14th century *H. 96.4 cm.*
The eighteen, or more, Lohans were enlightened holy men approaching the state of nirvana, and were often depicted as remote, ascetic figures. This sculpture however, portrays a robust, lively character, spontaneously turning to speak to his neighbour, and might equally well be the portrait of an abbot. The complete series would probably have been exhibited in a special hall of a temple. A.29–193

Game of polo by Li Lin   handscroll   Colours on silk   17th century   *H. 28 cm W. 91.5 cm*
In this detail the figures bend and sway, full of movement. The players resemble the horse-riding Mongols of the pre-Ming period, and this scroll, by a little-known artist, possibly reproduces an earlier work. Unlike the western framed picture or even the hanging scroll, the handscroll format enables events or scenery to be unfolded gradually before the viewer, giving a sense of the development of action and a changing viewpoint.   E.2601–1910

Travellers on a Mountain Pass   by Zhou Chen   active *c.*1500–35   fan   Ink on paper   *L. 51.8 cm*
With swift, wet calligraphic strokes, and a few liquid washes, the artist has brushed in the tortuous road and the immensity of the traveller's surroundings. Monochrome ink was often preferred for its directness, especially by the Ming scholar-painters whose work was associated closely with calligraphy. The fan format was used for small paintings which were often presented as gifts.   E.355–1956

Lacquer tray Ming 16th century *W. 19.3 cm*
As distinct from the plain lacquers found in Song tombs, this
elaborately-decorated dish may well have been preserved in a
Japanese temple storehouse. The design of a bird on a
flowering branch and surrounding borders are executed in
minutely-cut sections of mother-of-pearl set in the still-wet
lacquer, creating an effect of glittering elegance. FE.68–1974

Ivory figure of Zhongli Chuan
Ming 16th–17th century *H. 14.8 cm*
Small carvings in bamboo, horn or ivory
were increasingly prized during the Ming
period; this figure of a legendary Taoist
'Immortal' is remarkable for its apt
characterization and sensitive detail.

FE.4–1977

Carved red lacquer table Ming Xuande reign (1426–35)
H. 79.2 cm
Deeply carved in the thick lacquer top is a vigorous and fluid design
of five-clawed Imperial dragons and phoenixes among scrolling lotus,
and similar carving covers every other visible surface. Made for the
Ming Court, and inscribed with the Xuande reign mark, this
sumptuous and monumentally-conceived table is apparently the only
major example of its kind extant. Apart from furniture, dishes and
vessels of all kinds were made by this complex technique, in which up
to one hundred layers of lacquer might be applied before the carving
process. FE.6–1973

Chair *Huanghuali* wood Ming 16th century
H. 102.9 cm
This is one of a pair of chairs recently added by gift to the
Museum's collection of early Chinese furniture, and is
characteristically made of a very hard rosewood, carefully
selected for its golden colour and fine markings. Rooms
furnished with tables, chests, beds and other furniture in
this splendid style are to be seen in early paintings.
Distinguished by its skilled joinery and a restrained
simplicity in its design, which changed little over the
centuries, it was entirely suited to the Chinese interior, and
the well-ordered life of the scholar-official. FE.55–1977

Painted lacquer box Ming dated 1600 A.D. *L. 71.1 cm*
This cinnabar-red lacquer scroll box displays a style of
polychrome painted decoration which typifies the opulent
taste of late Ming times. Inside is a moonlit riverbank
picture with exotic birds executed partly in gold, while the
central scene on the cover depicts a legendary archery
competition at the Tang Court. A great variety of colours is
used and the sides of the box, as so often during this
period, are made of decorative basketwork. W.66–1925

283

Inlaid bronze phoenix Ming or earlier *c.*13th–15th century *H. 32 cm*
The symbolic phoenix appears in another form in this vessel. The decoration of bronze with intricate patterns in gold or silver strips, or wire, is characteristic of late Zhou work (*c.*4th–3rd century B.C.). This is the style which has been imitated in this accomplished object, but the motif of a cup-bearing phoenix is a conceit of later origin. M.306–1910

Jade stem cup Ming 15th century *H. 10.9 cm*
The dark streaks and light mottlings in this rare cup were probably appreciated for their aura of antiquity. A simple line decorates the rim and foot. The shape of the cup can be compared with those of the early Ming porcelain cups in the collection; its execution, however, in brittle jade, represents an altogether different skill. FE.71–1977

Cloisonné enamel incense burner Ming Early 15th century *W. 20.6 cm*
The techniques of cloisonné work were probably introduced into China in the Yuan period from Byzantium. Bronze wires soldered to the base shape the design which is filled in with molten glassy enamel; the metal is then gilded and polished. The archaic *gui* form with its two dragon handles has been adapted to later devotional use. The lotus scroll design displays an intensity of colour unmatched in any other craft. 507–1875

◁
Silk tapestry hanging Early Qing 17th century *H. 198 cm*
Silk production and weaving have been associated with China since antiquity. The delicate, luxurious tapestry-weaving known as *kesi* ('cut silk'), first developed in Song times, is usually very splendid; it was also used for making the Imperial robes. In this hanging a pair of mythical phoenixes, traditionally the emblem of the Empress, are seen perching and flying in a garden with a rockery and peonies. The hanging is woven in coloured silks and gold thread on a black background; despite years of fading, the effect is still one of glowing richness. T.844–1919

Porcelain dish Ming Hongzhi reign (1488–1505)
Diam. 26 cm
The handsome design of a jasmine-like flower surrounded by fruits—grapes, peaches, pomegranate, and lotus flower with its seedpod—is painted in underglaze blue, and the ground filled in with yellow enamel, creating a characteristically sumptuous effect. Porcelains of this quality were made for use at Court; the reign mark is finely written on the base.   C.320–1921

Blue-and-white porcelain vase Yuan Mid-14th century
H. 35.6 cm
The development of painting in cobalt pigment (before the glazing of the porcelain) created a revolution in ceramic style of the period, and opened the way to the immense variety of pictorial treatment deployed under the Ming. Vigorous and painterly, the Yuan style is devoted mainly to depicting mythical creatures such as the dragon, phoenix and *qilin*, and also a range of flower designs infused with symbolic meaning. In this dramatic scene from the celebrated *Story of the Western Chamber*, Lady Zheng rebukes Yingying's maid.   C.8–1952

Porcelain stemcup Ming Xuande reign (1426–35) *Diam. 10.1 cm*
Porcelains of the Xuande reign are famous for their refinement of material, form and design. This handsome cup, which is decorated with three swimming carp, is an example of the very rare underglaze copper-red ware of the period. The piece is distinguished by its fine shape, well-executed fish, and the orange-peel texture of the glaze. The mark is written in blue on the inside.   C.64–1935

Porcelain vase Ming Jiajing reign (1522–66)
H. 21.3 cm
The typical Ming scrolling floral designs set in decorative
bands round the vase show the lotus, the sacred flower of
Buddhism. The glowing red and green enamels are here used
like glazes to cover almost the entire surface. To keep the
colours from running together, the motifs were first incised in
the porcelain before being fired; the enamels were then baked
on at a much lower temperature.   C.943–1935

Porcelain vase Ming *c.*1500 *H. 38.1 cm*
This vase is decorated with cranes among
wind-blown flowering lotuses and other
plants growing out of the ruffled water. To
keep the coloured glazes apart, the design is
drawn out in applied ribbons or *cloisons* of
clay; applied to the porcelain in a second
firing, the colours acquire a singular richness.   C.996–1910

287

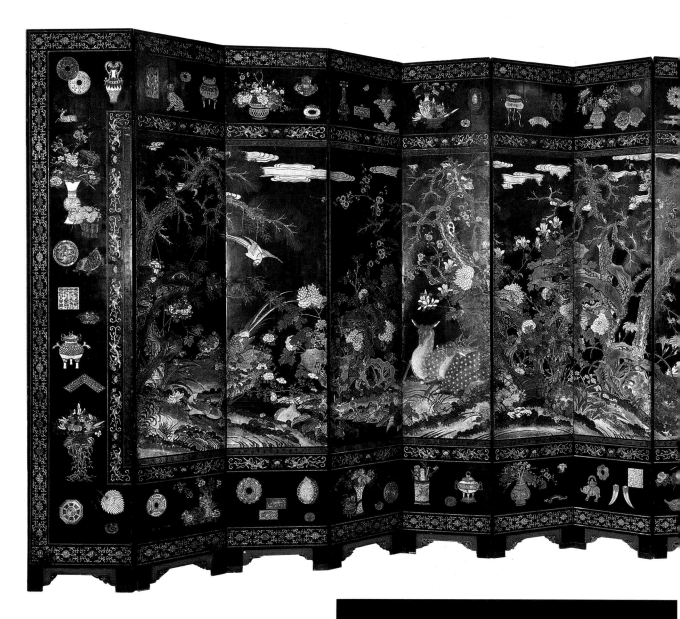

Imperial robe Qing First half of 19th century *H. 152 cm*
This splendid robe contains a full cosmological scheme, with a
cloud-filled sky representing the heavens, and rocks and
waves below, the earth. The bright yellow ground, the dynastic
colour of the Manchu, and the design of the Nine Dragons
and Twelve Symbols of Imperial Power, indicate that the robe
was made for the Emperor's use. The material is fine tapestry-
woven silk or *kesi*. This type of robe, *qifu*, was worn on semi-
formal occasions; the most formal court robe, *chaofu*, is closer
to Manchu national costume, but both share the characteristic
'horsehoof' cuffs.   T.190–1948

Coromandel lacquer screen   Qing   Early 18th century   *H. 269 cm W. 640 cm*
The trees, flowers, and animals shown on this eight-panelled folding screen have symbolic meaning in Taoist philosophy which is deeply rooted in the world of nature. Easily discernible are the pine, bamboo and prunus (the 'Three Friends of Winter') and pairs of pheasants, parrots, mandarin ducks, and deer. To the right, rising from a stormy sea strewn with precious emblems are mythical animals: the *longma*, or dragon-headed horse, and the divine tortoise, bearing on their backs ancient divination symbols; also, the legendary 'Pavilion of the Blest'. In this type of screen, the designs are cut through the black lacquer to a layer of composition, and then painted in brilliant colours. They were exported both to India—the 'Coromandel' coast—and to Europe, where they helped to furnish our great houses.   130–1885

Bodhisattva Guanyin   Woven silk   Qing   *c.*1700
H. 151.2 cm
This hanging is woven in *lampas* technique in various shades of blue, silver and golden-brown on a dark blue satin ground, with gold thread for the jewellery and nimbus. The four-armed deity is seated in a devout pose holding pearls in one hand and a lotus in the other; the iconography belongs to the esoteric, Tantric form of Buddhism and the hanging may have been intended for a Tibetan foundation in China.   T.97–1966

数枝梅向林梢出
一脉泉逆岭背来
做黄鹤山樵笔建南诗意
耕烟散人王翚

Pavilions under the pines by Wang Hui (1632-1717) Ink and slight colour on paper *H. 45.6 cm*
In this charming small hanging scroll scholars are shown engaged in their quiet pursuits near a waterfall. One of the 'Six Masters of the Qing dynasty', Wang Hui excelled in landscapes of mountain and river scenery which display a most fluent and accomplished brush style. More than lip service is paid to the great Yuan masters who pioneered this manner of painting; and in his inscription Wang Hui acknowledges his debt to the painter Wang Meng. FE.102–197

Blue chalcedony vase Qing 18th century *H. 9.9 cm*
The vase is in the form of a 'Buddha's hand' citron fruit, around which is entwined a spray of fruiting pomegranate in flowing lines. Hardstone carvers chose stones of the rarest colour and markings like this semi-opaque light blue chalcedony in order to show their skills to the full. C.1844–1910

Jade brush pot Qing 18th century
Diam. 20.3 cm
This massive cylindrical vessel makes use of a piece of pale 'mutton-fat' jade of a quality rarely obtainable until mining at Khotan in Central Asia was extended in the eighteenth century. The deep carving renders translucent the curvilinear design in which legendary figures of Taoism are assembled in a mountain retreat, while their horses water in the stream below. 1956–1882

Glass snuff bottle Qing 19th century
H. 7.9 cm
Snuff-taking was probably introduced into
China by the Jesuits at the early Qing Court.
The snuff bottles were carved in various
stones, ivory, and other materials, and were
usually equipped with an ivory spoon attached to the cap. This glass bottle with
multi-coloured overlays was wheel-cut with
a design of peaches. C.J535–1910

Rhinoceros horn cup Qing *c.*1700
H. 15.9 cm
From early times, the rhinoceros horn was
held to be endowed with magical properties,
and cups made of this finely-marked and
beautifully polished amber-brown material
were highly valued. This cup is elaborately
carved with writhing young dragons round
the rim after the manner of Song or Ming
jades. The rockwork stand may be original.
162 & A–1879

Nest of lacquer boxes Qianlong period
(1736–95) *H. 25.4 cm*
The various boxes uniting in the shape of a
silver ingot fit within an openwork cover of
red lacquer, carved with lotus scrollwork
which, when removed, forms a stand on six
feet. The black boxes are inlaid with green,
yellow, or red—an amazingly complex
work probably executed for the Palace.
FE.65–1974

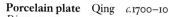

Porcelain plate Qing *c.*1700–10
Diam. 34 cm
The plate is decorated with a music party scene,
amusingly copied from a print by the Parisian
engraver Nicolas Bonnart, an early example of the
reproduction of European designs sent to Jingdezhen. The rich blue and the landscapes in panels
are typical of Kangxi period wares. The Chinese
accepted all types of commissions, thus swelling the
porcelain trade, which in the eighteenth century
reached massive proportions.　　　c.781–1910

Bottle *Flambé* red glaze Yongzheng
reign (1723–35) *H. 34.9 cm*
Among the porcelain glazes newly developed
at this period was a dense copper-red to
which vivid streaks of purplish-blue were
added: it was probably inspired by the Jun
wares of the Song period, which were also
copied with some success. The slender-
necked vase reproduces a bronze form. The
bottle has the reign-mark in stamped seal
characters on the bottom.　　　c.382–1910

Guanyin the Merciful *Blanc-de-Chine* porcelain Qing
*c.*1700 *H. 39.1 cm*
Many graceful figures were made in this fine *blanc-de-Chine*
porcelain, which was produced in the south-eastern coastal province
of Fujian. The more modern Guanyin is a very popular deity to
whom to address prayers, and is worshipped especially by mothers,
seamen, and merchants. In this version, she has assumed a quite
feminine appearance in her sinuous, flowing draperies.　　　c.548–1910

Famille jaune vase Qing *c.*1700
H. 52.1 cm
Many porcelains of the Kangxi reign were
decorated in the very popular enamelled
style of the *'famille verte'*, those with a yellow
ground being known as *'famille jaune'*; the
enamels—green, yellow, purple and black—
are painted on the 'biscuit' or unglazed
porcelain, which enhances their rich and
glowing effect. The ubiquitous floral designs
usually have a symbolic meaning: depicted
here are the 'Flowers of the Four Seasons',
the chrysanthemum, prunus, lotus, and
peony.   C.1284–1910

Famille rose dish Qing Yongzheng reign (1723–35) *Diam. 20.3 cm*
In Chinese painting, birds and flowers represent a category as distinct and meaningful as 'still life' in the art of the West. The quail, an emblem of courage, is shown with its usual spray of millet and flowering peach, possibly for colourful effect but more probably to add some further symbolic meaning. The *'famille rose'* palette developed at this time was ideally suited to presenting this type of subject on fine white porcelain. 646–1903

Famille rose vase Qing Qianlong reign (1736–95) *H. 32.1 cm*
In style, the vase is reminiscent of painted enamels on copper, a craft introduced at the Manchu Court early in the century by the Jesuits, who hoped to convert China to Christianity. In this way, the porcelain decorators became acquainted with the *yang-tsai*, or 'foreign colours' of the *famille rose*. The crowded design so incongruous to the traditional Chinese eye reflects Western influence, but also the eclectic taste of the Qianlong Emperor himself, who encouraged the imitation in porcelain of other kinds of works of art. C.1461–1910

Korea

Originally migrants from the Siberian region, the Korean people are of a different race from the Chinese; Korean culture was, nevertheless, inevitably shaped by its geographical situation between China and Japan, and the country has always been a natural bridge travelled by invaders, missionaries, and traders. In Han times, the north was colonized by China; but while the Silla kings rejected further subjugation, the sheer superiority of Tang culture and administrative systems could not be denied. The capital of United Silla (668–935) at Kyongju in the south became a centre of this cultural fusion in which Buddhism also played a dominant role.

The **Koryō** dynasty (918–1392) marks a high point in Korean artistic development; and the Museum's serenely graceful rare painted Buddhist hanging scroll of Samantabadhra on an elephant bears out this view. The Korean invention of moveable type for printing is reflected also in a Buddhist text (*sutra*) in the Department which dates from late in the period. Another art of which comparatively little survives is that of inlaid bronze work, represented here by an elegant vase depicting rural subjects with a characteristic delicacy and charm. The flowering of **Koryō** culture is nowhere more fully shown than in ceramics, where a celadon-glazed ware was produced that for refinement of design, nobility of form, and a gently-glowing brilliance of glaze was acknowledged to be outstanding even by the contemporary Song Chinese. The finest glaze tint is evocatively described by the term 'kingfisher'. Incised decoration and various kinds of moulded work are common, but more peculiarly Korean is a technique of inlaying designs in the body in black and white clays under the glaze, which produces a unique effect.

After the Mongol invasion which devastated the country, the Yi dynasty imposed a Chinese-style regime along Confucian lines. In pottery, an innate peasant artistry shines through in wares which, although sometimes roughly and even crudely made, display an outstanding vigour and expressive power.

Stoneware cup Late Silla 7th–10th century *L. 10.2 cm*
This cup is an example of the characteristic unglazed, ash-grey pottery found in numerous excavated tombs of this period. The forms are peculiarly Korean, and show accomplished potting which is sometimes relieved, although not in this case, by simple incised or stamped decoration. c.166–1926

Bodhisattva Samantabadhra hanging scroll
Colours and gold on silk Koryō period 13th–14th
century *H. 139 cm W. 56 cm*
The Bodhisattva is shown riding on a white elephant,
holding in his hands the blue lotus emblem, and with
the magic jewel set in his crown. The exceedingly rich
dress and caparison of the elephant are emphasized by
the bright colouring and abundant use of gold typical of
the Koryō style. Although many Buddhist temples have
survived the repeated invasions inflicted on the country,
only a handful of such paintings remains in Korea
today.   FE.51–1976

Inlaid bronze bottle Koryō period 12th century
H. 25 cm
This elegant little bottle is inlaid in silver wire with fine
linear designs, amongst which are shaped panels
containing a small figure and graceful willow trees and,
on the neck, phoenixes flying in clouds. Bronzes of this
type may well have inspired the typical Korean inlaid
pottery of the period.   M.1189–1926

Inlaid celadon ware bottle Koryō period 13th century ▷
H. 34.6 cm
Korean individuality finds expression in the unusual technique of
inlaying designs in white and black clays. Between the roundels with
their peony and chrysanthemum blooms, which are also touched with
copper-red, appear graceful willow trees, one of a number of oft-
repeated motifs which reflect quiet rural life. C.72–1911

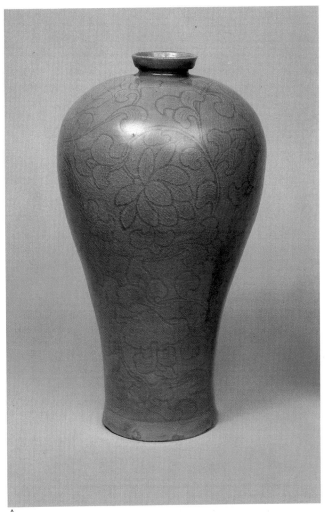

△
Celadon ware vase Koryō period 12th century *H. 34.1 cm*
The surface of the vase is decorated with a delicately-incised lotus
scroll pattern. Although plainly in debt to Song China in technique,
these Korean celadon wares have their own distinctive character. In
form, they show a serene dignity, while the glazes have at best a
shimmering brilliance—the so-called 'kingfisher tint'—which caused
them to be much admired even in China. C.70–1935

Porcelain jar Yi period 17th century *H. 28.9 cm*
This is one of several examples of the rare copper-red painted
porcelain in the collection. The lotus flower, drawn in a few simple
calligraphic strokes, is the Buddhist symbol of pure creativity. Its
inspired purity of line and the strong shape of the jar fully
compensate for the imperfection of the glaze. C.131–1913

297

Japan

Japan's history is coloured both by its location as an island chain close to a continental mainland—the Korean peninsula and China—and the origin of its people in successive migrations. Even early artefacts of the Neolithic Jōmon and metal-using Yayoi cultures show originality in skill and design; the primitive nature religion of Shinto was probably at its height at about this time.

The introduction of Buddhism from Korea at the Asuka court (552–645) under Prince Shōtoku accelerated the development of Japanese culture. The first great temples, such as Hōryūji near Nara, were founded and provided major encouragement and support, stimulating the growth of religious art; even today their wood-built structures remain great artistic treasure-houses. In the Nara period (645–794), contact with the Tang court introduced the ripe fruits of Chinese culture, and in Nara itself, the Imperial capital, are preserved numerous relics of that remarkable age in which Japanese craftsmen strove to raise their crafts to the standard of the mainland. The Heian court (794–1185), established at modern Kyoto, presided over a learned and sophisticated society; and the Kamakura rule (1185–1333) of military leaders also became worthy patrons. Throughout this period, Buddhist sculpture and painting were extremely refined and expressive, while the Tendai, Shingon and 'Pure Land' sects successively enlarged their figural repertoire. Secular painting followed Chinese models as well as developing the native *Yamato-e* style, in painted sliding screens and illustrated manuscript scrolls (*e-makemono*).

The Muromachi period (1392–1568), although plagued with internal strife, was one of expanding patronage. Ming China exerted its influence both on Japanese Court painting styles, and through the medium of the contemplative Buddhist sect of Zen (Chan), with its code of meditation and simple observances such as tea-drinking, which led to the purely Japanese cult of the Tea Ceremony. *Chanoyu* became a significant force, and in the Momoyama (1568–1615) and early Edo (1615–1912) periods, spread throughout the higher ranks of society, having a profound effect on the crafts. An adequate glazed stoneware pottery, influenced by Chinese wares, had been produced since the Nara period; the foremost of the 'Six Ancient Kilns' from Kamakura times onwards was Seto, which made a celadon ware. The Tea Masters appreciated a rustic style but while patronizing the rude vigour of Bizen and Shigaraki, they also commissioned the more refined 'painted Shino' and Oribe wares. From Kyoto itself came low-fired, coarse-grained *raku* bowls with glossy black or red glazes. Kyoto pottery became even more famous through the jewel-like enamelling of Ninsei, and his equally celebrated successor, Kenzan. Well-proportioned iron kettles came from Ashiya, while elegant lacquers were made for more delicate vessels.

The development of lacquer as a luxury art had begun in Nara times, with the Japanese outstripping even the Chinese in invention and skill. A rich example is the mid-seventeenth century '*Van Diemen*' box, made for a Dutch East India Company official, with its lavish gold and silver painting and inlay. Contact with Western traders is also recorded in a colourful screen showing the arrival of a Portuguese ship. The Dutch, too, soon became avid purchasers of Japanese porcelains.

The prosperity of late seventeenth- and eighteenth-century Edo (Tokyo) and Kyoto is reflected in the resplendent colour and daring design of their art. Painted screens of the Kano school, enamelled porcelains of Arita or Nabeshima, lacquers, and fine silk fabrics represent Court art, as well as the splendid woven or embroidered kimonos, and superbly finished accessories such as lacquered *inro* boxes and their minutely-carved *netsuke*. The more popular art of *ukiyo-e*, 'the floating world', depicts the colourful life of the capital and its entertainment districts.

Woodblock colour prints, ever more ingeniously designed, flourished throughout the eighteenth and nineteenth centuries, executed by such famous artists as Utamaro, Hiroshige (the master of landscape), and Kuniyoshi. The samurai's prowess is reflected in the work of celebrated swordsmiths and in suits of armour, and sword fittings themselves provided much artistic scope—the Department has a fine collection of these *tsuba*. Its holdings of late nineteenth- and twentieth-century arts, already considerable, are being further extended by contemporary purchases.

Bodhisattva Seishi Colours on silk Late Heian period 12th century *H. 100.2 cm W. 56.8 cm*
In the Heian period, Seishi is generally depicted attendant on Amida, the Buddha of the Pure Land of Rebirth whose cult was then at its height; here, he is seated on a lotus throne in a devout attitude ready to receive the soul of a believer. The painting may have formed part of a larger composition. The delicate outlines, rippling movement of the draperies, and exquisite colouring also call to mind the refinements of Heian courtly life which are pictured so vividly in Lady Murasaki's *Tale of Genji*.
FE.105–1970

Bodhisattva Jizō Wood Heian period 12th century *H. 140 cm*
Jizō, the Guardian and Saviour of Souls, is usually shown as a
mendicant priest holding a staff in his right hand and in his left a
jewel, both missing here. Much expressive wood sculpture was
produced in the Heian period, and although the front of this figure
has been much restored, the austere dignity of the overall concept
and the noble head still convey a sense of great spiritual power.

FE.14–1972

Buddha Amida Lacquered wood Kamakura period
13th century *H. 44.5 cm*
Realistic in its treatment, this Amida is a sculpture of unusual quality.
The slight figure is depicted seated cross-legged with hands in the
position of preaching; the features are carved with great sensitivity
and the rhythmic folds of the drapery suggest a mood of serenity. The
wood is lacquered black all over and the flesh areas are gilt. FE.5–1972

Seto stoneware vase Kamakura period 14th century *H. 26.7 cm*
The Seto kilns were foremost in following the achievements of Song
China in pottery, especially its celadon wares, and the *yingqing*
porcelains, from which the typical *meiping* form here is copied; the
impressed design and still unperfected yellowish-green glaze are,
however, quite Japanese. FE.6–1972

Bizen stoneware water jar Momoyama period Late 16th
century *H. 20.3 cm*
Originally a country ware, the rough-textured pots of Bizen are
striking for their refreshingly uninhibited and vigorous character.
These were qualities much admired by Tea Ceremony enthusiasts,
and the famous Tea Master, Furuta Oribe, is said to have started
using Bizen water jars for this purpose. Usually unglazed, the red
ware often develops an attractive kiln gloss. 191–1877

Two Shino ware cups Momoyama period Late 16th–
early 17th century *H. 9.5 cm*
Shino is typical of various early wares made for use in the Tea
Ceremony in its embodiment of quiet and rustic simplicity.
The material is hard and granular, and the thick near-white
glaze is bubbled and crazed. Plant sprays and insects are
depicted in simple iron-brown brushstrokes, an apparent
artlessness concealing the accuracy of observation. These
cups were used in the meal accompanying the Ceremony.
178A–1877

301

Arrival of a Portuguese Ship in Japan   Screen painted in colours
on paper   Momoyama period   *c.*1600   *H. 367 cm W. 160 cm*
The *namban*, or 'southern barbarians' who came to Japan in the
sixteenth century both to trade and to make Christian converts were
for some years a favourite subject of Japanese painters, who delighted
in their unfamiliar appearance and customs. The '*namban*'
screens often show the great black Portuguese carracks at anchor, and
strangely-dressed officers, crew, and missionary monks going on
shore, carrying gifts and objects with which to trade.   803–1892

***Raku* ware tea bowl**   by Honami Kōetsu
(1558–1637)   *Diam. 12.7 cm*
Raku wares were shaped by hand, in a light,
porous clay and baked at a low heat; they
were much prized for their subtle sensations
of touch and weight. Kōetsu was also celebrated as a sword specialist, calligrapher, and
designer of lacquer.   247–1877

Painted stoneware tea bowl by Ogata
Kenzan (1663–1743) *Diam. 11.4 cm*
A few leaves painted in brown and black on a
white 'slip' ground reveal the sure, almost
calligraphic hand of one of Japan's most
famous pottery decorators. C.610–1923

The Tea Ceremony

The Japanese Tea Ceremony (*chanoyu*) had
its origins in China among the monks of the
Zen (Chan) sect. Originally part of the
contemplative ritual, it was taken up in
Muromachi aristocratic circles, where it developed into a widely influential cult which
has profoundly affected Japanese manners,
customs, and arts. The carefully-designed
garden surrounding the tea house with its
rustic design and furnishings is the setting
for a simple ceremony, the essentials of
which in its purest form are serenity, respect
and decorum. Its aim is a kind of individual
and social enlightenment.

This taste for the natural and unsophisti-
cated gave new stimulus and direction to
many of the crafts; and in pottery, for
example, the wares of Shino, Bizen or the
raku masters, developed a new skill of ex-
ploiting accidental effects of the kiln and
transforming them into art.

303

Folding screen   Colours, gold, and silver on paper   Edo period   Late 17th–early 18th century   *H. 360 cm W. 138 cm*
The screen is decorated with the famous story of two rival Minamoto generals during the twelfth-century clan wars. Kajikawa Kagesue, seen in this detail fording the Uji river, stole a march on his colleague by telling him that his saddle-girth was undone; he was thus first to cross and attack the enemy. The artist has achieved an extremely dramatic composition with the two figures, bridge, and swirling clouds. The general's armour may be compared with the suit, see opposite.
                                                                                                                E.3054–1910

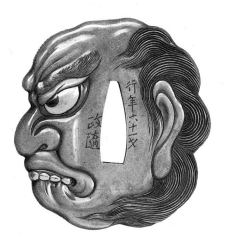

Two sword guards (*tsuba*)   *left:* signed *Shōzui* 18th century   *L. 7.4 cm   right:* signed *Iwamoto Konkan*, and dated 1780   *L. 7.5 cm*
Tsuba-making is only one of the specialized crafts surrounding the sword. At first somewhat plainly made in iron, they became increasingly complex and luxurious, seemingly endless in their variety of style and subject-matter. On the left is an unusual and humorous depiction of a Buddhist Guardian, in brass with other alloys and gold. The second *tsuba*, also in several metals, shows a riverbank by moonlight; the story goes that a magic fox hid there, disguised as a woman in order to attract men. Now mounted on a sword, it is among the finest *tsuba* in the collection.
                                                   614–1916
                                                   M.20–1949

'Akita' armour   *H. (overall) 142 cm*
Japanese armour, like the sword blade and its
various fittings, attracted over the centuries
the highest skills and choicest workmanship.
Constructed of overlapping layers of steel,
iron, and hide, it was the most practical
protection against the unique and terrible
qualities of the two-handed Japanese sword.
This famous suit was assembled to the order
of Lord Akita whose heraldic family badge, a
fan charged with crossed hawks' feathers,
forms the metal forecrest and is repeated
elsewhere on the suit in miniature; as is the
family's secondary badge, a lion and peony
medallion. It is mostly tailored in the *do-
maru* style adopted in the fourteenth century,
with the body-armour in a single piece
fastened at one side; the large shoulder-
guards, however, are more characteristic of
the earlier *oyoroi*, or 'great harness' style.
The helmet was certified in 1675 as being
twelfth-century work, but is now regarded as
being probably of the seventeenth century.
M.979–1928

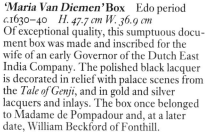

'Maria Van Diemen' Box Edo period
c.1630–40   H. 47.7 cm W. 36.9 cm
Of exceptional quality, this sumptuous document box was made and inscribed for the wife of an early Governor of the Dutch East India Company. The polished black lacquer is decorated in relief with palace scenes from the *Tale of Genji*, and in gold and silver lacquers and inlays. The box once belonged to Madame de Pompadour and, at a later date, William Beckford of Fonthill.

W.49–1916

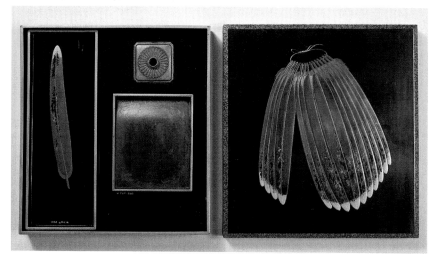

Lacquer writing-box Edo period 18th
century   H. 24.2 cm W. 21.9 cm
The top represents the tail feathers of a hawk tied together, in raised gold and silver lacquer (*takamakie*); inside are a tray, a brass water bottle of chrysanthemum design, and a stone for mixing the ink. Exquisite design and an extremely refined technique are hallmarks of lacquer produced at this period, when the art of falconry was also highly popular among the *daimyō*, or feudal vassal, class.

W.391–1910

Lacquer *inro* and two ivory *netsuke* 18th
century   H. inro, 7.6 cm; netsuke, 8.2 cm,
5.7 cm
Inro, boxes with several compartments, were worn by the Japanese as containers for seals and medicinal herbs, etcetera. A three-case *inro* is here enlivened in raised lacquer of red, brown, and gold with no less than one hundred and fifteen monkeys dancing, making music, wrestling, and portraying other human occupations and diversions. The same comic observation can be seen in the brilliant miniature art of *netsuke*— terminals by which the cords holding the *inro* hanging from the waist belt were held secure. The horse bending to graze is a marvellously sculptural concept. A more satirical subject is the archer with his bearded features, round eyes, and strange hat, apparently a Mongol, carrying a well-filled quiver, on his back.   W.222–1922; A.794–1910, 418–1904

Embroidered silk cover Edo period
19th century *H. 81.3 cm W. 63.5 cm*
The blue satin is magnificently embroidered
with a flight of cranes in skilfully-worked
gold and other coloured silks. Such cloths
(*fukusa*) were traditionally used as wrappers
for boxes containing a ceremonial gift; they
were later returned by the recipient.

T.20–1923

Embroidered silk kimono Edo period
19th century *H. 185.5 cm*
Of silvery-white figured silk, embroidered in
colours and gold with a design of flowering
plants growing by garden fences and trellis,
this sumptuous long-sleeved robe or *furisode*
(of which the back is shown) typifies the rich
and elegant taste of late Edo Japan. The
kimono was padded and lined with red satin
for winter wear. Worn with it, and of equally
splendid material, is the large waist band
known as an *obi*.   T.269–1960

Courtesan with attendants
Ascribed to Engetsudō
hanging scroll   Colours
on paper   Edo period
*c.*1750   *H. 103.2 cm W. 56.2 cm*
By the late seventeenth century,
Tokyo (Edo) was thronging with
a new middle class bent on
enjoying the pleasures and dis-
tractions of the city. Hence
there arose a market for *ukiyo-e*,
or pictures of everyday life, the
so-called 'floating world', which
extended to portrayals of the
leading beauties and courtesans
of the day.

The colourful work of the
Kaigetsudō school gives full play
to their lavish and costly dress,
and exhibits the genius of the
Japanese artist for splendidly
decorative design.   FE.2–1979

Sunrise on New Year's Day by Eishōsai
Chōki woodblock print *c*.1790–1800
I. 38.7 cm
A girl clasps her robe about her in a garden
as the sun rises orange out of a gently
rippling sea; the dark sky is coloured in
shining mica. The careful balance of the
composition and mood of the colouring
together produce an extremely vivid poetic
image. As the makers of *ukiyo-e* prints
extended their range in the eighteenth century, they were able to add the subtlety of
psychological interpretation to their list of
achievements.   E.3774–1953

**Scene in the Russo–Japanese War of
1904–05** by (?) Tsukioka Kōgyo Woodblock print dated 1904 *L. 76.2 cm*
The print shows a Japanese destroyer squad-
ron engaging a Russian battleship off Port
Arthur on 13 April 1904. It illustrates how
little of their former skill the printmakers had
lost in creating powerful and dramatic
images. Such was their speed of work that
the print went on sale in Tokyo within a
week of the battle.   E.3140–1905

Nabeshima porcelain dish   Edo period   Early 18th century ·
Diam. 20.3 cm
This rare porcelain dish was made at a private kiln near Arita, to the
order of the Nabeshima princes. The classic simplicity of the white
plate is relieved by the daring, assymetrical design of plants and
flowers outlined in underglaze blue, and filled in with coloured
enamels.   352–1877

Arita porcelain jar   Edo period   Late 17th century   *H. 38.8 cm*
A late starter in comparison with the Chinese, the Japanese porcelain
industry received a powerful boost when the Dutch transferred their
trade to Nagasaki after the fall of the Ming dynasty. It was in this way
that the 'blue-and-white' wares of the Arita factories, such as this
strongly-shaped jar with its 'tiger-and-bamboo' design, soon became
well-known in Western Europe.   1681–1876

Two Kakiemon porcelain ladies   Edo
period   *c.*1670–90   *H. 25.4 cm*
The characteristic tomato-red, sky-blue,
green, and yellow are used to fine effect on
the flowery kimonos of the two animated,
chatting 'ladies'. Enamelling on porcelain is
traditionally said to have been introduced to
Arita by the Kakiemon family and, by the late
seventeenth century, this palette was well
established, notably for wares exported to
Europe.   FE.33, 34–1980

Cloisonné enamel vase Meiji period *c.*1900 *H. 33.7 cm*
The long graceful sprays of wisteria hanging from the shoulder are treated in a naturalistic manner which almost resembles painted work, seeming to ignore the traditional limitations of the soldered-wire technique. 265–1903

Lacquer tea caddy by Tatsuoka Kuroda
Kyoto *c.*1977 *H. 12.5 cm*
By training a woodworker, Kuroda is among the select band who in Japan are officially honoured as 'Living National Treasures'. This finely-worked lacquer ware, overlaid with glittering, multi-coloured mother-of-pearl is typical of Kuroda's luxury products. FE.1–1978

Silver teapot by Kōnoike Yokohama Meiji period *c.*1900
H. 19.6 cm
This fine teapot is decorated with chased and repoussé chrysanthemum flowers, flower-buds, and leaves. The high-handled form is Japanese, but the teapot was nevertheless made for the Western market, as a product of the major craft revival of this time. M.2–1914

Stone Buddha   E. Indian   Pala school
Late 11th or 12 century   *H. 125 cm*
The historical Buddha himself lived the
simple life of a wandering monk, and in his
teaching discouraged the idea of a personal
cult. With the spread of Mahayana Buddhism, however, he became the object of a
more devotional religious attitude, and was
represented in an iconic form, with a fixed
range of postures and hand-signs (*mudras*).
Here the Buddha, wearing the crown and
ornaments of a monarch, makes the sign of
touching the earth as a witness to his Enlightenment. He is flanked by the Bodhisattvas
Avalokiteshvara and Maitreya.   617–1872

India, the Himalayas, and South-East Asia

The Indian sub-continent, now divided between the modern countries of India, Pakistan, Bangladesh, and Sri Lanka, has from the earliest times formed a distinct geographical and cultural entity, depending from the Asian landmass, but separated from it by the ocean and the world's highest mountain ranges. This relative isolation was relieved by periodic waves of immigration through the north-western passes, which tended to drive the existing populations further south. The first invaders in historical times were the Aryans during the second millennium B.C., who displaced what remained of the advanced protohistoric civilization of the Indus valley. They brought with them an Indo–European language and a religion which venerated gods embodying the elemental powers of nature. By a characteristically Indian process of gradual assimilation, this Vedic religion combined over many centuries with indigenous cults and forms of worship, giving rise to the phenomenon of Hinduism, with its prolific pantheon, its densely rich mythology, and its prescriptive social hierarchy dominated by the Brahmin priesthood. Around 500 B.C., the heterodox teachers, Gautama the Buddha and his near-contemporary Mahavira, who in different ways regarded salvation from the eternal cycle of rebirth as attainable by properly directed individual effort instead of by divine or priestly mediation, established the major religions known as Buddhism and Jainism. Buddhism, in particular, was to have a profound influence on most of Eastern Asia which may be counted as India's greatest contribution to world civilization.

It is difficult now to appreciate the full extent of the artistic achievement of classical India, for with only few exceptions, artefacts dating from before c.1000 A.D. in less permanent materials have been destroyed by India's severe climate. Only architectural remains and sculptures in stone, terracotta, and stucco, survive in any number from the third century B.C. onwards, almost all of them works of religious art made in the service of Buddhism, Jainism, and the various Hindu cults. These images and relief panels were the work of lay craftsmen, who imbued them with grace and vitality through a skilful combination of idealized forms, often emphasized by the sinuous *tribhanga* or triply flexed standing posture deriving from dance practice. At its finest, Indian sculpture offers a unique evocation of the transcendent bliss of highly developed beings, together with a joyous acceptance of the more sensuous worlds of minor gods, nature spirits, men, animals, and plants.

Even after the decline of this ancient tradition in the past millennium, and the ascendancy of Muslim dynasties and, more recently, of the British, Indian artists and craftsmen continued until the nineteenth century to show their remarkable skill in absorbing alien forms, whether Persian, Chinese or European, and transforming them in ever-new syntheses.

Gold plaque of Hariti   Pearls and cut garnet   Taxila   Kushan   3rd century
H. 4.5 cm
Hariti was a popular local goddess, or *yakshi*, of north-western India who was assimilated by the Buddhist and Hindu pantheons as a protectress of children, specifically from smallpox. In this repoussé gold plaque, perhaps worn as a pendant, she holds flowering stems in either hand. Her tunic is Hellenistic in origin.   I.S.9–1948

Hindu and Buddhist India

The adoption of Buddhism as a state religion by the Emperor Ashoka Maurya (c.269–232 B.C.) was followed by the rise of a vigorous school of stone sculpture, which produced the narrative reliefs of the Buddha's lives and the graceful guardian figures of nature spirits (*yakshis*) decorating the gateways and balustrades of the *stupas* or relic-mounds at Bharhut and Sanchi. The sculptural and architectural forms adopted at these sites often reveal lost antecedents in woodwork and ivory-carving. Under the invading Scythian dynasty of the Kushans in the first centuries A.D., the Buddha, who had himself disclaimed any divine or superhuman powers, began to be represented in an iconic form. This development occurred contemporaneously in the north-western province of Gandhara under strong Graeco–Roman influence, and at Mathura in Central India, where the indigenous models of Jain and *yaksha* figures were followed. Buddhism continued to develop in its more devotional Mahayana form, leading to the representation of Bodhisattvas, enlightened beings who compassionately foreswear liberation from the world until all other beings have also gained enlightenment. This iconography began to be formalized in the culturally rich period of the Gupta empire and its successors (c.350–650), when the Buddha figure also reached its most serene perfection. After this, Buddhism was increasingly in decline in its homeland. At the end of the twelfth century the great teaching monasteries which had flourished in eastern India under the Pala and Sena dynasties were finally destroyed by the invading Turks, and their tradition was preserved only in the Himalayan regions of Nepal and Tibet.

The decline of Buddhism was accompanied by a resurgence of Hindu devotional cults. In the Gupta and post-Gupta periods, the form of the Hindu temple underwent far-reaching developments. The temple itself became a symbolic microcosm of the universe, its exterior walls teeming with ranges of sculpted figures of gods, men, animals, and plant forms. The principal deities, especially Vishnu, Shiva, and the Goddess, acquired complex iconographies corresponding to their various aspects, themselves the result of earlier accretions of different popular myths and cults. The separate aspects of a god were often powerfully concentrated in a single, multiple-armed image, each hand holding a symbolic attribute such as a flower or weapon, or making a specific hand-sign (*mudra*). In India's fragmented political condition, different regional dynasties gave rise to distinct local styles of temple architecture and sculpture, showing a great diversity of expressive achievement. For example, the sleek forms of Pala figures from eastern India seem severe in comparison with the elaborate sculptures of the Hoyshala temples of Mysore, while the bronze images of the Tamil country in the south, made by the lost-wax process to be borne in ceremonial processions, are unequalled in their refined simplicity.

So little survives of the painting and decorative arts of classical India that it is now only possible to speculate as to their historical development, mainly on the basis of literary references. Painting was widely used to decorate palaces and houses, and was looked upon as a desirable accomplishment for cultured men and women. Fragmentary remains of wall-paintings in the Buddhist cave-temples of Ajanta offer a tantalizing glimpse of this lost art. Even by the time of the Muslim invasions, their sensuous naturalism had given way to an increasing linear stylization. The subsequent Muslim domination of northern India and the Deccan effectively disrupted the surviving Hindu artistic traditions, while even in the far south a growing loss of creative inspiration is evident after c.1500 A.D.

Stone *Yakshi* Mathura Kushan 2nd century A.D.
H. 51 cm
This *yakshi* or nymph, who clasps a branch of a tree, once formed part of a bracket from the ornamental gateway at the approach to a Jain *stupa* or relic-mound. Carved in the characteristic pink sandstone of the Mathura region, her frankly voluptuous form, emphasized by the stylized contrast of her full breasts and hips with her narrow waist and by her subtly balanced flexed posture, evokes the joyous fecundity of nature. The gathered folds of her diaphanous garment are seen hanging to the side. I.M.72–1927

Death of the Buddha Stone panel N.W. Indian Gandhara 2nd–4th century A.D.
L. 122 cm
Narrative relief panels showing scenes from the Buddha's past and present lives were made to cover the walls of the shrines and monasteries which were patronized by the wealthy Indian merchant classes. This fragment shows five disciples below the bier after the Buddha's *Parinirvana*, or final passing from the cycle of reincarnation into the extinction of nirvana. The four mourners on the left show strong Hellenistic influence in their demonstrative gestures, while the Buddha's last convert Subhadra, meditating beside a tripod, is a more typically Indian figure. I.S.7–1948

Head of the Buddha Stucco N.W. Indian Gandhara
5th century A.D. *H. 24.75 cm*
Towards the end of the Gandhara period, terracotta and
stucco increasingly replaced stone-carving as the principal
medium for *stupa* decoration. The angular inclination of this
Buddha head, and the linear emphasis of brow and nose and
the delicately elongated features together convey an extremely
graceful effect. Like much Gandhara sculpture, it would once
have been painted in naturalistic colours, and some traces of
pigment are still attached to it.   I.M.3–1931

Shiva Ekamukhalinga Mathura region Gupta *c.*400 A.D.
H. 58.5 cm
Shiva, the third deity in the Hindu triad, is conceived in
numerous different forms, both benign and awesomely des-
tructive, many of which are depicted in figurative sculptures.
His most common iconic form is the *lingam*, or phallus, often
set in the *yoni*, or female organ, symbolizing his primordial
power of creation and destruction of the universe. Here he is
shown in both phallic and human form, with his head
projecting from the *lingam*. His hair is tied in the fashion of
ascetics, while his third eye represents his divine insight.
                                                I.S.10–1969

Ascetic and other figures   Terracotta tile panel   Harwan
Kashmir   4th or 5th century A.D.   *H. 53.4 cm*
Moulded terracotta panels of this type, each numbered individually in
Kharoshthi characters, come from the Buddhist monastery of
Harwan overlooking the Dal Lake in Kashmir, where they served as
risers for the bench around a court. Their subject matter is both
unique and enigmatic, with strangely caricatured couples on a
balustraded terrace, aquatic birds, and ascetics who in their emaciated
nudity are unrepresentative of the moderate teachings of Buddhism.

I.S.9–1978

Stone torso of a Bodhisattva   Sanchi   *c.*900 A.D.   *H. 86.4 cm*
This famous torso was one of the first masterpieces of Indian
sculpture to be acquired by the Museum. It belonged to a figure of
the Bodhisattva Avalokiteshvara which originally stood in a small
temple at the Buddhist site of Sanchi in Central India. Carved of
fine-grained sandstone, its subtly flexed posture and combination of
sensuous modelling and stylized ornament evoke its subject's serene
and princely dignity.   I.M.184–1910

Adventures of Prince Kalyanakarin   Detail of a wall-painting   Ajanta   Cave I
5th-century A.D.   (Copy in oils on canvas by J. Griffiths and assistants.)
H. 210 cm W. 580 cm (whole)

The Buddhist cave site of Ajanta emerged from centuries of obscurity after its chance
discovery by a party of British officers on a hunting expedition in 1819. Its uniquely extensive
remains of wall-paintings dating from *c.*100 B.C. to 600 A.D. later excited a widespread
interest, which has unfortunately since led to much loss and deterioration caused by
vandalism and misguided conservation methods. Several series of copies of the paintings were
made in the nineteenth and early twentieth centuries, although many of these have now been
lost by fire. The Museum possesses the surviving residue of those made by J. Griffiths and
his pupils at the Bombay School of Art in *c.*1872–85; even through the medium of these late
nineteenth-century copies, it is possible to appreciate the refined vision and technique of this
otherwise vanished classical art. This particular composition was long thought to show scenes
from the *Mahajanaka Jataka*, one of the stories of the Buddha's past lives; but it has recently
been suggested that it in fact depicts a popular story of the noble Prince Kalyanakarin who,
after being shipwrecked and then blinded and robbed by his evil younger brother, eventually
had his sight and his kingdom restored through the love of a king's daughter.   I.S.31–1885

Mother Goddess Ambika Stone Orissa
c.1100 A.D. *H. 51.5 cm*
Although the central teaching of Jainism was
one of strict asceticism directed towards the
cessation of rebirth, lay worshippers, as so
often in India, continued to pay homage to
the minor deities controlling the natural
forces of fertility. Ambika, the patroness of
motherhood, thus became a tutelary deity
associated with the twenty-second Jain
Tirthankara or Saviour, Neminatha. She sits
under a mango tree, protecting a child with
one hand and holding a branch in the
other. I.S.61–1963

Durga killing the Buffalo-demon
Stone Mysore Hoyshala Early 13th
century *H. 143 cm*
The Goddess is worshipped in many forms
in India, from the benignly maternal to the
awesomely predatory. In one of her fiercer
aspects as Durga, she was implored by the
gods to rid the world of a troublesome
buffalo-demon, Mahishasura. In her four
hands she holds a bow, bell, sword, and
spear with which she serenely transfixes the
demon. The highly elaborate carving of her
headdress and ornaments, and of the decorated arch above, is typical of Hoyshala
sculpture; it was helped by the quality of the
local stone, which was soft and easy to work
when first quarried, but later turned extremely hard. I.S.77–1965

Shiva Nataraja Bronze Madras Chola 11th century *H. 89 cm*
Ringed by a circle of flames, Shiva as 'Lord of the Dance' dances on the back of the prostrate
dwarf Apasmara, who signifies the power of ignorance and materialism. In two of his hands he
carries the drum and a tongue of flame, symbolizing the complementary universal principles
of Creation and Destruction. His two lower hands make the gesture of protection and point to
his raised left foot, the worship of which leads to salvation. The highly developed language of
sacred dance played an important part in Hindu temple ritual in many regions until quite
recent times, and it exercised a profound influence on the iconography of sculpture.

I.M.2–1934

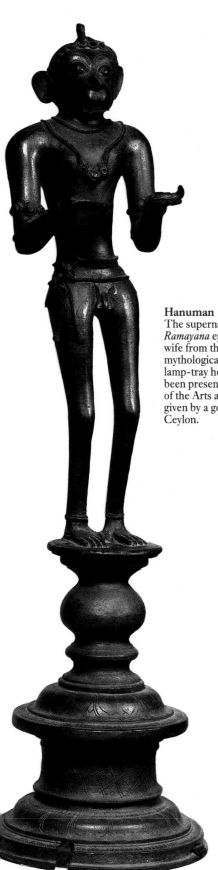

Bodhisattva Padmapani From a palm-leaf manuscript of *Ashtasahasrika Prajnaparamita* Pala school E. Indian *c.*1120 *H. 7.2 cm W. 5.8 cm*
Padmapani, a form of Avalokiteshvara, holds a white lotus and is attended by the goddess Tara and the guardian deity Hayagriva. Pictures of deities served an auspiciously protective rather than illustrative function when included in manuscripts of Buddhist wisdom literature. The Pala style of the great teaching monasteries of eastern India shows strong continuity from the earlier classical style of Ajanta.   I.S.8–1958

Hanuman Bronze Ceylon *c.*14th century *H. 76.2 cm*
The supernatural exploits of the monkey chief Hanuman in the *Ramayana* epic, in which he helps the hero Rama to recapture his wife from the wicked King Ravana, made him a popular Hindu mythological figure. This bronze originally served as an oil-lamp; the lamp-tray held by Hanuman is now missing. Once thought to have been presented to the Museum by William Morris, the leading figure of the Arts and Crafts Movement, it is now believed to have been given by a government official of the same name who had served in Ceylon.   275–1869

Jina (Jain Saviour) Bronze W. Indian 9th–10th century *H. 25 cm*
In keeping with the ascetic and world-denying tenor of Jainism, images of the twenty-four Jain Saviours tend to be hieratically formal in character, and to lack the sensuousness and elegance of much Indian figure sculpture. They are usually shown as standing or seated ascetics, absorbed in profound meditation. This Jina is attended by saintly and celestial figures, while two devotees kneel below his throne.   I.S.10–1968

Mughal and British India

The Muslim Sultans, who dominated northern India from the thirteenth century, brought with them a Persian court culture, whose most distinguished field of expression was mosque and tomb architecture. Their cultural achievement has, however, been overshadowed by that of the Mughals, whose Indian empire, first established by the Central Asian prince Babur in 1527, was later consolidated and extended by his brilliant and forceful grandson Akbar (r. 1556–1605). An energetic and wide-ranging patron of the arts, Akbar established a large atelier of native artists under the direction of two master-painters from the Safavid court of Persia. A dynamic eclectic style of poetical and historical manuscript illustration rapidly evolved. Its vivid naturalism showed a debt to European art which became more evident in the period of Jahangir (r. 1605–27), notable for its finely painted court portraits and animal studies. The arts of hardstone carving, glass manufacture, carpet weaving, textile embroidery, jewellery, metalwork, and enamelling all flourished under the Mughals; they show a masterly synthesis of Persian, Indian, and European elements, characterized above all by a delight in floral motifs. Many of these arts reached their maturity in the opulent reign of Shah Jahan (r. 1628–58), builder of the Taj Mahal. But under the puritanical Aurangzeb (r. 1658–1707) and his effete successors, Mughal art lost its vital, early inspiration, although accomplished work was produced until the nineteenth century.

The Muslim courts of the Deccan maintained their independent traditions of painting and decorative arts, although their quality and individuality were diminished after Aurangzeb's conquest in the 1680s. The Rajput courts of Rajasthan and the Punjab Hills, despite their submission to Akbar and Jahangir, continued to preserve earlier Hindu cultural traditions. The numerous local schools of Rajput painting kept their own bold and poetic vision, both in traditional illustrations of devotional and poetical texts, and in their versions of the Mughal-inspired art of portraiture.

European trade with India expanded from the early seventeenth century: the Portuguese were followed by the competing Dutch, English, and French East India Companies. European motifs began to form an exotic element in Indian decorative design, especially in export items such as the chintzes of the Coromandel coast. The disappearance of court patronage and growth of British power from the mid-eighteenth century were ultimately the undoing of Indian craftsmen, particularly the weavers, whose work was imitated and then undercut by the Manchester mill-owners. By the end of the nineteenth century, the traditional arts of India were either greatly impoverished or extinct.

Emperor Jahangir's Zebra by Mans Gouache on paper Mughal 1621 *H. 18.3 cm W. 24.1 cm*
In his Memoirs, Jahangir reveals himsel as a keen amateur naturalist, always rea to note the peculiarities of the flowers, birds, and animals he encountered. He would often have a visual record made b specialist artists, the most accomplishe of whom was Mansur. Jahangir mention the astonishment at court after the presentation of this zebra: 'As it was strang some people imagined that it had been coloured. After minute inquiry into the truth, it became known that the Lord of the world was the Creator thereof.'

I.M.23–19:

Babur supervises the laying out of th Garden of Fidelity by Bishan Das an Nanha Gouache on paper Mughal *c.1590 H. 21.9 cm W. 14.4 cm; H. 22.2 cm W. 13.6 cm*
Among the illustrated manuscripts commissioned by the Emperor Akbar were several versions of the *Baburnama* or Memoirs of his illustrious grandfathe Babur, who had first established Mugha power in India. Babur's vivid descriptive writing, full of incidental detail, was matched by the imaginative power of the imperial artists. In this double-page painting, Babur lays out one of the many gardens he created in his wanderings, in this case the Garden of Fidelity near Jalalabad in modern Afghanistan.

I.M.276 & A–1913

Marriage of Krishna's parents Gouache on paper Rajasthan (?) *c.1525–50 H. 17.5 cm W. 23.5 cm*
This scene of a Hindu wedding belongs to a famous dispersed *Bhagavata Purana* manuscript, narrating events from Krishna's life. It is painted in the bold and vivacious Early Rajput style, which was to form the basis for the development of numerous local schools o painting at the courts of Rajasthan from the early seventeenth century onwards. The future parents of Krishna stand before the sacrificial fire on which a priest pours clarified butter; they are attended by maid and male relatives.

I.S.I–197

Emperor Akbar receives a nobleman   Gouache on paper, from a manuscript of the
Akbarnama   Mughal   *c.*1590   *H. 38 cm W. 24 cm*   Outline and painting by Husain Naqqash,
faces by Kesu.
One of the most outstanding illustrated manuscripts produced by Akbar's studio was the
chronicle of his reign written by his friend and confidant Abu'l Fazl. The Museum has more than
one hundred pages of it in its collection, covering the years 1560–77. Vigorously naturalistic, they
illustrate scenes from the Emperor's daily life, as well as his military campaigns and events of
state. This scene, in which Akbar receives Husain Quli Khan Jahan, shows the splendour of the
Mughal court at Agra.
                                                                    I.S.2–1896 (113/117)

Krishna's combat with Indra   Gouache on paper, from a *Harivamsa* manuscript   Mughal
*c.*1590   *H. 29.6 cm W. 18.4 cm*
Unlike most Muslim rulers, Akbar was deeply interested in the teaching of other religions, and even
initiated a short-lived eclectic faith centred on his own person. He also commissioned Persian
translations of the Hindu epics, illustrated by his artists, many of whom were themselves Hindus. This
dramatic composition shows the aerial combat in which Krishna on the bird Garuda overcomes Indra on
his elephant, watched from above by other gods and celestial beings; below is a coastal landscape scene
deriving from Flemish painting.   I.S.5–1970

Emperor Shah Jahan by Bichitr   Gouache on paper   Mughal
1630   *H. 22.2 cm W. 13.4 cm*
Before the Mughal period, naturalistic portraiture was almost unknown
in Indian art, with its predilection for ideal forms. By the reign of
Jahangir, who is known to have admired English miniatures, it had
displaced manuscript illustration as the mainstream of Mughal painting.
Under Shah Jahan and his successors, portraiture became more stiffly
official in character. This painting is inscribed by Shah Jahan himself as
'a good portrait of me in my fortieth year'.   I.M.17–1925

*Nobleman with companions listening to
music* Gouache on paper   Mughal
*c.*1620–30   *H. 20 cm W. 14.5 cm*
This tranquil study of an open air music
party, in which a young nobleman and
companions seated under a pipal tree listen
to a singer accompanied by a *tanpura* player,
is an example of Mughal portraiture in its
more relaxed and informal aspect. In the
foreground appears one of the earliest representations of a *huqqa* in Indian painting.   I.S.89–1965

Jade wine-cup of Emperor Shah Jahan
Mughal 1657 *L. 18.7 cm*
Like their Timurid ancestors, the Mughal Emperors were patrons of jade-carving. The finest pieces date from Shah Jahan's reign when the earlier use of dark jades, and relatively austere forms deriving from metal-work, gave way to more organic and imaginatively eclectic conceptions carved in paler jade. This exquisite cup is of a lobed half-gourd shape, tapering into a curving handle in the form of a wild goat's head, with a base of open lotus petals with radiating leaves. It shows a masterly integration of Persian, Indian, Chinese, and European decorative elements. I.S.12–1962

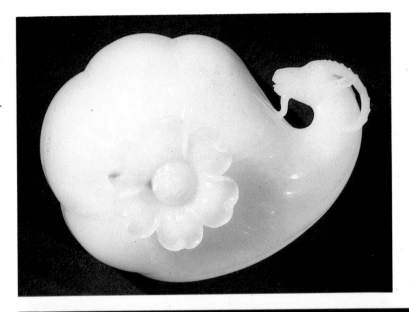

Satin coat with pictorial embroidery
Mughal Period of Jahangir (1605–27)
L. 100 cm
This is thought to be a unique surviving example of an especially fine type of Mughal court coat referred to as *nadiri* by Jahangir in his Memoirs. Embroidered in chain-stitch in blue, yellow, green, gold, and brown silks, its pattern consists of hillocks, flowering trees and plants, peacocks, storks, ducks, butter-flies, and animals, including tigers, deer, and rabbits. I.S.18–1947

Jewelled spoon Mughal Late 16th century *L. 18.5 cm*
Surviving early examples of Mughal jewel-lery and goldsmiths' work are very rare. The shape of this gold spoon, set with ruby and emerald pieces and a diamond, can be related to late sixteenth-century European designs. I.M.173–1910

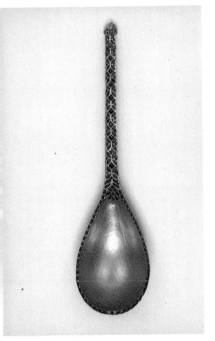

Pile carpet Agra or Lahore *c.*1640
L. 141 cm W. 90 cm
The art of pile-carpet weaving was introduced into India by Akbar, who brought
craftsmen from eastern Persia to teach their
skills. By the reign of Shah Jahan, when this
carpet fragment was woven, the ubiquitous
floral motifs found in contemporary architectural ornament, metalwork, and textiles
had strongly influenced carpet design; the
use of the trellis pattern suggests Italian
influence.   T.403–1910

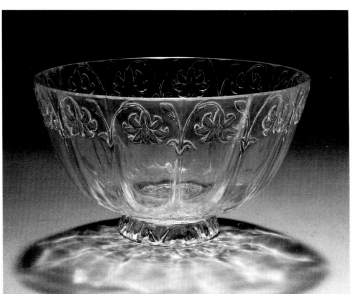

Crystal bowl Mughal *c.*1650 *H. 8.5 cm*
Rock crystal has been carved in India for at
least two thousand years; it was used from an
early period for making amulets, Buddhist
reliquaries, and luxury items such as wine-
cups. Its clear, ice-like appearance had a
great appeal for the Mughals, to whom good
quality glass was almost unknown. This very
delicately carved bowl, divided into compartments by attenuated lily stems, can be attributed to the reign of Shah Jahan.   986–1875

Silver beaker and cover Mughal *c.1650–1700* *H. 14 cm*
The form of this beaker appears to have been copied by the Mughal craftsman from a Dutch or German model, which had perhaps been among the gifts presented to the Emperor by Dutch merchants negotiating trading rights. The shallow flowering plant forms were probably originally intended to be filled with coloured enamels, but this was not carried out. I.S.31–1961

Bidri huqqa **bowl** Bidar Deccan Late 17th century *H. 16.5 cm*
In the Muslim kingdom of Bidar in the Deccan, a distinct technique was developed of inlaying silver (or occasionally brass) in a heavy pewter-like base metal, an alloy of zinc, copper, tin, and lead. The colour contrast between the often very elaborate floral and abstract silver ornamentation and its background was enhanced by chemically blackening the base metal. I.S.181–1965

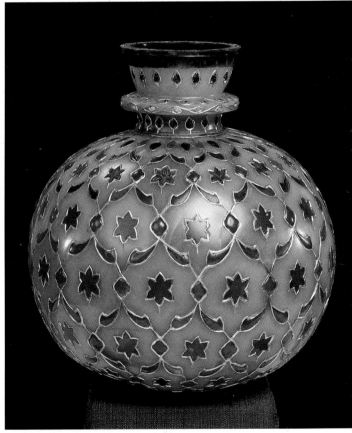

Jade inlaid *huqqa* bowl with precious stones in a gold setting
Mughal 17th or 18th century *H. 18.5 cm*
The habit of smoking tobacco appears to have been introduced into India by the Portuguese in the Deccan towards the end of Akbar's reign. Despite being banned for a time by Jahangir, it became popular among all classes of society. As elsewhere in the East, the smoke was cooled and purified by passing it through a water-pipe (*huqqa*), which might have a bowl of glass, jade, ceramic, or various metals. I.S.02593

A European   Gouache on paper   Mughal   *c.*1590   *H. 30 cm W. 18.3 cm*
The Mughals' earliest contacts with European culture occurred when the Jesuits in Goa sent several missions to Akbar's Court in the hope of converting him to Christianity. They were followed by the representatives of the Portuguese, Dutch, and English East India Companies. This Mughal view of a European is probably based on an engraving, perhaps of the Emperor Charles v; the Christian ladies in the landscape background, however, appear to be worshipping at a Shiva temple.   I.M.386–1914

Painted cotton wall-hanging Golconda (under Dutch patronage) *c.1640 L. 259 cm W. 152 cm*

The hand-painted and resist-dyed cotton fabrics or chintzes of the Coromandel coast were exported to Europe in great numbers during the seventeenth and eighteenth centuries, and had a profound effect on European decorative design. They were painted freehand in a laborious dyeing process which imparted brilliant, non-fugitive colours. The artists improvised from models provided by their European clients, who favoured quaint subject matter. This composition depicts two native potentates with youths above and two Dutch traders with serving-women below.

687–1898

Painted cotton floor-spread Golconda *c.1630 Whole: H. 325 cm W. 246 cm*

This detail of a large floor-spread made for the Persian or Indo–Persian taste shows two men in Persian costume shooting black partridges amid fanciful flowering plants and trees. The Golconda cotton-painters have imaginatively transformed the Persian and Italianate forms in the overall design of the floor-spread, thought to have once belonged to the Maharajas of Amber in Rajasthan.

I.M.160–1929

Gamecock Deccan, probably Golconda _c._1610–2c
_H. 17.4 cm W. 11.2 cm_
While the Mughal style of painting was developing
from a fusion of Persian and native Indian elements in
the north in the late sixteenth century, analogous style
were also evolving at the independent Muslim courts c
Ahmadnagar, Golconda, and Bijapur in the Deccan. I
contrast to the sober realism of the Mughal school, the
Deccani painters at their best achieved more subtle an
poignant effects. Although this fighting-cock lacks the
anatomical naturalism of a study by Mansur, its bold
colouring and strutting attitude express its real
nature. I.S.92–19

Ivory cabinet Ceylon _c._1700 _H. 24 cm_
Ivory carving is of great antiquity in India, although
little survives from early times; some examples from th
first centuries A.D. have been excavated at Pompeii in
Italy and Begram in Afghanistan. Ceylon, where ivory
was plentiful, was a major centre of production. This
cabinet was made under Dutch influence and its panel
designs showing Adam and Eve in the Garden with
birds and animals, including elephants and camels, wa
probably adapted from a seventeenth-century Dutch
engraving. 1067–185

Cotton girdle (patka) Golconda 17th or 18th century *W. 71 cm L. 540 cm*
Long girdles, tied round the waist with the hanging ends displaying decorative border designs, were commonly worn by noblemen in Mughal times. Floral borders were especially popular, and in this example the cypress is used as a motif. As with the larger chintzes, the pattern was first drawn freehand on paper and stencilled on to the material, and the mordants used in the dyeing process to fix the colours were applied directly by brush. I.S.94–1948

Papier-mâché casket Painted and lacquered Deccan *c.*1660 *H. 8 cm*
Like many other Mughal crafts, the technique of painting and lacquering papier-mâché came from Persia, perhaps by way of Kashmir, which remained a prolific centre until recently. It was first used for book-covers, and later extended to luxury items such as mirror-backs and boxes. This jewel casket is one of the most famous surviving seventeenth-century examples. Its finely painted scenes of a prince and noblewomen in garden surroundings, and a European gallant in Restoration costume playing a flute have been attributed to the artist Rahim Deccani. 851–1889

Inlaid wooden casket Sind, possibly Tatta 17th century *H. 12.7 cm*
Like their counterparts working in metal, Indian woodworkers achieved rich effects of surface decoration through inlaying with contrasting materials. This wooden casket, with falling front and internal fittings, is inlaid with trees, birds, and male and female figures in stained and incised ivory and brass wire. 1090–1875

Bhairava Raga Gouache on paper Malwa
*c.*1600 *H. 22.6 cm W. 16.7 cm*
This leaf from a series of *ragamala* paintings,
or pictorial representations of the supposed
character of the major musical modes (*ragas*),
shows Bhairava in the form of Krishna
conversing with a lady. Its glowing colours,
stylized drawing, and schematic architectural
forms are typical of seventeenth-century
painting in Malwa and Bundelkhand, where
the robust Early Rajput tradition continued
with little dilution by Mughal influences.
I.S.55–1952

***Thakur Padam Singh of Ghanerao and
companions*** by Manna Gouache on
paper Ajmer 1721 *H. 24.3 cm W. 31 cm*
By the early eighteenth century, the Mughal
art of court portraiture had become well
established at the major courts of Rajasthan,
and even minor Rajput chiefs, or Thakurs,
were patronizing it. Rajasthani artists
adapted the genre to their own poetic and
strictly hierarchical vision; hence the relative
diminution of the serving-girl compared with
the noblemen and their dogs. I.S.12–1978

Maharaja Umed Singh of Kotah shooting tiger   Gouache on paper   Kotah
*c.*1790   *H. 33 cm W. 40 cm*
Among the various local schools of Rajasthani painting, that of Kotah was outstanding for its
powerful renderings of animals and landscape, especially in hunting scenes. Raja Umed
Singh and his minister Zalim Singh are seen in a tree-hide firing at the tiger which has been
lured by a tethered buffalo. The moonlit jungle with distant rocky outcrops is invested with a
dramatic and unearthly quality.   I.S.563–1952

Resourceful Radha   Gouache on
paper   Basohli   *c.*1660–70   *H. 18 cm*
W. 27.5 cm
By the late seventeenth century, a vigorous and expressive style of manuscript
illustration had become established in the
Punjab Hill state of Basohli: this can be
seen in the series of illustrations to the
Rasamanjari, a Sanskrit treatise classify-
ing ideal types of lovers and their emotions, to which this painting belongs. The
nayika or heroine, here interpreted as
Radha, seeing a boy-servant about to cut
the tree under which she used to meet
Krishna, seizes his axe and throws it in
the pond. Krishna is seen seated inside
the house.   I.S.48–1953

Radha and Krishna on a lakeside terrace Gouache
on paper Garhwal *c.*1780–90 *H. 18.8 cm W. 13.4 cm*
The spread of the poetic Guler–Kangra idiom among the
Punjab Hill courts gave rise to a number of variant styles,
one of which is associated with Garhwal. This painting
belongs to a series of *Baramasa*, or illustrations of the
twelve months of the year seen through the activities of
idealized lovers; it represents the winter month of *Aghan*
(November–December). Two lovers, personified as Radha
and Krishna, stand gazing at one another on a terrace,
while two cranes soar into the sky behind them.   I.S.6–1960

Radha and Krishna in the grove Gouache on paper
Kangra *c.*1780 *H. 12.3 cm W. 17.2 cm*
At Guler and Kangra, in the middle to late eighteenth
century, a remarkable final flowering of Punjab Hill
painting took place, in which the technical skills brought by
Mughal-trained artists returning from the plains were
transformed by the poetic and devotional feeling of the
native Rajput tradition. At Kangra in particular, episodes
from the youth of Krishna, including scenes of his love
affair with Radha, were set in an idyllic version of the local
landscape and rendered with rare delicacy.   I.S.15–1949

William Fullarton giving directions to a servant
by Dip Chand Gouache on paper Murshidabad
1760–63 *H. 26.5 cm W. 22.8 cm*
An East India Company officer sits in the attitude of a
Mughal nobleman, smoking a *huqqa* on his terrace,
attended by servants with yak-tail fly whisks. He is
probably William Fullarton, who practised as a surgeon
in Bengal and Bihar in the mid-eighteenth century, and
was on intimate terms with the local nobility. He lived
in the native quarter at Patna and while there commissioned portraits of members of his household and others
from the Murshidabad artist Dip Chand. I.M.33–1912

Women selling grains and vegetables by Shiva
Dayal Lal Gouache on paper Patna Mid-19th
century *H. 20 cm W. 33 cm*
British patronage of Indian artists in the late eighteenth
and nineteenth centuries gave rise to the hybrid, so-
called Company style, which combined traditional
pictorial conventions with effects borrowed from European art, such as shadow, modelling, and perspective.
Its subject matter reflected British interest in the
picturesque aspects of Indian life: common themes
were topographical views, popular festivals, portraits of
different castes and native types, and scenes of street
and bazaar life such as this statuesque tableau of
vegetable sellers. I.S.66–1949

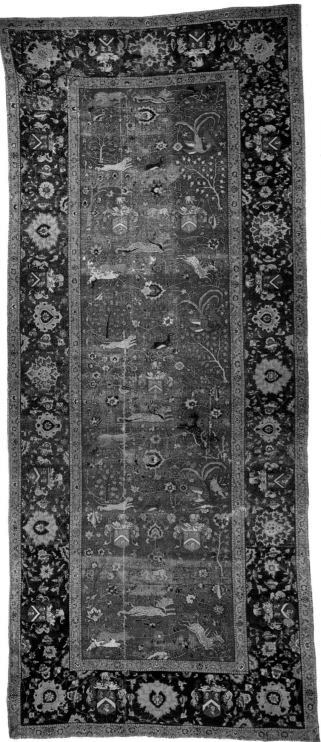

Fremlin carpet Lahore or Agra *c*.1640 *L. 579 cm W. 248 cm*
Sir Thomas Roe, the ambassador of King James I to the court of
Jahangir, is known to have brought home with him 'a great carpet
with my arms thereon'. His initiative was followed by other
Englishmen, including William Fremlin, a prominent Company
official in India, for whom this carpet was woven. Its design, mainly
Persian in conception, contains mythical beasts such as winged deer
and *simurgh* birds, and the Fremlin arms. It was probably used as a
table-cover rather than a floor-covering, which accounts for its
narrow proportions.   I.M.1–1936

Writing-cabinet and table-stand Vizagapatam *c*.1725–50
H. 156.8 cm
The Portuguese, Dutch, and English traders in India were impressed
by the ease with which local craftsmen in wood and ivory were able to
imitate European furniture designs, embellishing them with mainly
indigenous ornament. One of the two main types of furniture made
for European patrons at Vizagapatam on the east coast relied on the
inlaying of hardwoods (rosewood, ebony, or teak) with ivory, which in
turn was inlaid with black lac for decorative effect. The most
common design was a border of stylized flowers, deriving from Indo–
Persian textiles.   I.S.19–1968

'Burgomaster' chair Vizagapatam *c.*1770 *H. 82 cm*
The other principal technique of the Vizagapatam furniture-makers was to veneer ivory sheets on a wooden—usually teak—core, the ivory being decorated with lac inlay as with the inlaid pieces (see opposite). This chair of the Burgomaster type, with a revolving upper half, shows European influence in its floral ornament. According to a silver plate screwed to its frame, the chair came from the palace of Tipu Sultan after the fall of Seringapatam (see below), and was given to Queen Charlotte by Warren Hastings; however, this statement is otherwise uncorroborated. I.S.25–1970

Shawl border Kashmir *c.*1750–1800 *L. 284.5 cm*
W. 132.1 cm
The shawls of Kashmir, woven from the fleece of mountain goats, were celebrated for their extreme fineness and warmth, and for the beauty of their colours and designs; this detail shows one form of the traditional *buta* motif. By the late eighteenth century, Kashmir shawls had become fashionable wear in Europe, and were exported in great numbers. But the weavers' concessions to foreign taste, encouraged by French agents especially, led to artistic decline. By the 1870s, changing European fashions and the undermining of the weavers' market by cheaper French and British machine-made imitations quickly brought about the final decline of the shawl industry. I.M.17–1915

Golden throne of Ranjit Singh
Lahore   *c.*1830   *H. 92 cm*
Although furniture was little used before the
coming of Europeans to India, thrones had
been a symbolic appurtenance of royalty
from early times. This impressive throne of
wood overlaid with gold is traditionally associated with Maharaja Ranjit Singh (1780–
1839), an astute and colourful ruler who
united the Sikh community of the Punjab
into a formidable power. The Anglo–Sikh
wars which followed his death ended in the
British annexation of the Punjab and the
dispersal of the effects of the court of
Lahore. The throne was brought to England
and displayed in the East India Company's
museum.   I.S.2518

Tipu's Tiger   Seringapatam   Mysore state   *c.*1790   *L. 177.8 cm*
This painted wooden effigy of a tiger mauling a prostrate British officer was made for Tipu
Sultan, the ruler of Mysore, as an expression both of his fascination with tigers and
his loathing of the British. The tiger's body contains a miniature organ, probably of French
manufacture, which ingeniously simulates its roars as well as the groans of its victim.
Captured in 1799 at the fall of Seringapatam, in which Tipu himself died, it became a
favourite exhibit in the East India Company's museum in London. Keats alludes to it in a
satirical poem, *The Cap and Bells*.   I.S.2545

Nepal and Tibet

The birth of the Buddha, and early Buddhism, were closely associated with what is now southern Nepal, but it was not until about the middle of the seventh century that Buddhism reached Tibet. Each country looked on India as the source of its religious culture with which its art was closely concerned. While Buddhism flourished in India, pilgrims and teachers travelled across the high passes of the Himalayas to visit its holy places. Going in the other direction, to monasteries in Nepal and Tibet, they took with them scriptures, as well as information about the latest religious developments, their rituals, and the objects, such as sculpture and painting, needed for the performance of those rituals. The final Muslim invasion of northern India cut off this source of religious knowledge, and forced the craftsmen who relied on it for their living to emigrate. They went to Nepal and Tibet, and on to the Mongol Court of China, where Tibet also found sympathetic support for her religious doctrines. As a result, Tibet absorbed elements of Chinese and Central Asian culture while Nepal continued to orientate herself more towards the south of the Himalayas. Tibet and Newar Nepal never lost their common religious link, however, and their art shared a style, technique, and subject matter that were in many ways similar. It is likely that the Nepalese style was the more dominant at first but gradually Tibet evolved her own form of artistic expression, which became almost indistinguishable at times from that of Nepal as craftsmen and patrons visited each country. Although, therefore, some objects are unquestionably Tibetan (see p. 342), or Nepalese (see pp. 344 and 347), there are others (see p. 343, below) to which it is more difficult to assign a precise place of origin. At its best, the art of Nepal and Tibet combines grace and vigour to express deep spiritual power.

Gilt bronze figure of the Buddha Partly painted Tibetan Perhaps 14th century A.D.
H. 34.3 cm
Although the veneration of the Buddha is basic to all forms of Buddhism, in Tibet many other deities demand the worshipper's attentions so that Buddha icons are less common than might be expected. This one, seated on a stylized lotus throne, shows one of the origins of Tibetan metal sculpture in the Pala art of eastern India, and also its conservatism in preserving a style which remained almost unaltered several centuries later. Religious force and ethereal calm are brilliantly combined in the facial expression.
I.M.121–1910

Padmasambhava, with his wives and disciples Gouache on prepared cotton cloth
Tibetan *c.*14th century *H. 58 cm*
Tibetan religious paintings are usually hanging scrolls (*tangkas*) executed in opaque colour on prepared cotton cloth, and mounted on textile, often silk, borders. They usually show a central deity drawn on a larger scale than the minor figures which surround it. Here, the central figure is that of a famous teacher who was invited from south of the Himalayas to go to Tibet in the second half of the eighth century A.D. to help found Samye, the first Tibetan Buddhist monastery.
I.S.20–1970

Tantric monk and his female assistant Gilt bronze
Tibetan 16th or 17th century *H. 22.7 cm*
Tibetan religious life has been strongly affected by Tantrism, the cult of magic and elaborate ritual. This is reflected in the appearance of many images which are endowed with much esoteric symbolism including the use of skulls, blood, animal skins, and postures such as the one shown here. It covers a wide spectrum of thought from ideas about the nature of the soul to the ritual performance of the sexual act.
I.M.61–1929

Bodhisattva Avalokiteshvara Gouache on prepared cotton cloth Tibetan 18th century *H. 58 cm W. 41 cm*
This Bodhisattva has many forms, one of which is said to be the spiritual ancestor of all the Dalai Lamas. The one shown here has eleven heads and a thousand arms, and represents the god of compassion and mercy. By the religious merit he has built up through many previous lives, he has qualified to escape rebirth but has chosen to remain to help all mortals achieve enlightenment.

I.M.412–1914

Four *mandalas* Gouache on prepared cotton cloth Tibetan *c.*1450 *H. 73.7 cm*
A *mandala* is a formal arrangement of a main deity, surrounded by its retinue of subordinate deities. Of any material and size, it is used for special rituals and meditation. Here, the central deities are surrounded by a stylized building with a door in each side, and then by circles of flames, thunderbolts, cemeteries, and lotus petals. The painting, showing a fusion of Tibetan and Nepalese styles, was probably executed in Tibet by a Nepalese painter.

I.S.167–1964

Bodhisattva Amoghapasha   Gouache on prepared cotton cloth   Nepalese   *c.*1450
H. 97 cm W. 74.5 cm
This scroll painting is similar to a *tangka* in Tibet, but usually called a *paubha* in Nepal; it
shows another form of Avalokiteshvara as Lord of the World. He is a popular deity among
Buddhist Newars in Nepal, who commission images of him in metal and paint. The fresh and
vigorous execution is emphasized by the gilt niche surrounding the central figure.   I.S.58–1977

Portrait figure of a monk Gilt bronze inlaid with silver and copper Tibetan Probably 13th century *H. 18.5 cm*

The highly individualized facial treatment leaves no doubt that this image was a portrait of a living person. Tibetan craftsmen were trained to keep to the strict rules for making images for worship or stylized portraits of historical figures; there was also a tradition for making more individual likenesses in paintings and bronzes some of which, as here, achieved a powerful characterization. Although a name is given in the inscription, the sitter has not been positively identified. I.S.13–1971

Carved ivory lions Tibetan or Nepalese *c.*12th century *H. 17.8 cm*

These probably belonged to a set of four (a third is in the British Museum) which supported a throne, where they implied that its occupant possessed the qualities of a lion. The stylization of the mane, fierce expression of the face, and broad chest skilfully convey the beast's majesty. Lions similar to these are found carved on the thrones of Buddhist images, and the joist-ends of Tibetan buildings. I.S.269 & A–1960

Painted and gilt copper head of Bhairava Nepalese 17th century
H. 69.2 cm
The formidable expression, flaming hair, skulls in the crown, and snake necklace, are intended as much to frighten the enemies of religion as to overawe the worshipper of this deity. The form of its image shown here was used in a ritual during which devotees took liquid through the hole in the mouth which was piped down from behind. A sumptuous effect is created by the characteristic Nepalese inlaying of imitation gems. I.M.172–1913

Embroidered dancer's apron Tibetan 19th century *H. 81 cm W. 87.5 cm*
This apron was used as part of the costume of a dancer taking part in the religious dances—often wrongly called devil dances—which were performed outside monasteries. In many cases expressing allegories of the struggle between good and evil, and accompanied by music, they took place towards the end of the year. The appliqué work of which the apron is made is also used in Tibet for religious pictures. 499B–1905

Silver butter lamp Tibetan 18th or
19th century *H. 22.8 cm*
No altar in Tibet is complete without at least
one butter lamp, preferably kept burning
continuously. Offerings are made to the
monks or monasteries of lamps made of
beautifully worked silver or gold, and carrying a commemorative inscription.   527–1905

Bodhisattva Avalokiteshvara Gilt copper Nepalese 13th
or 14th century *H. 91.5 cm*
Bodhisattvas usually wear crowns and jewellery similar to the way
in which the Buddha was thought to have worn them as a prince
before he took up the religious life. The name of this deity is Lord
of Compassion, and this is symbolized by the gesture of his right
hand which signifies charity, and emphasized by the sacred cord
over his left shoulder, his flexed position, and the gentle
expression on his face.   I.M.239–1922

Libation jug Tibetan 17th or 18th century *H. 14 cm*
This jug probably formed part of a four-
piece set of ritual objects. Two main motifs
appear, the lotus bud and petals for lid and
base, and the Indian mythical water animal,
makara, for handle and spout. The exquisite
craftsmanship of the gilt copper mounts and
rock crystal body places the jug almost in the
class of jewellery.   I.M.379–1914

South-East Asia

Except for the areas which came under Chinese political control, the early history of South-East Asia is obscure. The earliest evidence of Indian culture in the region is found on the mainland, and belongs to about the second century A.D. From that time onwards, it spread steadily and peacefully, except to northern Vietnam. Before being carried up the valleys of the large rivers such as the Mekong, it was largely confined to the deltas and coastal strip, suggesting that it was brought by sea traders who, as well as selling their goods, may have been allowed to settle and marry into the local population. Where the land was rich, as in Cambodia and Java, powerful states arose which built huge temples for the worship of Buddhist and Hindu gods, and the glory of the kings, such as Angkor and Borobodur. Many sculpture workshops were needed to decorate these buildings, whose craftsmen followed as best they could the designs then being used in India. These were interpreted according to local traditions which, while maintaining a recognizable Indian origin, gradually evolved into distinct regional styles. Within these, many sub-divisions arose during the long art history of many different peoples inhabiting the vast area of the mainland, peninsular, and islands of South-East Asia. The most influential styles, between the seventh and thirteenth centuries, were the Cambodian (Khmer), Javanese, and Thai. The first two combine a sensitive refinement and strength to produce an art whose purpose is to overawe in the service of religion. Whereas this was usually monumental, and carried out in stone, Thai sculpture was often more intimate and took the form of small bronze images. Decorative arts flourished everywhere, with Indonesia and Malaysia making some superb textiles and Burma excellent lacquerwork and silverware.

Embossed gold betel nut container Set with rubies and emeralds Burmese 19th century *H. 41.5 cm*
The sacred goose (*hamsa*) has been an important motif in Burmese art since the seventh century A.D., and was regarded as possessing the ideal Buddhist qualities of purity and gentleness. Containers in this form are still popular and are often made of lacquered wood set with pieces of mirror and coloured glass. The one shown here formed part of the Burmese regalia belonging to King Thibaw, the last representative of the Burmese monarchy. I.S.246–1964

Buddhist shrine Carved and gilt wood inlaid with semi-precious stones, coloured glass, and pieces of mirror Burmese *c.*1850 *H. 285.7 cm*

Until comparatively recently, much of Burmese art was religious, and craftsmen such as wood carvers and lacquer workers produced shrines which provided a focal point for worship. The rich design, the sculpted figures, and use of much gold leaf and imitation gems, were intended to glorify the Buddha figure and intensify the worshipper's spiritual awareness. The deity is placed in a niche similar to the decorative portal at the back of some Burmese royal thrones; the structure supporting the Buddha is also not unlike a throne. The umbrellas, symbols of sovereignty, shown at the top of the shrine, are sanctioned by long tradition in this context, but the lions placed in niches below are a more direct reference to the form of a royal throne. Containers for offerings, including two *hamsas* similar to the one shown opposite, are placed near the shrine, along with a box containing volumes of scriptures. I.S.II–1969

Sandstone head of the Buddha Cambodian (Khmer) Early
13th century *H. 27.9 cm*
This head beautifully illustrates the impassive smile present on many
Khmer Buddha figures. It is intended to convey the remoteness of
the deity tempered with its humanity and compassion. The versatility
of Khmer sculptors enabled them to execute with equal facility low
reliefs or figures almost in the round, portraits of kings and Hindu
deities; the serene expression of the Buddha figures probably has the
widest appeal.   I.S.15–1968

Volcanic stone figure of Uma Javanese Early 15th century
H. 53.9 cm
Despite the inferior status which was usually assigned to women in
South-East Asia, the cult of female deities was adopted along with
the other gods of the two great Indian religions. Here Uma (her name
means Light), one of the consorts of Shiva, stands on a lotus base
wearing the crown and jewellery of royalty; in her upper right hand
she holds a lotus flower, and in the left a fly whisk; her other two
hands are clasped together in a gesture of respectful salutation.
                                                                I.M.147–1921

Bronze figure of the Buddha North Thai Early 16th century *H. 42.5 cm*
The Thais brought the craft of casting bronze images to a high level of perfection, both technically and aesthetically, which reached its zenith at about the end of the fifteenth century. They took Indian traditions and moulded them into a distinct style that admirably suited their own forms of religious expression. At its best it is remarkable for its persuasive spirituality, and for its idealization of form, derived from the simplified anatomy.   I.S.90–1958

Scenes from the Buddha's life Steatite Burmese 12th or 13th century
H. 8.5 cm
Based directly on contemporary Indian examples, the scenes represent clockwise, from the bottom left: the nativity, in which the Buddha was born from his standing mother's right-hand side; the first sermon, which the Buddha gave in the deer park; the encounter with the elephant which the Buddha overcame with love; the Buddha passing into nirvana; the descent from the Tavatimsa heaven; the miracles of flames rising from his shoulders and water pouring from his feet; the monkey's gift of honey and, centre, the Buddha's enlightenment.   I.M.378–1914

Dancer's headdress Lacquered and gilt wood, sheet metal with mirror glass and imitation stones Burmese Late 19th century *H. 36.8 cm*
Burmese theatre includes orchestral music, songs, and dances, even though the story may have a religious theme. A single performance can last all night, and it sometimes takes three performances to complete a play. I.S.06207

Lacquer bowl Burmese *c.*1910–1920 *H. 34 cm*
The versatility of lacquer is amply illustrated in the Museum's collections. Used in making shrines and images, it was also employed in the manufacture of book pages and covers, headdresses, musical instruments, furniture, architectural details, and boxes and bowls such as the one illustrated here. I.M.57–1932

Puppet figure Carved and painted wood, with costume of silk embroidered with gold thread, sequins, pieces of mirror, and glass beads Burmese Late 19th century *H. 63.5 cm*
Puppet shows were patronized by the Burmese kings, and an official at court was in charge of performances. The themes of the plays were taken from the stories of Buddha's previous births, and incidents in Burmese history. As well as providing entertainment, they had a moral element, such as the triumph of virtue over vice, and included extemporizations which were used as outlets for comment on current affairs. I.S.33–1966

celadon-glazed jar Thai 14th–15th century *H. 16.3 cm*
Strongly individual celadon-glazed stonewares were made at Sawan-kalok in Central Thailand during this period; rather heavily made, they have thick, glassy glazes influenced by Chinese prototypes. Quantities were also exported throughout the Archipelago.
C.238–1927

Blue-and-white *kendi* N. Vietnamese 15th–16th century *L. 16.3 cm*
From kilns in this region, also known as Annam, comes a type of light stoneware pottery painted in underglaze cobalt after the early Ming style; it largely imitates the Chinese designs, but also has a distinctive local flavour. The *kendi*, a form of drinking vessel, is of South-East Asian origin.
C.97–1967

Brown-glazed stoneware jar Cambodian 12th century *H. 59.1 cm*
The course of pottery-making in the Khmer kingdom is still decidedly obscure; but excavations at the great Angkor temple have helped to identify and date olive-brown glazed wares of this type, with their bands of simple combed decoration, in which monumentality of form is skilfully combined with delicacy.
C.65–1939

Illustration from a folding book Gouache on paper Burmese Late 19th century *H. 20 cm*
Usually of a religious nature, Burmese painting consists of wall-paintings or illustrations to texts. This book, in the form of a long horizontal strip of paper folded vertically, has the text along the bottom and the illustrations above. It shows a disciple of the Buddha seated with a king in his palace, and also flying with the king's gift for the Buddha. The illustrations are simple and direct and a highly decorative effect is achieved by using bright colours (mostly red, yellow, blue, and green) and gold paint. I.S.8–195

Shoulder cloth (*selendang*) Cotton with tie-dyed (*ikat*) pattern Malaysian Late 19th century *H. 82 cm W. 221 cm*
This shoulder-cloth was probably made on the north-east coast of Malaysia, which is famous for its beautiful hand-woven textiles. Thrown across the bare shoulders rather like a stole, it was used both for decoration and protection from the chill of the evening. I.S.83–197

old ear ornaments E. Javanese 13th–
th century *H. 2.5 cm*
arrings are among the most popular forms
f Javanese jewellery, and are made in a great
riety of shapes. The ones shown here are
the shapes of a mythological bird and sea-
onster, a conch shell, and a flower bud.

I.S.15–18–1978

Skirt cloth (kain panjang) Woven cotton with wax-resist dyed (batik) pattern Central
Javanese Late 19th century *H. 256.5 cm W. 109 cm*
Java has used the technique of batik for at least two hundred years, during which time many
beautiful patterns have been produced. They have strong, lively, designs which often combine
foliage and geometrical motifs executed in harmonious colours. A slight crackle, caused by
the partial breaking of the wax resist, sometimes adds to their attraction. There are many
versions of this one, which was originally only worn by persons of princely rank.

I.M.265–1921

agger (kris) Gold mounts Malaysian
erak) Probably 19th century *H. 49 cm*
his weapon is particularly characteristic of
Malaysia and Indonesia. Usually wavy in
ape, the blade is sometimes inlaid with
old. Much magic lore has grown up around
e making of *kris*, and many blades were
garded as having supernatural powers.

I.S.371 & A–1950

Sword (dha) Mounts of gold and spinel rubies Burmese
Late 19th century *L. 94 cm*
There are several types of *dha*, from those used for clearing
undergrowth to efficient weapons of self-defence. This one is
similar to the latter type but was intended more for ceremonial
use than for battle. Its sumptuous decoration lends support to
the tradition that it was given by King Mindon of Burma to
Lord Dalhousie (Governor-general of India) in about 1854.

I.S.2574

Inlaid brass ewer   W. Persian   13th century   *H. 37.8 cm*
Richly inlaid metalwork is among the most characteristic of crafts practised in the Islamic world.
The technique lends itself well to the intricate arabesques and geometric abstractions which play
so effective a part in Islamic decorative design. The silver and copper inlays are unusually well
preserved on this magnificent ewer from Persia. Including bands of figure motifs and, on the
shoulder, cursive calligraphy in which the strong uprights terminate in human heads, they are set
in a ground of black composition which makes the contrast even more striking.   381–1897

The Islamic World

The faith of Islam is centred on the revelations of the Arab Prophet Mohammed which are recorded in the Koran. In A.D. 622 he travelled from Mecca to Medina to set about building the first Muslim state; soon after his death came the swift conquest of Syria, Egypt, Iraq, and Iran, followed by others, which established the reign of militant power from Central Asia westwards to Spain and Atlantic North Africa. Thus came about the firm association of many peoples in religion, since progressively expanded, which today remains a major cultural and political world force.

Despite their underlying diversity, the arts of the Near East gradually evolved many features in common that can only be called Islamic. The mosque itself is a leading example, deriving its architectural layout from its role as a Muslim house of prayer, and remaining always orientated both physically and metaphorically towards Mecca. Its interior furnishings show to Western eyes a characteristic plainness and simplicity which springs directly from the prohibition of the Koran against imagery, whether in god-like, human, or animal form. The effects of this rejection of figure sculpture and painting are strongly felt also in the secular arts of Islam, even though its application was variable and, at times, minimal. The often monumentally splendid architecture of the mosque was, however, complemented in other ways: by the rich texture and colour of carpets, intricately carved and inlaid woodwork, and sumptuously tiled walls; and these and other crafts achieved an unrivalled development of pattern and design in which plant and geometrical motifs are woven together in infinitely subtle variations of arabesque, interlace, and tracery. Among the most important means of spreading the message of the Koran was the written word: thus the art of calligraphy performed a dual role since in various forms the nobly-stylized Arabic script is everywhere prominent in design; in a very real sense it is the word of the Prophet himself which gives Islamic art much of its identity and character.

The rich variety of its development nevertheless owes much to differing national traditions, and to the repeated shifts of power often brought about through conquest or intrigue. It was only with the flowering of the Baghdad Caliphate that a distinctive Islamic style began to emerge, notably in Mesopotamia and Persia from the ninth century. The ancient and flourishing crafts of architectural decoration, stone, wood, and ivory-carving, glass-making and weaving underwent a change of emphasis, while important advances were made in the technology of ceramics and metalwork, and in their decorative design. The Seljuk Turks, who in 1056 assumed the Caliphate, were great builders and patrons of art, and gave fresh impetus to these developments. More brutal in its consequence was the invasion of the Mongols in the thirteenth century, followed scarcely a century later by that of Tamerlane; yet it was in Persia that the arts flourished most abundantly from this period, notably in architecture and book illustration, and in the following Safavid age also, in textiles and woven carpets.

Meanwhile, Egypt and Syria under the Mamluks (1250–1517) also prospered, with much fine craftsmanship particularly in inlaid metalwork, pottery, and enamelled glass. The new emerging force, however, was that of the Ottoman Turks, established in Asia Minor, who took Constantinople in 1453. Their mosque architecture, based on that of the inherited Byzantine churches such as Santa Sophia, was magnificent, and may be said to have inspired the superb tile-work of Isnik pottery with which it was decorated. They also showed a remarkably uninhibited approach to colour and design in textile and carpet-weaving.

Early Islamic Art

Of the more significant aspects of early Islamic art, one in particular—architecture—is for obvious reasons barely represented in the collection, while relatively few paintings have survived intact. Early textiles and metalwork from Persia reflect the Imperial splendour of the preceding Sasanian Persian age: there are rare, fragmentary silks with lions, birds of prey, and other motifs in classic roundel designs, and bronze or brass vessels showing an assurance of form reminiscent of that time. In the same way, in Syria and in Egypt under the Fatimids (969–1171), the acanthus and vine-scroll of Hellenistic tradition remain prominent, notably in wall decoration and such crafts as ivory-carving.

Under the Abbasid Caliphate in Baghdad (750–1258), both Eastern and Arab–Islamic influences were able to contribute towards the formation of a distinct Islamic style: typical of this are intricate geometric patterns which tend towards a flat abstraction, and an increasing use of formalized calligraphy. Certain crafts also underwent major changes, with pottery, for example, breaking new ground with developments such as painting on a white ground, especially in a new golden lustre pigment, in which animals and even humans are depicted in lively silhouette. Parallel to this in eastern or northern Persia is the bold use of contrasting coloured slips with painted or carved designs. After the Seljuk conquest, ceramic techniques blossomed further at Rayy and Kashan, with various lustre or polychrome-painted and relief-moulded or carved styles, in which elegant courtly figure subjects appear. The influence of imported Chinese porcelains also led to the introduction of a superior hard white material and more refined forms. Resplendent colour is everywhere, and never to more effect than in the extensive glazed tilework now used to decorate the walls of mosques and palaces. Metalworkers brought to perfection an art of cast and inlaid designs in costly gold and silver; Khorasan and Mosul were major centres of this intricate craft, which indeed characterized the entire region.

Essential to the arts was their association with the mosque. The rich elaboration of Islamic woodcarving is represented by a fine Egyptian pulpit of a slightly later, Mamluk date. Inlaid bronze candlesticks and censers, and splendid enamelled glass lamps from Syria are among other works which illustrate this aspect.

Page from a Koran Ink and colours on paper Persian 11th century *H. 19 cm* Calligraphy occupies a central place in Islamic art, both as an independent art form and through its recurrent use in decorative design. More fundamental still is its role as a means of disseminating the faith as codified in the Koran. Of various scripts developed in Islam that known as Kufic (after Kufa in Mesopotamia) was especially influential, and in the hands of early Persian calligraphers this formal, upright style combines dignity with elegance. L.1920–193

Woven silk   E. Persian   8th–9th century
H. 62 cm W. 46 cm
The many silks with roundel designs of
confronted animals or birds illustrate the
extent to which the art of Sasanian Persia
remained influential in early Islam, and are a
reflection of the grandeur and nobility of that
style. This example is ascribed to a Soghdian
workshop.   763–1893

Engraved brass ewer   E. Persian   8th century   *H. 44.2 cm*
The ewer is one of the rare surviving examples of early Islamic
metalwork, which at this time was still strongly influenced by the
preceding Sasanian style. The partly-cast shape is graceful in form,
and the fluted neck is engraved with simple designs; the high curving
handle is characteristically Sasanian.   434–1906

Cut glass bottle   Persian   9th–10th century   *H. 23.5 cm*
This attractive bottle is decorated with formal plant-like designs and
birds, with galloping horses on the shoulder and palmettes on the
neck. The art of glass was born in the Near East and remained one of
its glories in Islamic times. The designs are here cut in relief on the
wheel after the manner of lapidary art, and recall similar work in rock
crystal.   20–1965

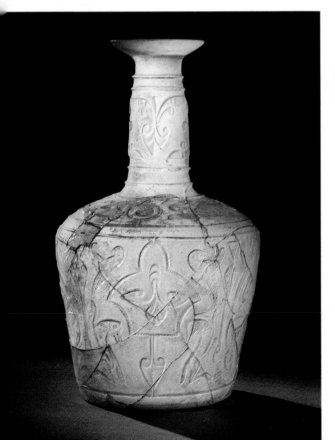

Pottery dish Mesopotamian 9th century
Diam. 37.5 cm
Under the rule of the Abbasid Caliphs in
their capital Baghdad, the exploration of new
techniques brought a new distinction to the
art of pottery. Among these was the use of a
white tin-oxide glaze as a smooth surface for
painting. The beauty of this dish lies in its
simplicity, and the combination of soft green
splashes with its blue frond-like design.

C.65-1934

Slip-painted pottery bowl **E. Persian** 9th–10th century
Diam. 25.1 cm
A striking style of ceramic painting was invented far to the east under
the Samanid rulers of Samarkand, in which the colours were
stabilized by mixing with clay 'slip'. A vivid red, olive-green, and
brown-black are used mainly for plant designs or calligraphic
inscriptions. The bold, uninhibited style reflects the Turkic element
in the populations of this region. C.47-1952

Lustred pottery dish Mesopotamian
9th–10th century *Diam. 19.1 cm*
Although the technique may have originated
in Cairo, it was at Baghdad that painting on
pottery in the typically Islamic golden lustre
was developed. The metallic deposit resulted
from a combination of sulphur with oxides of
silver and copper. The designs of human
figures or, as in this case, animals reserved
on a dotted ground, have a somewhat flat,
heraldic quality; the inscriptions are words of
blessing. C.56-1930

Pottery dish N. Persian 10th century
Diam. 25.4 cm
On this dish the design of a falcon with wings
outstretched is merely incised in outline in
the underglaze 'slip', and touched here and
there with green, brown, and purple. The
style is spirited and rustic, and the effect
surprisingly modern. C.725–1923

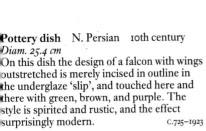

Pottery jar N.W. Persian Garrus district 12th century
H. 43.2 cm
In this remote north-western region of Kurdistan a type of pottery is
found which is decorated by carving through a layer of white 'slip' so
as to reveal the darker body beneath. On this fine loop-handled jar,
the design of animals and strongly-stylized Kufic inscriptions (the
early angular form of Arabic Script) is covered with a pleasing green
glaze. C.9–1952

361

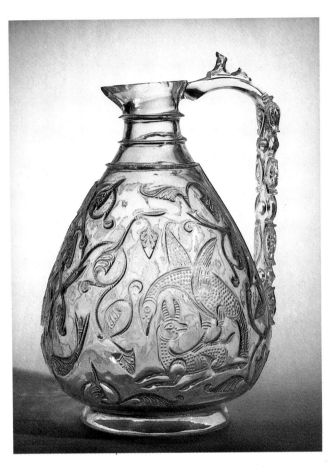

Rock crystal ewer Egyptian (Fatimid) Late 10th century
H. 21.6 cm
A large bird of prey is perched on the back of an ibex among the leafy
plant scrolls. Traditional Near Eastern skill in lapidary arts is
reflected in this group of shapely crystal ewers and other objects from
Egypt, which are wheel cut with designs in relief. The many examples
preserved in European church treasuries show that such wares, along
with contemporary Islamic textiles, were much in demand there.

7904–1862

Ivory horn Sicilian (?) 11th–12th century *L. 61 cm*
Finely-decorated caskets as well as drinking-horns are among the
works in carved ivory produced in Sicily, Spain, and other parts of the
northern Mediterranean under Arab influence. Whether or not the
workshops concerned were Muslim, the effect of their style is
apparent in the deeply-carved scrollwork set with animals and birds,
which has links with both Islam and Byzantium. The mouthpiece and
rim and bands of loose silver rings are of much later date.   7953–1862

Woven silk Persian 11th–12th century
H. 34 cm W. 30 cm
Early silk fabrics have generally survived either in Europe, where they were greatly prized, or in burials: this fine example was unearthed near Rayy. It illustrates the Islamic fondness for calligraphy as decoration, the pairs of seated figures being framed in a verse on the impermanence of life by the sixth-century poet Ka'b ibn Zuhair.

T.94–1937

Woven silk Egyptian 14th century
This fragment of tabby-woven silk was excavated near Asyut in Upper Egypt. Incorporating pairs of winged lions and birds in a formal pattern of tracery, it represents the powerful continuity of a tradition of textile design that may be traced back to Sasanian Persia.

704–1878

Lustred pottery bowl Egyptian (Fatimid) 1st half of the 12th century *Diam. 30.8 cm*
The subject of a Coptic priest carrying a censer is a reminder that Christianity still survived in Egypt. The Fatimid lustre-ware, which probably derived from that of Mesopotamia, is somewhat inferior technically, but shows here a particularly fine colour; the painting, although flat and stylized, is executed with an entertaining eye for detail such as the rhythmic movement of the swinging censer and scimitar. The piece bears the signature of the potter, Sa'd.   C.49–1952

Pottery jar Mesopotamian Late 12th–early 13th century *H. 26.7 cm*
An effective style of pottery decoration involved painting in black under a clear or, as in this case, a turquoise glaze; it is associated especially with Rakka in Northern Mesopotamia. The wares were decorated with birds and human figures and, as here, calligraphy and silhouetted plants, executed in a vigorous line.   C.137–1929

Bronze mortar Persian 12th century *H. 17.8 cm*
This massive octagonal vessel was probably based on a stone original, and used for pounding foods or medicines. The entire piece was cast together with the human heads and ox-head with ring handle which stand out in relief. The engraved designs include benedictory inscriptions and the name of the original owner, Umar ibn Mahdi.   M.24–1963

Lustred pottery dish Persian   dated 604 A.H.
(A.D. 1207)   *Diam. 34.9 cm*
The dish is decorated with the figure of a
courtly polo player dressed in a flowered
robe, riding a piebald horse; the ground is
filled with a variety of birds and plants.
Lustre painting from Kashan at this time
employs a magnificently refined and creative
line to achieve effects that are essentially
poetic. The long inscribed verse surrounding
this also contains the date.   C.51–1952

Pottery dish Persian   12th century   *Diam. 18.4 cm*
This dish shows developments in Persian pottery under
Seljuk rule resulting from the influence of imported
Chinese porcelain. The ware is hard, white, and
compact enough to be translucent when thin; the
sharply-curved rim is also a Chinese feature. A lively
rhythm is created by the incised leafy scroll under the
cobalt-blue glaze.   C.68–1931

Pottery tankard Persian   12th century   *H. 13.3 cm*
Found at Feraghan, near the pottery centre of Sultanabad where it may have been
made, this tankard has a typically elegant Persian form, the stylishly-striped design
being achieved by carving through a layer of black slip. The covering glaze of
turquoise-blue completes the glowing effect so well suited to the brilliant light of
the region.   C.725–1909

365

Minai style painted bowl Persian Late 12th century
Diam. 18.4 cm
The interior of the bowl shows a seated princely figure holding
a cup, surrounded by courtiers and musicians, while the
outside is decorated with Kufic lettering. The late Seljuk
potters of Persia achieved a full, jewel-like polychrome
through the use of low-temperature enamels to supplement
existing pigments, and the effect, heightened by touches of
gold, resembles that of the exquisite painted miniatures of the
period. C.52–1952

Kashan lustred tile Persian Early 14th century
31.8 cm sq
The Sasanian king Bahrum Gur is shown out hunting with
his favourite Azada, who sits behind him on the camel,
playing a harp; the episode comes from Firdausi's
Shahnameh or 'Book of Kings'. The wall tile is said to
come from a palace in Mazanderan. The Mohameddan
veto on representing living things, while upheld in religious
buildings, was less well observed elsewhere, and such
designs imply a view of life in which austerity was hardly
the rule. 1841–1876

Inlaid bronze bowl Persian Late 13th century *H. 14 cm*
Made of white bronze, so-called because of its high tin
content, this high-footed bowl is typical of the north-west
Persia area, as is the style of the decorative roundels engraved
and inlaid in silver and the repetitive inscription which records
good wishes. It was probably used as a wine bowl. M.28–1968

Tilework frieze   Persian (Bokhara)   *c.1360   H. 23.5 cm*
A striking style of tilework developed in eastern Persia after the
manner of carved stucco decoration. The elegant inscriptions are cut
in such a way as to project above the carved ground of whirling
foliage, the effect being heightened by the contrast of deep green and
white glazes. The frieze came from the walls of the tomb mosque of
Buyan Kuli Khan, built in about 1358.   2031A–1899

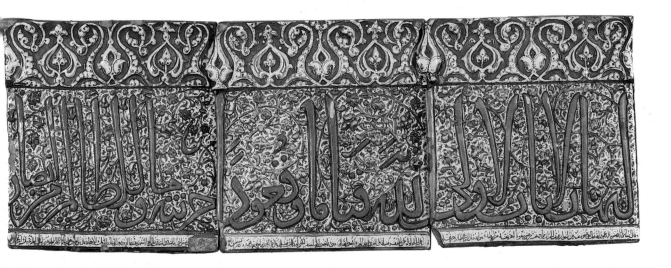

Lustred tilework frieze   Persian
(Kashan)   Early 13th century   *H. 43.8 cm*
This is an example of early lustred work
from the Kashan potteries, with particularly
fine calligraphic inscriptions moulded in
relief, and coloured blue on a ground of
brownish-gold scrollwork. The leafy arabesques are unusually intricate. It once
formed part of an extensive scheme covering
the walls of a mosque at Meshed.   1481–1876

Marble basin   Syrian   dated 676 A.H.
(A.D. 1277)   *Diam. 85.2 cm*
The basin is pierced in the centre and was
formerly part of a fountain; rounded in form,
it is topped by a twelve-sided polygonal rim.
The sides present a handsome continuous
pattern of formal interlaced scrollwork. It
was brought from Hama, and the inscription
gives the name and titles of the local ruler,
al-Malik al-Mansur Mohammed (1244–84),
as well as the date, calculated from the
Hejira or migration of Mohammed to
Medina from Mecca.   335–1903

Pulpit (*mimbar*) Egyptian Late 15th century *H. 732 cm*

The priest addresses the faithful at prayer from the *mimbar*, a familiar sight in mosques throughout the Islamic world.
Fine carving ornaments every surface with geometric patterns, hypnotic in their intricacy and effect of endless, cell-
like creation; ivory inlays also enrich the design, while 'stalactite' borders crown the doorway and pulpit itself.
Although relatively late in date this pulpit, erected by Sultan Qaitbay (1468–96) in his mosque in Cairo, follows the
traditional style, and typifies the rich extravagance of Mamluk taste.   1050–1869

368

[G]lass mosque lamp Syrian 1309–10
[H.] 28.9 cm
[Th]e lamp was made for the upstart Mamluk
[Su]ltan Baybars II, to whom it is dedicated in
[th]e splendid inscriptions, which also incor-
[po]rate passages from the Koran. Such
[hig]hly-enamelled decoration represents an
[im]portant development in the art of glass and
[thi]s is among the finest of its kind. The
[la]mps, with oil-burners inside, were sus-
[pe]nded on chains from the ceiling. The glass
[its]elf is brownish in colour and the enamels
[thi]ck and brilliant.   322–1900

[In]laid brass incense burner Syrian 2nd
[ha]lf of 13th century *H. 19.5 cm*
[La]vishly damascened with silver and gold,
[wh]ich remain in almost mint state, the
[bur]ner has a hinged cover with three open-
[wo]rk roundels to let out the smoke. The
[de]signs represent hunting, falconry, music-
[m]aking, drinking, and other pleasures of the
[co]urt. The piece is distinctively Syrian both
[in] its three-footed form and overall refine-
[me]nt of style.   M.709–1910

[In]laid bronze candlestick Egyptian ▷
[1]300 *H. 35.8 cm*
[Ca]ndlesticks of this impressive form were
[m]ade throughout Islam. The well-preserved
[sil]ver inlays are in a broad, Egyptian style; as
[we]ll as bold decorative inscriptions, they
[in]clude elegant large roundels with a tra-
[dit]ional design of birds and animals, arranged
[aro]und an animal-head on a scrollwork
[gro]und. It was made for an unknown patron,
[Ru]kn al-Dīn Muhammad ibn Qaratāy, of
[Ba]ghdad.   M.716–1910

369

Pottery bowl Persian (Kashan) Early 13th century *Diam. 19.7 cm*
The bowl is decorated in underglaze black with an unusually naturalistic representation of water weeds. A band of swimming fish on a blue ground decorates the upper part of the bowl's interior, the swift, sure hand of the painter ensuring a lively design. C.721–1909

The Luck of Edenhall Syrian Mid-13th century *H. 15.9 cm*
Furnished with a case of French stamped leather dating from the fourteenth century, this famous glass, enamelled with arabesque designs, was possibly brought from the Holy Land by a crusader. It belonged thereafter to the Musgrave family, of Edenhall in Cumberland, from whom it was acquired in 1959. Longfellow wrote a poem around its story in 1834. C.1 to B–1959

Pottery jar Syrian 14th century
H. 38.1 cm
Bold design is a feature of these Syrian wares which are painted in blue and black under a thick, glassy glaze with birds and debased calligraphic motifs. Jars of this kind were apparently exported from Damascus to Europe as containers for exotic fruits and spices. 483–1864

Later Islamic Art

In the thirteenth century, a natural division occurred with the Mongol conquest, which caused widespread devastation. The Il-Khans eventually became converts and patrons of art, their domination of Asia itself helping to introduce fresh ideas, including Chinese styles and motifs, which enlivened painting and changed decorative design.

In Persia, the succeeding Timurids (1380–1502) and Safavids (1502–1736) assiduously cultivated the arts, with notable effect on the book and book-illustration and at Herat and Shiraz in particular the painted miniature was raised to a surpassing level. Carpet-weaving achieved major importance in Safavid Persia. The 'Ardabil' carpet in the Museum is perhaps the most famous early surviving example and in its great size, harmonious colour, and near-symmetrical design, is a work of extraordinary impact. More luxurious still are the so-called 'polonaise' silk carpets, a name underlining the trade by which increasing contact was now being forged with Europe.

Turkey was also a major source of carpets, its peoples being descended from the migrant Turks of Central Asia where the craft had its origins. Many small prayer rugs were produced here; and Ottoman court weavers also won fame for their richly-coloured, boldly patterned silks and velvets, mostly with stylized floral arabesques. No less characteristic of Ottoman art is the pottery of Isnik, with its brilliantly-glazed white body, which from the late fifteenth century developed a robust style of arabesque and floral designs painted in strong, clear colours of unprecedented intensity. The need for wall-tiles to decorate the many fine mosques and palaces gave further stimulus to this art. Military requirements also encouraged metalworkers in the arts of arms and armour, and here a fine scimitar and helmet represent the Museum's sizeable study collection.

The elegance and charm of Persian art contrasts with the near-barbaric vigour of these Turkish designs. The Safavid court silks of the sixteenth and seventeenth centuries are of extraordinary quality, sumptuous in their use of gold and silver threads and subtle colour. In pottery, a near-porcelain imitating the Chinese blue-and-white is complemented by plain wares in soft green, blue, or amber; the thinly-blown glasses in these colours are also extremely refined.

Astrolabe Brass Persian dated 1666 *L. 17 cm*
This astrolabe is important for its handsomely decorated *rete*, the openwork disc which carries a star map. Astrolabes were used to determine, among other things, the advance positions of celestial bodies, and they were also used in mosques to establish the proper hours of prayer. The piece is signed by the maker Khalil, and decorator Mohammad Mahdi, of Yazd.   M.38–1916

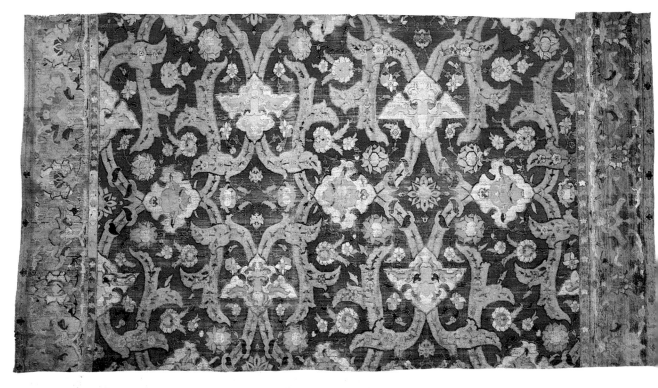

'Polonaise' silk carpet Persian *c.*1600-20 *H. 259 cm W. 145 cm*
This is a fragment of one of a group of early seventeenth-century carpets, woven in
silk and brocaded in gold and silver thread, of which a number were ordered by
European princely patrons—hence their one-time mistaken attribution to Poland.
In this example, the bold arabesque designs are essentially floral in character.
Probably from the royal workshops in Isfahan or from Kashan, they are among the
most luxurious ever produced.   36–1854

Carpet Persian 16th–17th century
H. 226 cm W. 170 cm
The Safavid period is the classic age of the
Persian carpet. Made later than the celebrated 'medallion' carpets of the sixteenth
century (see p. 117) and woven in wool pile
on cotton, the carpet, of which this is a detail
is from one of the group of so-called 'vase'
carpets; the main design, however, is floral,
with an interlacing trellis of stems in which
the vases of flowers are subsidiary. It is
characterized by rich colouring and boldness
of design.   453–188

'Ardabil' carpet   Persian   dated 1540
l. 1043 cm W. 585 cm
Possibly the world's most famous carpet,
it is one of the pair formerly in the
mosque at Ardabil, the ancestral shrine of
the Safavid rulers. It is certainly among
the largest and also one of the most
beautiful carpets, superb in its design and
rich dark colours. The inscribed date
makes it a landmark in the history of early
carpet-weaving. The design, with a large
central medallion surrounded by others
on an arabesque ground of flowers and
their interlaced curving stems is entirely
symmetrical, and bears a clear correlation
with decorated book covers and miniature paintings of the Safavid period. The
carpet is woven in silk on a wool pile with
about three hundred knots to the square
inch.   272–1893

Painted miniature Persian *c.*1430 *H. 17.8 cm*
After the conquests of Tamerlane, there followed a fresh flowering of
the arts in Persia, and miniature painting in particular reached a peak
of excellence. At Herat, under the patronage of his son, Shah Rukh,
some brilliantly illustrated manuscripts were produced. From the
rare *History of Hafiz i Abru* comes this page with a scene of the defeat
of Pir Padishah of Khurasan by forces of Shah Rukh himself, filled
with gory detail and the excitement of victory.   E.5499–1958

'Kubachi' pottery dish N.W. Persian *c.*1600 *Diam. 34.6 cm*
Various examples of this type of pottery were found in the town of
Kubachi in a remote part of Daghestan, which has hence given them
its name. They range in date from the mid-fifteenth century, when
Chinese porcelain designs were copied, to about 1630, and consist
mainly of decorative dishes, although some tiles also appear in the
collection. Despite the somewhat inferior manufacture, they are
justly admired for their spontaneity of colour and drawing.

C.58–1952

Silver gilt tankard Turkish 16th century *H. 15.9 cm*
Very little Islamic silver and gold work has survived. This sumptuous tankard has cast decoration, comprising mainly interlaced leafy tracery raised in relief on a matted ground, which is typically Turkish in its bold vigour. The tankard form has forerunners in Persian metalwork as well as in finely-worked Persian jade. The lid is a later addition.
158–1894

High-footed Isnik bowl Turkish *c.*1545 *H. 42.6 cm*
From the late fifteenth century onwards, under the inspiration of the Ottoman Sultans, a superior form of pottery was developed at Isnik in Turkey, formerly Nicaea. The ware, which is technically excellent, has a fine white body and brilliant glaze under which it is painted in an unusually brilliant range of colours. This splendid large bowl has a striking pattern of repeating spiral stems in the blue, turquoise, and black typical of the Isnik palette.
243–1876

375

Isnik tile panel Turkish *c.*1575 ▷
W. 109.3 cm
With the maturity of the Isnik potteries in the
sixteenth century came the manufacture of
extensive series of wall-tiles for the many
splendid buildings under construction in
Constantinople and elsewhere. The effect of
the repeated leafy patterns and brilliant
colour harmonies in the great mosques and
palaces of the Sultans is quite overwhelming.
This panel of tiles from the baths at the
Mosque of Eyub Ensari ranks with the finest
work of the time.   401–1900

Isnik pottery dish Turkish 2nd half of 16th century
Diam. 29.2 cm
This dish is in a relatively unusual Isnik style in which a deep
lavender-blue is used as a ground for the design of carnations,
tulips, and other flowers, ingeniously arranged over the surface.
The white and red pigments are thickly applied and the colour
effect is one of extreme richness.   276–1893

Isnik pottery mug Turkish Late 16th century *H. 26.7 cm*
The 'Armenian bole' red of Isnik ware, seen here in its richest
'sealing-wax' tint, is counterbalanced by fresh green and blue.
The rhythmic interlaced patterns of plant-like forms have a
strange disconcerting vitality. The pattern shown here is relatively
abstract, but other pieces show designs with flowers, human
figures—even ships and houses—in the same lively style.
                    1708–1855

Helmet Turkish *c.*1500 *H. 35.5 cm*
This helmet of iron finely damascened with
silver, and originally also with gilt, was
obviously made for a very senior officer; it is
inscribed with the title of an unnamed sultan,
and bears the mark of the Constantinople
armoury. The helmet was raised from a
single sheet, and has typically Turkish spiral
fluting. The nasal guard in front was lowered
for protection, and a veil of mail would also
have been attached. 399–1888

Velvet Turkish 16th or early 17th century *H. 154 cm*
The fabric is woven with a strong ogival lattice pattern framing
floral elements in gold and silver on a ground of red silk pile. It is
typical of many such Turkish silks of this period, rich and
splendid, which were used not only for hangings and cushion
covers in the divan, or council-chamber, but also for clothing.
800–1897

Scimitar (*gilij*) Turkish dated
1025 A.H. (A.D. 1616) *L. 80.5 cm*
The blade, like that of most Islamic swords,
is of extremely tough watered steel; it bears
inscriptions in gold overlay, which include
invocations to the angels of the Prophet and
names of former owners. Uniquely Turkish
features are the noticeably angled blade, and
its thickened and channelled back. The cast
silver guard and ivory handle are later
replacements. M.31–1965

Prayer rug Turkish 18th century *H. 188 cm W. 125 cm*
The rug has incorporated into it the design of a *mihrab* or prayer niche similar to those found in mosques, so that it could be laid out and used for this purpose at the appointed times. Of wool and cotton pile, and rather simple and austere in style, it is typical of many in the collection. The colouring is characteristic of Kula rugs, which are generally of coarser weave than those of Ghiordes, both with higher pile and softer wool. Both towns are in the southern part of Turkey.   844–1901

Silk brocade Persian 16th–17th century *H. 176 cm W. 110 cm*
This luxurious silk hanging is woven with a highly stylized plant design beneath a niche with hovering butterflies, the threads of silvery gold, silver, buff, and blue standing out against a dark blue satin ground. There is a similar panel at Lyons with a red ground, bearing a signature.   T.9–1915

Tile picture Persian *c.*1600 *H. 109.3 cm*
The tile shows a picnic scene in a garden with elegant youths and ladies reclining among
flowering trees. Probably produced in the reign of Shah Abbas I, it was said to have come
from the Hall of the Forty Columns (Chehil Sutun) at Isfahan, although this is uncertain. In
brilliant colours on a white ground with bright blue sky, it makes use of the *cuerda seca* or 'dry
cord' technique of waxy lines which keep the colours from running.   139–1891

Khusraw and the Lion Painted miniature Persian dated 1632
H. 26.7 cm W. 15.3 cm
This miniature, from a manuscript of *The Romance of Chosroes and
Shirin* by Ganjavi Nizami, shows Khusraw stunning the lion with a
blow. The illuminations are by Riza Abbasi, and the text was
transcribed in 1680; the border was added in the late nineteenth
century. In late Safavid times, the Persian arts of the book show
increasing virtuosity: here the sense of formal design, pointing to the
dramatic moment, is reinforced by harmonious colour and heightened by a loving eye for incidental detail, such as the tile decoration
behind Chosroes and curtains blowing in the wind.   L.1613–1964

Pottery bottle Persian Early 17th century *H. 37.5 cm*
This elegantly tall-necked, white-bodied flask has a transparent green glaze,
its shape reflecting the languid grace of much art of this period. The design
in relief shows a tribesman with a lion on a leash on one side and curious,
winged creatures on the other.   C.1975–1910

Blue-and-white pottery dish Persian 17th century
Diam. 37.5 cm
As with pottery in Europe, the later Islamic wares were powerfully
influenced by imported Chinese porcelains. Similar to a Wan Li style
blue-and-white dish with a river landscape with islands, pavilions,
and ducks on a bank in the foreground, they were often directly
copied or adapted, and made at Kirman or, as here, at Meshed. The
material is fine and white, and the blue brilliant; the dish also has a
well-carved ornamental border.   1152–1876

Glass bottle Persian 17th–18th century *H. 33 cm*
Although its technique is inspired by Venice, this sprinkler bottle with
ribbed neck of pale brownish glass mirrors the graceful forms of the Safavid
age. Attractive tones of green, blue, violet, and yellow were also used in the
Persian glassworks.   99–1877

Velvet Persian Late 16th–early 17th century *H. 160 cm W. 76 cm*
The panel shows graceful youths in a garden with cypresses and a
flower-bordered pool: they stand in pairs alternately leaning towards
each other and turned away, thus creating a strange effect of
counterpoint. This magical scene is executed in a complex technique
of silk pile with colours and silver on a gold ground. A masterpiece of
Safavid weaving, it was formerly preserved in the Treasury at Jaipur
in India. T.226–1923

Silk Persian Late 16th century *H. 105 cm W. 68 cm*
The cloth is finely woven in soft colours on a yellow satin ground.
The delicately-outlined repeating design shows a figure holding a
flask and bowl in a garden with cypresses and a fishpond with
rockery, various animals, and birds. Its refinement of design and
workmanship alike reflect the great flowering of the textile arts at the
court of Shah Abbas I (1587–1629), and its concern with the poetic
view of the world of nature. 282–1906

Index